Ac

America's Covert Border War

"Todd Bensman is one of the last remaining authentic counterter-rorism experts and investigators on jihadist terrorism, whose new book will mesmerize, shock, inform, and totally enlighten you on the covert war against Islamist militants fought by the government inside the U.S., as well as around the world. Bensman is also an amazingly gifted writer whose book unfolds as though one were reading a great crime novel—with a plot line made for a Netflix series. Even though I have specialized in terrorism for more than twenty-five years, I have learned more from reading the work of Todd Bensman than any other counter terrorist official or 'expert' in the world, bar none. I guarantee you that once you open the first page, you won't put it down till the last."

—Steven Emerson, Executive Director of the
Investigative Project on Terrorism; author of seven books
on terrorism and national security, and the executive
producer of two award-winning documentaries on jihadist
terrorism (the 1994 PBS documentary *Jihad in America*
and the 2013 documentary *The Grand Deception*)

"Amidst multiple international crises, most of the media have lost sight of the jihadi threat to America. Todd Bensman is a welcome exception. His investigative reporting on continuing terrorist attempts to infiltrate the United States deserves wide attention from specialists and the general public alike."

—Clifford D. May, Founder and President, The
Foundation for Defense of Democracies

"Drawing upon his unique experience, both as a counterterrorism professional within the Texas Department of Public Safety, as well as his many years as an investigative journalist, Bensman utilizes a vast range of primary sources to provide an unmatched, richly detailed account of the vulnerabilities to terrorist infiltration that exist at the

United States' southern border. Timely and engaging, this book cuts through the otherwise deeply politicized debate that surrounds this topic to give a clear-eyed, factually based account of the threat as we know it, the counterterrorism machinery that was put in place after 9/11 to defeat it, and the worrisome holes in the system that persist to this day. Simply put, it is a must-read for anyone wishing to get to grips with this issue."

—Sam Mullins, professor at Daniel K. Inouye Asia-Pacific Center for Security Studies and author of *Jihadist Infiltration of Migrant Flows to Europe: Perpetrators, Modus Operandi and Policy Implications*

"Journalist and former counterterrorism intelligence manager Todd Bensman shines a spotlight into a complex issue that few truly understand. Trust me when I say this: Bensman has been in the trenches and behind the scenes to safeguard Texas. He deserves our thanks."

—Fred Burton, former Diplomatic Security Service Special Agent and *New York Times* bestselling author of *Beirut Rules*, *Chasing Shadows*, and *Ghost*

"Progressives on the cultural and political left harbor a lot of dangerous and seditious ideas about illegal immigration. Chief among them is that lax border enforcement and massive waves of third-world migrants are *not* an invitation to terrorist infiltration. But Todd Bensman's new book, *America's Covert Border War*, is even more dangerous and seditious because it speaks plain, powerful truth about the very real problem of jihadi infiltration, backed up by the kind of deep reporting that will challenge the assumptions of even the most willfully ignorant, glib, or smug. The book is a well-grounded warning from a longtime veteran of the War on Terror, as well as a bold rebuke to the media's unfortunate culture of denial, avoidance, and resistance."

—William McGowan, author, *Coloring The News* and *Gray Lady Down*

"Todd Bensman provides a deeply disturbing national security perspective of failed immigration controls from Panama through Mexico, to the southern borders of Mexico to which we were blind. Bensman now examines the threat of lone jihadists and organized groups moving through those countries to the United States. He knows this world from his reporting on the ground in Central America and Mexico, and as a government intelligence worker. With this book, we are far less blind."

—Dr. Michael Lauderdale, University of Texas at Austin,
Clara Pope Willoughby Centennial Professor

"Bensman draws on his many years studying the U.S.-Mexican border to establish the presence of a major, but secret, national counterterrorism project; then to show the serious neglect that hobbles it; and finally, to recommend solutions. He needs urgently to be heeded, lest disaster come via the Rio Grande."

—Daniel Pipes, founder of The Middle East Forum,
thought leader of U.S. foreign policy in the region, and
author of sixteen books on Islam and the Middle East

AMERICA'S COVERT BORDER WAR

THE UNTOLD STORY OF THE NATION'S BATTLE TO PREVENT JIHADIST INFILTRATION

TODD BENSMAN

BOMBARDIER
BOOKS

BOMBARDIER BOOKS
An Imprint of Post Hill Press
ISBN: 978-1-64293-725-1
ISBN (eBook): 978-1-64293-726-8

America's Covert Border War:
The Untold Story of the Nation's Battle to Prevent Jihadist Infiltration
© 2021 by Todd Bensman
All Rights Reserved

Post Hill Press
New York • Nashville
posthillpress.com

Published in the United States of America
1 2 3 4 5 6 7 8 9 10

I dedicate this book to my father, Roger G. Bensman.
Thanks for staying around so long.

CONTENTS

INTRODUCTION

SMALL NUMBERS, BIG CONSEQUENCES

In October 2018, President Donald Trump claimed that he had "very good information" that Middle Eastern migrants had been traveling through Latin America and that "there could very well be" Islamic terrorists in the massive migrant caravan of Central Americans that was forcing its way through Mexico to the American border.[1] In fact, the president warned, the US Border Patrol had intercepted "some real bad ones." At one point, the president tweeted an older news story about Muslim prayer rugs ostensibly left behind at the border by Muslim migrants. Trump, of course, had his reasons for raising this obscure threat specter; he was chumming up support for his promised border wall, still not funded at that time, as huge migrant caravans were heading for the US southern border from Central America.

An epic firestorm of challenge and pushback erupted over this rare presidential claim of terrorist border infiltration. The *Washington Post* concluded that prayer rugs associated with southern border migration from Muslim countries counted as "similar to the claims of a conspiracy theory that has long been popular with far-right and anti-Muslim figures and publications."[2] The *New York Times* published a "Fact Check" column determining as "an unproved rumor" the notion that Muslim migrants were sneaking over the border and posed a terrorism threat.[3] Elected leaders and some retired homeland security practitioners went on air to contradict the president's claims of terrorist land border infiltration as outlandish, a flat-out lie, or just wrong. El Paso Congressman Robert Francis "Beto" O'Rourke insisted in a column that "precisely zero terrorists, terrorist groups or terror plots" had ever been connected to the border.[4] Even Republican Senator Jeff Flake, from the border state of Arizona, dismissed the idea of Middle Eastern travelers through Latin America and potential terrorists among them as "pretty much a canard and a fear tactic."[5] Vox Media said apprehensions of people from Muslim-majority countries only happened at "vanishingly small rates."[6]

The melee only ended when Trump stopped talking and tweeting about the issue in the spring of 2019, leaving the matter hanging, unresolved and probably discredited in the broader public mind.

The intensity of reaction to Trump's claims was nothing new. Counterclaims, rebuttals, and false narratives break out almost every time the claim is made that infiltrating terrorists could or have come in over the southern US border. This predictable cycle of claim-rebuttal testifies to the notion's sheer latent political power. Were the assertion ever to be decided as true, it would unleash tougher national immigration policy that would negatively impact a broad diversity of stakeholders that *want* illegal Hispanic immigration, even need it—agribusiness, the non-profit migrant advocacy industry, foreign governments dependent on remittance money, and US politicians interested in the Latino vote, not to mention the immigrants themselves. Trump's claim caused its momentary havoc because he and his opponents well understood the idea held real political might, in this case to unchain funding for his border wall.

Among all of the more indisputably established threat issues along the southern border that draw appropriations and resources—uncontrolled illegal immigration, cartel violence, sex trafficking, and drug smuggling—none are more muscular than the one that has violent Islamists stealing over the border. Fights break out over this infiltration notion because agendas are served when the American public is left hanging in fact-or-fiction suspense about this topic, without resolution or ever any serious journalistic effort to explore the question to an end.

This book endeavors to provide such a resolution. It gores oxen on both sides of the question to get there. But this book discloses that America built and deployed an internationally expansive, ambitious, and somehow almost entirely unreported counterterrorism enterprise at the border and along its Latin American approaches. Why would political leadership on both sides of the partisan divide start and perpetuate a counterterrorism war to address an enemy that supposedly does not exist except as a dismissible phantom?

The short answer is that professional homeland security leadership under both Democrats and Republicans, with access to intelligence reporting most Americans don't have, regarded the threat of terrorist infiltration as quite real. How could such a stark disconnect between ground reality and public perception have developed?

One answer is that homeland security leaders and professionals, no matter which party occupied the White House, saw things the American public can't, or won't. One purpose of this book is to make visible what *they* see so that we can all move on.

Through confidential records and stories shared with me, collections of public court records, interviews with the covert border war fighters, and my own experiences among those professionals, this book not only shows how this last great unknown American counterterrorism enterprise of the 9/11 era has operated in America's backyard and across the globe, but also poses a novel proposition: that these secret programs have repeatedly prevented terror attacks through America's back gates. For years.

The 9/11 hijackers and others have entered the United States by simply flying into its airports on legal visas and fraudulent identity documents. The country, of course, has, rather famously and infamously, worked hard to sew up those more conventional entry methods to mostly widespread approbation. But of all the pathways left for enterprising terrorist travelers looking for a way in, none has proven so contentious and politically consequential as the one by land border. That would be because, in using Mexicans and Central Americans as cloaking, jihadists draw that population into a national security vortex that can lead to deeply unwanted restrictions on their movement across the border. Hence, the forcible, almost desperate, pushback when Trump asserted that jihadists would or could use Spanish-speaking migrants as camouflage.

But jihadists and their sympathizers *have* used them and their routes. In telling the fullest possible story of America's covert border war against this especially nefarious method of terrorist travel, this book cannot help but also clear the air of some of the debunking pushback of the sort Donald Trump's claims drew: first, a river of migrants from the Middle East and Muslim-majority countries, never dry, does indeed flow through Latin America and over the US southern border as he said.

The US government labels migrants from places like these as "special interest aliens" (SIAs), a term with which readers will soon become very familiar. SIAs is the government parlance most often used to reference these unique ultra-distance immigrants. At several thousand per year in recent times, SIAs make up less than a percent of the federal government's roughly half a million annual apprehensions within one hundred miles of the southern border. They travel incredible distances along surprising routes that will be detailed in this book. However, because hard-bitten jihadists too often travel the routes among them, SIAs are regarded as posing a higher, different risk than that posed by almost all other nationalities. This river deposits real Middle Easterners on the American side, not prayer rugs. Real terrorists—though a minority of a minority—have ridden it in, as I will show in the following pages. They will do so again and perhaps not only to conduct attacks but also to provide money, intelligence about their American hosts, and logistical and propaganda supporting their brethren and greater cause abroad. They are needles in the SIA haystack—ignored or dismissed at national peril.

The presence and purpose of the American counterterrorism effort to find them in SIA traffic and reduce their threat will be shown as beyond dispute. Perhaps more arguable is my thesis that the secret border programs described in these pages have prevented terror attacks from the southern land border to date, and that shuttering the efforts would immediately imperil Americans. Here, I hope to persuade. But if a public discussion over my thesis finally ensues, this book's other purpose will have been served, which is to finally propel this threat issue into the same national border policy debate space that all the other more "respectable" land border problems occupy, hopefully free of the sort of hyperbole and polemics that have diminished any national discussion of jihadist infiltration in past years.

I know about America's covert border war from my unique perches as both a Texas-based counterterrorism manager and analyst who worked inside the project with federal security clearance and also as a journalist traveling the migrant trails.

My odyssey into this subject began in 2006, when I worked as an investigative reporter for Hearst News in San Antonio, Texas, covering counterterrorism and national security issues such as Mexico's bloody civil drug war at the time. Reporters in my south Texas space often heard rumors that Middle Easterners were crossing the border, sometimes leaving behind ostensible trace evidence like prayer rugs. I noticed that other reporters and editors who would normally check out leads—however skeptically—always dismissed these reports and my questions about them with an axiomatic wave of hand. To entertain the possibility that not everyone crossing our southern border was Mexican or Central American was to perpetuate right-wing Republican conspiracy theories. Even a few of my FBI sources, albeit stationed far from the borderlands, dismissed them as unconfirmed.

The prayer rug rumors never panned out. But like footprints on a dusty trail, migrant trace evidence embodied by supposedly abandoned prayer rugs and Korans became irrelevant once I began meeting and interviewing real migrants who probably used such items back home. Curiosity generated leads that eventually led me to Brownsville, Texas, where after some bartering with an immigration attorney, I spent seven hours interviewing a Middle Eastern migrant who had crossed the border. His name was Aamir Bahnan Boles, a twenty-four-year-old Iraqi, and unlike the fabled prayer rugs, he was quite real. In subsequent years, I would meet, photograph, and videotape a great many more real-life SIA migrants who crossed the border and also on their way to it, Syrians, Bangladeshis, Iranians, Uzbeks, Lebanese, Jordanians, Saudis, and Pakistanis. But the meeting with Boles, a living, breathing, border-crossing Iraqi, started my own long journey of learning, literally. It took me to Syria and Jordan, Guatemala, Nicaragua, Panama, Costa Rica, and Mexico. I wrote a five-part series on SIA traffic, which was published in May 2007 and earned plaudits from the likes of the National Press Club and the Inter-American Press Association.

Iraqi war refugee Aamir Boles in 2007. Photo by Todd Bensman

Significantly to me at the time, my series was old news to members of the US homeland security establishment. Many were working on the supposed fable in full-time jobs. They were part of a far-flung counterterrorism campaign—at and south of the border—about which the American public knew nothing. Homeland security professionals who built and operated the programs, Democrat and Republican appointees and their presidents on both sides of the aisle, had access to often foreign intelligence information the general public never saw, by design, but which helps to explain the longevity of the covert American border war, with its fairly disparate components.

Eventually, I would work among those executing it. In 2009, I left my journalism career and joined the Texas Department of Public Safety's Intelligence and Counterterrorism Division, where I became a senior intelligence analyst.

Given a federal security clearance, I was stationed in the State of Texas's multiagency intelligence "fusion center" in Austin and worked with a dozen federal agencies' employees. Guided by my earlier journalism, I soon tracked down those stationed in different parts of the national homeland security enterprise who were working on the SIA migration issue. I discovered an informal "collective" of kindred subject matter experts in the military intelligence services, the FBI, Immigration and Customs Enforcement, and Customs and Border Protection. In time, I launched a program whereby my analysts would interview SIAs in ICE detention centers on our state's long border with Mexico, mining their recent experiences for intelligence and providing it to these federal agency partners working in the SIA game. I conducted many of the interviews myself, spending untold hours face-to-face with the actual migrants at the heart of this book.

A word about sourcing. Some of the information presented here derives from both journalism and intelligence universes. I draw some from my recollections and direct observation as an intelligence practitioner for nine years. Other material was shared by active-duty Intelligence Community colleagues after I left state service in 2018—provided verbally during interviews and from government documents on the condition that I protect their provenance from disclosure.

I mined the recollections of several former ranking homeland security officials who were there at the beginning of construction, so to speak. The bulk of this book is based on my pre– and post–law enforcement field reporting as a journalist from the smuggling routes and from the excavation of public records of all sorts that, only after being put together, paint the complete portrait. I collected one trove of public records while still in my intelligence job, studying for a Department of Homeland Security–sponsored master's degree from the Naval Postgraduate School's Center for Homeland Defense and Security. My unrestricted thesis about SIA smuggling drew from thousands of federal court prosecution records, all of them generated by the covert border war at the center of this book.

The thesis publication in September 2015 coincided with the long series of attacks by border-crossing jihadists who posed as migrants to enter Europe through its unguarded back gates. When President Trump's floated suggestions about border-crossing terrorists drew furled-eyebrow disbelief, laboratory-worthy land border infiltration by terrorists was happening right then, on an almost industrial scale. As will be detailed at length in Chapter One, it was happening to Europe, with inexplicably little public acknowledgment in the United States. The migrant-terrorists who upended America's closest allies did not only physically attack and kill; many engaged in nonviolent activities, like recruitment and the provision of material and intelligence support that made the attacking and killing possible. The reporting from Europe's terrorist border infiltration laboratory shows that the threat covers a broader variety of dangerous Islamist sympathizers and supporters who do not necessarily kill but who developed nations would always want to detect and repel with equal urgency. Some were mass murderers in hiding.

Europe's calamity struck me as powerful affirmation—tragic proof of concept—of what can happen when targeted Western societies fail to adequately recognize and prepare to manage this terrorism travel method when it happens. The tactic becomes not only calculable in body count but also as a present, ongoing danger unless recognized and arduously prepared for ahead of time because the bad guys tend to naturally repeat tactics that worked. The world is blessed—and cursed—with knowing now that terrorist infiltrations over the European Union's long external land and marine borders worked there, just as it will work at the US southern border should America's covert war falter under mocking disregard.

Small numbers and diminutive looks prove deceiving in the inexact art of calculating threat and risk. Between 100 and 150 terrorists and their helpful acolytes were among the three million migrants who stole over European borders during the 2014–2017 migrant crisis, the best research to date suggests. Those numbers may seem inauspicious at first blush, absent thought as to the vast damages they have wrought on almost every European institution. Remember that the 9/11 attacks required a mere nineteen al-Qaeda hijackers to kill some 3,000 people. But these few killers set off a cascading chain reaction of costs far beyond their initial victims. They cost the blood of thousands of soldiers, along with trillions of dollars fighting both foreign wars and managing future domestic homeland security risk.

Europe's catastrophic experience with terrorist border penetrations that happened during its migrant crisis, which resulted in years of attacks and plots that continued on through 2020, confirms that objects in the rearview mirror appear smaller than they are, posing outsized danger in their ongoing consequences. The impacts of these attacks, plots, and discoveries of hiding war criminals and terrorists who came over the borders with refugee-migrants extended far beyond mere body count in Europe; the relative handful of jihadists altered societies there just as dramatically as they did in America after 9/11. The wrong way to think about homeland security risk and threat is to conclude that smallness of number equates to smallness of threat, and especially the absence of attack, as the recent European experience shows so painfully. Yet this flawed reasoning has taken hold among American media and politicians, selectively, it seems, when it suits politically.

The small-numbers/big-consequences paradigm is not limited to terrorism, of course, and applies to risks such as pandemics. Though experts predicted COVID-19 would kill only a sliver of a percent of America's 350 million people, the entire nation sacrificed and suffered emotionally and economically to suppress a fractionally tiny body count when compared to total population. Like a pandemic, SIA migration happens out of sight and can too easily be put out of mind, catching unprepared, naïve, or overly idealistic government leaders flatfooted as it did in Europe. But those few of us who study the migration of SIAs will not be surprised when disaster next strikes or that the consequences of only a few will vastly outsize the initial footprint.

If it's fair to conclude Europe did not learn the lessons of September 11 until migrant jihadists struck widely there, neither has America learned the lessons of Europe since 2015.

If the past predicts the future, I expect pushback and challenge over the meaning of facts presented in this book. But after reading it, few should be able to deny the presence of a secret national counterterrorism project built to address terrorist border proliferation. This American enterprise was operating long before Trump arrived to tweet about its purpose and will need to go on long after he is gone—hence another purpose for this book: to show that the counterterrorism border project has suffered from denialism-related neglect and requires program-wide evaluation, repair, and reform to meet a threat that appears to be escalating. Significant holes in the net, or imperfections in the cordon, persist. These will be described in the following pages along with recommendations for improvement.

With government infrastructure to be described in the following pages built and working, the notion of the terrorist infiltration threat warrants an upgrade in the public discussion from outlandish or discreditable to a proper seat at the civil debate as to what should be done about it. This book, in staking a position that the machine America built has done its job incredibly well but needs an overhaul, is intended to serve at least the modest purpose of opening a normal discourse about it, without the hyperbole and denialism that has warped it on both sides of the partisan divide. The threat of terror travel over the US land borders is certainly not outlandish to homeland security professionals hard at work in classified shadows to keep the country safe from it. As this book will show, luck has been with them so far in preventing an attack. But all dice eventually roll up sevens.

CHAPTER ONE

PROOF OF CONCEPT: WEAPONIZED HUMAN PROLIFERATION IN EUROPE

We have sent many operatives to Europe with the refugees. Some of our brothers have fulfilled their mission, but others are still waiting to be activated.

—Islamic State commander in encrypted data service interview with the *Washington Post*, April 2016.[1]

Almost as soon as the bombs went off in Brussels on Tuesday morning, the new act of terrorism in the heart of Europe was employed in the bitter debate about the influx of migrants from the Middle East and North Africa. Even before the identities and nationalities of the attackers were known, there was an immediate association in popular discourse between the attacks…and the migrant crisis. Right-wing politicians and average citizens alike raised concerns that groups like the Islamic State…are slipping radicalized recruits…through the vast migrant stream and into unprepared Europe.

—Steven Erlanger, writing in the *New York Times*, March 2016.[2]

On November 13, 2015, just twelve weeks after Europe's leaders declared their countries open to millions of migrants and refugees from Muslim-majority nations like Syria and Iraq, teams of Islamic State terrorist operatives staged six coordinated suicide attacks throughout Paris. More than 130 concertgoers and restaurant patrons lay dead and at least 500 more were wounded in a panicking city, not to mention seven dead suicide bombers. In the rubble of the Stade de France, outside gate D, forensic investigators discovered a bloodied fake Syrian passport not far from one of the three dismembered suicide bombers who detonated themselves there.[3] Another fake Syrian identity document was discovered near the remains of another assailant at the Bataclan concert hall attack site.

Unbeknownst to anyone at that busy moment and still much of the world even now, the documents were the first hard evidence that a once hypothetical bogeyman, one often disparaged in the United States and Europe as not real, had just struck.

The dead suicide bombers, Islamic State operatives from Iraq, had carried the fake identification documents through the Greek island of Leros near the coast of Turkey, a touchpoint of the so-called Balkans Route migrant trail that saw hundreds of thousands pass northward to Hungary, then westward into Europe's heartlands.[4] And soon, there it was: Islamist terrorists had infiltrated land borders. They had done it to reach their targets undetected until they could kill. Almost all of the Paris attackers, it turned out, were part of a large cell that ISIS sent incognito among the hundreds of thousands of migrants moving away from Middle East wars, "Arab Springs," and ruined states.[5] Just four months later, in March 2016, surviving Paris attack cell members who stowed themselves inside the mass migration Trojan Horse, ironically into Greece first and then a long overland journey through the Balkans and Hungary, conducted three suicide bombings in Brussels, Belgium, which killed 32 and injured 320 more.[6]

Their attacks in Paris and Brussels revealed in the first public way that terrorist operatives had reached their targets by posing as smuggled refugees who sneaked in over the land borders camouflaged well among greater numbers of the benevolent. But actually, ISIS had been sending in murderous operatives among the migrants nearly two years earlier. These earlier migrant-terrorists had entirely escaped public reporting or official recognition, and so barriers—physical and political—to the many attacks to come later in Paris, Brussels, and many more besides remained in lowered position.

Among the earliest missed clues that ISIS was sending its operatives into the migrant flow came on January 3, 2014, long before Paris in November 2015 and Brussels in March 2016. Greek police pulled over a taxi in the town of Oresteia and found twenty-three-year-old French citizen Ibrahim Boudina, who grew up in Cannes, France, and was returning among the migrants from fighting the jihad with ISIS in Syria.[7] The Greeks found a French-language manual in Boudina's luggage titled *How to Make Artisanal Bombs in the Name of Allah.*

The Greeks released him but let French intelligence know of the encounter. Boudina couldn't just fly home under his own name; he was already on a French terrorism watch list, and his family and friends in Cannes were under surveillance, the *New York Times* much later reported. Several weeks after his release in Greece, Boudina's mother received a phone call from Syria informing her that her son had been "sent on a mission."

It turned out that this mission was to conduct bombings on the French Riviera, where he arrived to link up with other extremists known as the "Cannes-Torcy group."[8] One fellow traveler on the migrant trail from Syria apparently never made it: Abdelkader Tilba, who had fought alongside Boudina in Syria. The battlefield comrades had joined the jihad together, fought, and were to reconnect back home in Europe for the planned French Riviera attacks. But thirteen days after Boudina's tangle with Greek police, on January 16, 2014, Italian port officials in the town of Acona arrested Tilba after an identity check. This led police the next month, in February 2014, to surround the Boudina family apartment near Cannes and bust him. Inside they found Red Bull soda cans filled with 600 grams of TATP, a signature ISIS explosive that would later be used in Paris and Brussels.

About a year later, on January 15, 2015, the remainder of Boudina's crew was on the verge of carrying out a sophisticated plan to dress in police uniforms, attack Belgian police stations, and ambush officers on patrol. Instead, police were able to preemptively storm a hideout in Verviers. A fierce gun battle broke out, during which two of the terrorists died and a third was severely wounded. Anti-terrorism police recovered stockpiles of automatic rifles, explosives, communications equipment, and the police uniforms that were to be worn.[9]

In the United States at the time and now too, these organized terrorist border infiltrations, rather than the old method of flying into international airports on various kinds of visas, somehow passed barely acknowledged, the idea was marginalized as an anti-immigrant xenophobic trope favored by right-wingers to demonize foreigners and migration generally.

Since a terrorist border infiltration from international migration routes had never happened, it *could* not and also maybe should not warrant attention, or so the reasoning went.[10] But the Cannes-Torcy plots, and the Paris and Brussels attacks, realizations of a long-mythologized form of terrorist mobility, were just the beginning.

The worst was yet to come from the terrorist border infiltrators, years more and to the present, of stunning gore, fear, and drama in a dozen European countries as migrant terrorists attacked well-intentioned hosts who had welcomed all who got over the borders to resettle. White-knuckle fear rippled through European Union populations for years to the present. Life for hundreds of millions contended with sudden running gun battles in the streets anywhere and anytime, with hours-long sieges, funeral processions, public trials featuring handcuffed migrants, hysterical witnesses on television, garlands of flowers at slaughter scenes, and concrete barricades that transformed major cities from one end of the continent to the other into seemingly permanent securitized green zones.

Other house guests who defied the popularly imagined caricatures of the desperately needy migrant came in over the border from the trails, hiding histories as war criminals, perpetrators of barbaric atrocities, slavers, kidnappers, ethnic cleansers, executioners, and indoctrinated terrorist operatives with hard combat experience.

For years, precious few national security professionals and academics have explicitly acknowledged that long-haul migration and terrorist border infiltration of developed Western nations had happened on an unremitting scale not experienced in contemporary times. As a result, few have yet even to study and mine the extraordinary experience for homeland security lessons or as a new prism through which to view international migration in a more balanced way.

Not until four more bloody years after Paris did any terrorism scholar, Sam Mullins in this case, then of the George C. Marshall European Center for Security Studies in Germany, get around to mounting a first quantitative tally of the phenomenon, a baseline necessary for future study that still has yet to happen. The landmark Mullins snapshot study found that at least 140 border-crossing refugees and migrants, likely an undercount, migrated across the borders, gamed asylum systems, and carried out attacks that killed and maimed over a thousand Europeans between the Arab Spring uprisings of 2011 to 2018.[11] Among the 140 in the Mullins count were dozens of foiled plots in addition to those that ended with spilled blood. My own Center for Immigration Studies tally published a few months later in 2019, of the shorter but headier 2014–2018 period of the migrant crisis, identified a likely undercounted 104 border-crossing migrant terrorists, terrorist sympathizers and supporters of the cause, and war criminals who exploited asylum systems.[12] My study found that approximately 27 formed a single large cell of trained operatives deployed by ISIS's "External Operations Division" into the migration flows to conduct the French and Belgium attacks, as well as others.[13]

Both Mullins's study and my own confirmed 2018 research by Heritage Foundation scholar Robin Simcox in establishing an equally nefarious, if complementary, tactic exploited by these undesirable guests: Europe's legal asylum systems proved indispensable to the success of these migratory terrorists.[14] The jihadists systematically exploited an overwhelmed, backlogged European asylum system, not unlike the one used by the United States, to achieve entry, temporary legal status, and ample time to set up attacks and plots. My own study found that asylum processes provided an average of eleven months of freedom and public assistance support for fifty-five jihadist migrants. Conversely, the systems ferreted out no terrorist links; they seemed designed only to usher them in, characteristics of the American asylum system that I will describe at greater length in Chapter Four.

AN UNRELENTING ASSAULT BY BORDER INFILTRATION

Attacks, plots, and arrests of terrorist border infiltrators never let up after Mullins, Simcox, and I published our numbers in 2018 and 2019. The terror blazed its way well through 2020 and throughout the writing of this book. It went on (our terrible initial numbers ever rising) despite Europe's many efforts to reduce overall mass migration flows from Muslim-majority countries, the idea being that this would also reduce the seedling terror threat it carried. But nothing seemed to bring relief to the beleaguered continent.

One of the 2020 cases almost brought the issue home to the American public in tragic fashion. In April of that year, German authorities arrested five Tajik migrant asylum seekers organized by senior ISIS operatives to attack two US Air Force bases. They had used their asylum statuses to best advantage: the five had entered Germany as refugees and claimed asylum, which provided the time and cover for them to acquire machine guns, ammunition, bomb-building instructions, and explosive materials.[15] The men had joined ISIS in January 2019 and were directed by ISIS commanders from afar—a so-called "remote-control" operation—for what was clearly envisioned as a mass-casualty event. But since American service members were spared, how the Tajikistani plotters had gotten so close to them, using a newly minted terror-travel tactic, went largely unnoticed yet again.

Despite Europe's successful efforts to reduce the human flows and also the poisons within it, terrorists continued to disguise themselves as migrants and get through the cordons, even the most wanted terrorists among them. In April 2020, three years after the migrant crisis ended, Spanish police arrested the so-called "ISIS Rapper" Abdel-Majed Abdel Bary, an Egyptborn British subject who once posted a photograph of himself holding a severed head in Syria and whose father had bombed American embassies in Africa in 1998. Fortunately, they caught Bary several days after he arrived in Spain on a wooden migrant boat carrying a bogus Algerian passport, the days plenty of time for him and the two jihadists with whom he was hiding out to have done some damage.[16]

Other Europeans weren't so lucky in 2020. Also that April, a Sudanese asylum seeker granted French residency in June 2017 on an asylum claim struck his benefactors in the seaside town of Romans-sur-Isére.[17] Police arrested Abdallah Ahmed-Osman on his knees praying to Allah following a knife rampage during which he allegedly was shouting "Allahu Akbar" as he stabbed to death two passersby and slashed eight more on the street. Authorities found writings at the assailant's home in which he complained of living in a "country of disbelievers."[18]

The march of attacks from 2014 onward proved unremitting. In August 2020, an Iraqi asylum seeker thought to have radicalized while living in a Berlin refugee center "purposefully hunted" motorcyclists in a Opel Astra sedan, crushing two riders and severely injuring three passengers in another car while bulldozing one of the motorbikes into it.[19] The thirty year-old

Iraqi identified as "Sarmad A." gave German anti-terrorism investigators plenty of reason to initially conclude he harbored an "Islamist motive" for the attack, despite past psychological treatment. Initial reporting had it that Sarmad allegedly shouted "Allahu Akbar" during his attack, laid a prayer rug on the street, and began praying afterward.[20] He also maintained a Facebook page where he supported ISIS and seemed to foretell that he planned to become a martyr in a way that involved a car.

A NEW TERROR TACTIC IS BORN AND HERE TO STAY

Terrorist border infiltration must now be regarded as an established—and highly dangerous—new method of surprise attack on the global stage that will not go away anytime soon because, simply, it works too well. The method is as cynically underhanded as any terrorist could conceive in that it derives great tactical advantage from camouflaging malevolent travelers within numerically greater benevolent ones. Most deviously, the tactic exploits almost natural host-nation compulsions to welcome those camouflaging noncombatants out of humanitarian sentiment and overriding reluctance to ever regard suffering migrants, crying on televisions and computer screens, as potentially dangerous. The jihadist infiltrations in Europe did eventually taint the camouflaging human herd in much the same way that migrant advocates and agribusiness interests in the United States fear would happen to Spanish-speaking migrants.

Europe's face-off with both camouflaged terrorists and camouflaging non-terrorists presents a laboratory-perfect opportunity to dissect a modern-day Trojan Horse, how it was built and used.

For the United States, Europe's ongoing contortions under the onslaught should have spoken loudly as proof of concept: Migrants known in government parlance as "special interest aliens" from the very same countries, though in lower volumes, flow continuously over the southern border and over the northern border from Canada too. Jihadists are among them here the same as they were in Europe, as these pages will reveal.

The following questions should finally be viewed as fair and reasonable in light of the ongoing European experience: Could organized terror groups or lone terrorist entrepreneurs replicate the success they had to have seen in Europe? Could they too walk across the US land border, also game the highly similar US asylum system, and devise ways to slaughter their hosts in their own home on their own timetables? How does the institution of American homeland security even think about this threat? But as the Trump example so profoundly demonstrated, answers to questions like these are to be drowned out by professed outrage that they would even be asked.

To answer questions like these—and this book very much will—first requires acknowledgment and comprehension of what, exactly, happened to Europe, how terrorist border infiltrations and years of fear and chaos felt and looked like after those first Paris attacks in November 2015 revealed that this long-feared tactic was no longer a theoretical notion favored by far-right political parties. It was actually happening.

Differences obviously exist between the United States and Europe—in distances that must be traversed by commercial aircraft, the higher associated expenses and risk of detection, and ever-shifting geopolitical situations in transit countries—and must be reflected in any comparative risk analysis. But many of the main factors that enabled Europe's costly catastrophe with migrant terrorist infiltrators bear a striking resemblance to the American circumstance as 2021 gives way to the future.

Chief among the similarities to keep in mind as Europe's experience becomes clear below are asylum systems that seem almost engineered to *usher in* jihadists rather than to deter and detect their many easy frauds. Also worth keeping in mind is an inherent inability of the American system to confidently learn the hearts, minds, and backgrounds of strangers arriving from often anti-American cultures in countries with stone-age information systems. Perhaps the most important similarity is the liberal progressive politics of virtue that embrace mass migration, that are insistently unmoored from security considerations, automatically regarded as racist, and that are always eager to wave the migrant caravans through with all benefit of doubt.

MAYHEM AT GROUND ZERO: GERMANY

They (ISIS) have taken advantage of, to some extent, the migrant crisis in Europe, something which the nations have a growing awareness of.

—James Clapper, US Director of National Intelligence, appointed by President Barack Obama, speaking at a *Christian Science Monitor* breakfast April 25, 2016.[21]

All of the previous year, 2014, the mass migration from the Islamic world had penetrated the twenty-seven-member European Union's common external land and sea borders and were pooling up inside member countries. Their numbers had been rising from various Arab Springs, Syria's war, and general economic malaise in Afghanistan, the Horn of Africa, the Caucuses, and throughout sub-Saharan Africa. Tens of thousands were backed up at a dam of the EU's wealthiest interior countries, like Germany, asking for asylum and building tension for an answer to the question: Will Europe let them in or turn them back?

An EU rule known as "the Dublin Agreement" required that those seeking international protections request it in the first EU country they entered. Hungary, Poland, and Italy, as the first countries many of these refugees transited, were not only less generous and welcoming but had less-developed economies. Would Germany and other wealthier interior EU nations throw them back to those first transit countries was the big question that, on August 24, 2015, German Chancellor Angela Merkel answered. Her words were heard throughout the Muslim world: Germany will take one million.

Embedded in her explanation was that this was a progressive, new, virtuous Germany that, pointedly *unlike* the old one, felt empathy toward suffering humankind and would boldly accept religious and racial diversity. The spillway was opened. Millions poured through to join the tens of thousands who had already pooled up at the borders.[22] The media punditocracy amply rewarded Merkel for this, her repudiation of old Germany's ideal of citizenship as rooted in one race, blood birthright, language, and religion.[23]

Time magazine's naming of Merkel as Person of the Year in December 2015 was emblematic of the sentiment.[24] The magazine regaled her decision as "astounding" in that "the most generous, openhearted gesture of recent history blossomed from Germany, the country that within living memory blew apart the European continent and then the world by taking to gruesome extremes all the forces its Chancellor strives to hold in check: Nationalism, nativism, self-righteousness, reversion to arms."

Scattered warnings about importing a terrorism threat over the borders, mostly from conservative politicians and their parties, were quickly brushed off as the xenophobia Merkel meant to vanquish.[25] A senior official of Hungary's right-of-center nationalist government, which strongly opposed the move, for instance, complained that Germany sought to impose "moral imperialism" and that "the Germans think they're the Americans of Europe."[26] The reference to the United States, of course, harkened to fairly widespread political tolerance among Democrats of similar mass migration over the American southern border.

Merkel doubled down on the open-doors policy even days after the Paris attacks.[27]

"The strongest response to terrorists is to carry on living our lives and our values as we have until now—self-confident and free, considerate and engaged," Merkel said during a forty-minute speech to the Bundestag's lower house, to prolonged applause just days after the Paris attacks.[28]

A kind of border-shaming ensued as reporters put other European leaders to the virtue test, pressing the question: Would they, too, rise to the occasion, lower the drawbridge, and demonstrate a humanitarian embrace to a watching world? Or would they showcase the intolerant, cruel, white tribalism of Old World Europe? Under this glare of virtue expectation, Sweden, Austria, Finland, France, and other wealthy nations followed suit in a kind of herd-think, their leaders averse to social condemnations that would follow should they fail to prioritize selfless tolerance over selfish security.

Very soon after Europe let three million resettle, ominous clues began to surface as to the true feelings many of the migrants privately harbored about their eager hosts.

"She gives us food only so that we can turn against the Muslims," the boy identified only as "Mohammed J.," in line with European privacy laws, posted on his social media about the German leader some were calling "Mother Merkel," or "the Refugee Chancellor."[29] "Surround and kill the unbelievers" was how Mohammad planned to return the favors of his kindly hosts.

Mohammed had traveled with his parents and sister from Damascus, then Lebanon, and from there to Turkey, where the family caught a smuggler's boat for the journey over the Aegean Sea to Greece. From there, the family followed the surging humanity along the same route the Paris and Brussels bombers took. With some variation, the infamous "Balkans Route" from Greece took a majority of the terrorist-migrants through Macedonia, Serbia, Croatia, Hungary, Slovenia, and Austria, and then into more prosperous interior nations of the EU. Eventually, Hungary would spoil the party when it put up electrified fencing along its border, drawing widespread condemnation from the other EU partners but also, unbeknownst to them and completely unappreciated later, ending one of the most trammeled of the terrorist travel routes.

Housed in a city of Cologne refugee center, Mohammed spent his time chatting online with an ISIS recruiter back in Syria named "Bilal" and searching the internet for shops that sold swords, the phrase "we kill German people," and also "military airport in Cologne." By September 2016, he had amassed sewing needles for shrapnel, a battery holder, 700 grams of gunpowder from legal fireworks, 300 grams of sulfur, and butane gas cartridges. Police came for him at his mosque before he could strike, after he wrote on his Facebook page, "My future, God willing, will be in heaven, in paradise with the martyrs."

Having taken in more migrants than most of Europe, Germany suffered the brunt of attacks and plots. The killing, plotting, and trauma of the ongoing surprise attacks, after Paris and Brussels, spread across Germany with migrant resettlement distribution and went on for years, to the present day. They varied widely in tactics, sophistication, scope, and casualties. They did not always involve deployed operatives; often, the attackers qualified as lone offenders. Sometimes, like in the case involving the five Tajikistanis in April 2020 planning to attack American military targets, they formed small cells directed from afar, "remote-control" affairs.

Those to be described here are representative, rather than comprehensive, to provide a sense of how it happened—and what it would look like if even some of this happened on American soil.

Some attacks were globally reported (though almost never how the perpetrators arrived), such as the 2016 pre-Christmas vehicle ramming attack on a Berlin Christmas market by Anis Amri, a Tunisian failed asylum seeker who killed twelve and injured dozens more. Amri had illegally entered the

EU in 2011 by posing as an underage refugee on a smuggler's migrant boat that landed initially on Italy's resort island of Lampedusa.[30] He did what he did for the global jihad while Germany dithered on deporting him. Police later shot him dead following a dramatic car chase.

But the majority of plots and attacks, like the one by Mohammed J. in Cologne, inexplicably dodged international notoriety and broader realization that something new and different was afoot in the world.

From 2014 through 2018, German antiterrorism police snared eighteen other migrant jihadists for eleven distinct attack plots that envisioned the use of bombs, axes, knives, guns, and motor vehicles, and which were thwarted. Among the migrants who got into Germany and killed, tried to kill, or helped to kill was Mohammad Daleel, a twenty-seven-year-old Syrian asylum seeker who would claim the mantle as Germany's first jihadist suicide bomber—blowing himself up and injuring fifteen at a Bavarian wine bar—and whom ISIS claimed as a sleeper.

Daleel, a burly, fit young soldier of Allah who asked friends at the refugee center to call him "Rambo," had trekked the Balkans Route from Turkey to Greece before making his way north to Bulgaria and then over to Germany. ISIS later claimed it deployed him for the attack. Nine days before Germany planned to deport him back to Bulgaria, where he had been found to have already applied for asylum, Daleel videotaped a message on his cell phone pledging allegiance to ISIS and explaining that his martyrdom operation was for "revenge" against German participation in allied operations against ISIS. He blew himself up, along with fifteen patrons at the bar he picked.

Shortly after Daleel's "martyrdom," twenty-six-year-old Palestinian asylum seeker Ahmad Alhaw waged a bloody "Allahu Akbar" knifing spree in a supermarket in July 2017, killing a fifty-year-old German man and slashing a fifty-year-old woman and four other men who tried to stop him. Alhaw was living in a Hamburg refugee shelter pending a deportation to the West Bank territory.

Hamburg's mayor, Olaf Scholz, seemed surprised and angry that "the attacker is someone who sought protection here in Germany and then turned his hate against us."[31]

He should not have been surprised, not by then. Antiterrorism police were perpetually frantic. Headlines about attacks and plots, not just in Germany but elsewhere in Europe, were generating hundreds of new terrorism tips and leads about the migrants. Alhaw had been on a German list of radicalized potential terrorist suspects that quickly reached 800—just in Mayor Scholz's Hamburg and surrounding area.[32] As of 2017, Germany's domestic intelligence service was estimating the national list of radical Islamist suspects at 1,600, up from a mere 100 three years earlier.[33] The police couldn't catch them all.

Mohammed Riyadh, a.k.a. Riaz Khan Ahmadzai, used a knife and axe to slash twenty trapped passengers inside a moving Bavarian commuter train after writing his father, "Now pray for me that I can take revenge on these infidels, and that I go to heaven."[34] Riyadh had traveled the Balkans Route behind the Paris and Brussels attackers, though he was apparently a lone freelancer and not deployed like his predecessors. By most accounts, he was the perfect sleeper.

Riyadh was adjusting well, having been placed in a German foster home as an unaccompanied minor who claimed to be seventeen and fleeing the Afghan war.[35] (Minors and refugees from known war zones got special asylum consideration and public benefits.) He played soccer with locals and went to school. A local bakery had given him an internship. He liked to go on rides around the serene Bavarian town of Ochsenfurt, population 11,000, on the bicycle given to him by a kindly group of refugee assistance volunteers in town.

However, in the privacy of the bedroom his foster family assigned him, the teenager marinated in a pungent hatred for all those infidel Germans around him. In there, he cultivated a double life online featuring ISIS propaganda and ideology. The name he gave on his asylum application (Riaz Khan Ahmadzai) was fake and so was the country he claimed as home; he was actually from Pakistan, a country not as likely as Afghanistan to justify the asylum Riyadh was granted.[36] His personal history had been easy to obscure in the crush of humanity that carried him over the border with hundreds of thousands of Afghans, a testament to the vulnerability that nations accommodate in accepting complete strangers who arrive at their borders with unverifiable tales of woe.

An unaccompanied sixteen-year-old minor given the name "Jawad S." arrived in the migrant river in November 2015 and was assigned by his German hosts to a center for other parentless refugee youths in the small village of Piesport. German authorities had rejected his asylum claim in August 2017, and he reportedly turned out to be older than he claimed, but he was allowed to stay while his appeal worked its way through the system.

He hopped a train to Amsterdam, got off, and stabbed two American tourists at the central train station, apparently chosen at random. Police shot and wounded Jawad, who survived to tell his interrogators he chose that country to attack because there "the Prophet Muhammad, the Koran, Islam and Allah are often offended."[37] The Americans recovered.

Over a year, ISIS dispatched a four-man attack squad to Germany. They were Syrian nationals—Salah A., Hamza C., Abd Arahman A.K., and Mahood B.—who had fought for ISIS in Syria. First into the migrant caravans went the crew's explosives man, Abd Arahman A.K. in October 2014.[38] He set off from Turkey through the Balkans to Germany after completing an extensive explosives training course for the mission.

Following their bomb man, separately, in March and July of 2015 were Salah A. (sometimes reported as "Saleh A.") and Hamza C., also along the Balkans Route (the journey took Hamza two months). ISIS leadership sent them "to kill as many passersby as possible" in Dusseldorf's trendy downtown, prosecutors later said. Bringing up the rear, in January 2016, was Mahood B., who made his way in among the migrants too. All dutifully applied for German asylum. And while they waited, they plotted the attack from their respective refugee centers. The plan was for two of the bombers to detonate on the Heinrich-Heine-Allee, Dusseldorf's version of the Champs-Elysée. Then, the other attackers were to fire their automatic weapons and throw grenades at those fleeing. But Salah A. experienced a serendipitous change of heart while visiting Paris. He turned himself in to police and told them everything.[39] Police promptly arrested the others. But this had been a close call.

By the middle of 2016, a national German counterterrorism task force, part intelligence and part boots-on-ground assault brigade, had strengthened to more than 200 officers. It roved the nation hunting migrant terrorists. It broke up other such plots, several to bomb targets in Berlin. In August 2016, for instance, the brigades picked off Syrian national Khaled H. in a refugee center among 700 other asylum seekers.[40] Khaled was a former ISIS fighter deployed into the migrant flows with a mission to conduct a "spectacular atrocity" on a crowded German sports stadium. Khaled had traveled the Balkans Route.

Other migrant-terrorist plots broken up in time included one to shoot up the Russian embassy in Berlin for Russia's support of Syria's Assad regime, and yet another one to bomb Cologne.

Some of the migrant jihadists were stone-cold killers; others, like "Bilal C.," did the indispensable groundwork that made the killing happen.

The Algerian-born ISIS fighter watched the Paris attack he enabled from Germany, where he had settled and applied for asylum just months before. He started fighting for ISIS in 2014, and when the group decided to migrate teams of killers into Europe that year, he became one of the cell's chief scouts. He ranged far ahead of the pack to locate the best refugee travel routes to safe houses in Belgium, to note shifting border openings, border control procedures, security presences, wait times, and smuggling opportunities.[41] Bilal C. sent all this back to the Paris cell's ringleader, who would lead much of the actual smuggling along the routes Bilal identified.[42]

From June to August 2015, Bilal traveled widely, spotting and ironing out best ways forward—and also reverse-engineering overland routes back to Syria. He explored from Syria to Greece and up the Balkans Route through Hungary and into Austria, sending back the topographic information necessary for the teams to know where to go and how. He remained under the radar until his July 2016 arrest, likely in the country on a German residency permit.

Bilal's return routes proved useful later too. One who used it from Germany was Ahmad Alkhald, the cell's "explosives chief" who built all the suicide bomb belts used in the Paris and Brussels attacks.[43] Alkhald originally entered Europe in September 2015 by posing as a refugee migrating via the Greek island of Leros and then up through the Balkans to Hungary and then Austria and Germany.[44] Alkhald spent some time under the noses of German authorities, probably incognito as a Syrian asylum seeker since he had a fake Syrian passport of the sort all the team members had. Shortly before the Paris attacks, Alkhald met with key cell leaders in the city of Ulm. And it was from Ulm that the explosives chief used Bilal's return route to get back into Syria. His whereabouts for international arrest warrants in connection with the Paris attacks remained unknown as of this writing.[45]

The German counterterrorism task force went on disrupting migrant-terror plots into 2019 and 2020, like the arrest of three Iraqi refugees in Dithmarschen, near the border with Denmark, on January 30, 2020. The refugees had carried out test explosions using nine ounces of gunpowder they'd extracted from fireworks, a familiar source by now, and ordered a detonator from a British contact in allegedly preparing a car-bomb attack on an unspecified German location.[46] British law enforcement intercepted the detonator.

Other malevolent migrants slipped the task force's desperate grasps, like the Syrian who in October 2019, perhaps hoping to replicate Anis Amri's Christmas market attack of a few years earlier, hijacked a lorry in Frankfurt and ploughed it hard and repeatedly into vehicles at a traffic light, critically injuring eight people.

From the time of Amri's terrible 2016 Christmas market truck-ramming attack through the summer of 2020, German authorities foiled a dozen other vehicle–ramming attacks, including two in November 2019.[47] German police thwarted a biological bomb attack in June 2018 by a Tunisian migrant linked to ISIS. As of the summer of 2020, the number of Islamists considered dangerous in Germany had increased five-fold since 2013 to stand at 680. The number of conservative Salafist Muslims in the country stood at an estimated 11,000—twice as many as in 2013.[48]

THE SPREADING CANCER: FRANCE

Within this mix, ISIL…is spreading like a cancer, taking advantage of paths of least resistance, threatening European nations and our own with terrorist attacks.

—Air Force Gen. Philip M. Breedlove,
NATO Supreme Allied Commander for Europe
and Commander of US European Command,
speaking of the migration flows before the Senate
Armed Services Committee, March 1, 2016.[49]

Few EU countries were entirely immune from attacks and plot tries, from Poland in the east to Great Britain in the west and from Sweden in the north to Spain in the south. For a time, many took advantage of the Schengen Area's permissive absence of border checks to move among countries once inside on claims for asylum and refugee status. The Schengen Area, or "zone," which generally encompasses the European Union, consists of two dozen countries that in 1995 agreed to combine internal and external immigration enforcement and strategies. The Schengen Zone treaty agreement eliminated internal border controls, such as passport and commerce checks for member citizens, to facilitate interior economic activity, while creating one common external border of 27,000 sea miles and 5,500 land miles.[50] Think interstate travel within the United States. Between just 2014 and 2017, the thirteen member states lining just the zone's external land borders recorded more than 2.5 million detections of illegal border crossings along several land and sea routes during the migrant crisis.[51] In 2016, once the European members realized the Paris and Brussels attackers had exploited this internal border laxity to plot and equip those attacks with lethal munitions, seven of the countries reimposed border controls for the first time since the agreement was penned two decades earlier.[52] Many of the border controls remained through 2020 so as not to so easily enable terrorist planning.

Despite whatever he knew of how the Cannes-Torcy group operatives reached France in early 2014, French President François Hollande was unhesitatingly quick to show his "solidarity" with Merkel on the refugee issue. Amid thousands of his constituents demonstrating in cities around France, carrying banners such as "refugees welcome," the French president proudly announced his country would take 100,000 migrants and more later. No less than France's image and standing in the world were at stake, he explained.[53]

"Everyone must understand: you can't ask for solidarity when there's a problem and then exempt yourself from doing your duty when there's a solution," Hollande said.

Whether the knowledge about how the Cannes-Torcy terrorists traveled reached Hollande, Merkel, or other European leaders before they opened the gates is not known. Perhaps their intelligence agencies never realized a Trojan Horse was inside the wire or, if they did, failed to send word up. Or maybe leaders chose to dismiss these as insignificant outlier events.

But more were coming or were already in, even as these leaders spoke. Many of these early infiltrators were European-born citizens of France and Belgium who had illegally joined the ISIS fight and could not return openly because of warrants for their arrests, terror watch-listings, or convictions in absentia. That's why they chose the almost perfect cover of fake war refugees.

The cell's boss and planning mastermind was a Belgian-Moroccan named Abdelhamid Abaaoud who held rank in ISIS's external operations division. The young man from the Molenbeek district of Brussels could never have simply flown home to Belgium in any normal way, not after a gruesome ISIS propaganda video showed him driving a pickup truck dragging mutilated bodies through an occupied Syrian village. Or after he recruited his thirteen-year-old brother to join him in Syria (who would die in one of the Paris attacks).[54]

Dodging an international arrest warrant, Abaaoud returned undercover among the migrants in probably mid-2014 by traveling through Greece and up the Balkans Route and then to his home country of Belgium. He spent his time there organizing a cell of returned jihadists of European citizenship who'd likewise camouflaged among the migrants returning from Syria. Into France and neighboring Belgium, Austria, and Germany, Abaaoud imported jihadists on the migrant trail, even picking up some at the Budapest train station himself and driving them back to Belgium apartments he had rented with ISIS cash. He nurtured his crew. He saw to it that they had some of that money to live on while they built their bombs, stockpiled automatic weapons and ammunition, and steeled themselves for an elaborate campaign of terror on France for participating in a coalition air war against ISIS. It was a boon that the 1995 Schengen Zone agreement's abolition of internal borders allowed him to drive at will over international borders, with never a papers or vehicle check coming or going, to organize the team and their weapons.

Among those Abaaoud personally escorted from Syria all the way to Belgium for a non-Paris attack was Ayoub el-Khazzani, a twenty-five-year-old Moroccan who, within a few weeks of his arrival in August 2015, would attempt a massacre on the high-speed Paris-to-Amsterdam train. El-Khazzani had legally lived mainly in Spain, a hashish pusher, but also hustled a meager living in Germany, Belgium, and, for eight or nine months, France. In 2014, he, like Abaaoud, was among hundreds of young Muslim European men who answered the local mosque calls to fight with ISIS in Syria. Since el-Khazzani ended up on the radar of Spanish intelligence services and could no longer return the normal way, he and Abaaoud traveled the migration route together among refugees moving from Turkey into Greece and then the Balkans.[55] They reached Hungary and headed toward Belgium, later telling a court that Abaaoud had ordered him to conduct an attack once he got there.[56]

Some three weeks into his sojourn in Brussels, el-Khazzani boarded the Paris-bound train armed with a Kalashnikov assault rifle, 270 rounds of ammunition, a Luger pistol, a bottle of gasoline, a box cutter, and a hammer. He entered the passenger car bathroom, took off his shirt, and slung the rifle over a shoulder. He then exited and launched what he hoped would be a mass murder. Instead, three American tourists, two of them off-duty US servicemen, spotted el-Khazzani, wrestled him to the ground, and held him for police despite their own wounds.[57] The Hollywood actor and film producer Clint Eastwood would later make a movie lionizing their heroics, *The 15:17 to Paris.*

Ignorance about all this among Europe's leaders, if that is what it was, would be short-lived. Just two months out from his speech declaring the country a resettlement zone for migrants, the Paris attacks having exposed the border infiltrations, Hollande had to declare a state of emergency, and the pattern of border infiltration could no longer be denied or entirely ignored.

Abaaoud and his remaining cell members weren't long for the world. After his imported team carried out the Paris attacks, he went on the run. One night, Abaaoud met a relative in a field and confided that he had imported ninety jihadists on the migrant trails and that they were now "scattered" throughout Europe. Five days after the Paris attacks, police tracked Abaaoud to a Saint-Denis suburb apartment building north of Paris and tried to take him.[58] But Abaaoud and two other jihadists in the apartment opened up with automatic weapons. In the wild daylight gun battle of the densely populated suburb, police got the upper hand and killed Abaaoud and his two fellow jihadists. Five police officers were wounded.

The following weeks, months, and—significantly—*years* featured similarly chaotic public scenes of extreme violence. Militarized French police foiled a number of attacks in the nick of time, staging dramatic raids, blocking off streets, and diverting traffic to make seventy-five arrests and to jail twenty-eight suspects through the spring of 2016 and beyond.[59]

Terrorist plots, small-scale attacks, and war criminals who came in on the migrant trails may have slowed in pace over the years but nevertheless continued to torment parts of Europe. On October 1, 2017, a Tunisian jihadist with a fresh residence permit, screaming "Allahu Akbar," took a long knife to two young women in front of the Saint-Charles train station in the Mediterranean port city of Marseille. The women were cousins in their twenties. Both died bloody deaths in front of a crowd of screaming, running people. A police patrol who heard the screaming responded and shot the assailant dead on the spot.[60]

Police later identified the attacker as twenty-nine-year-old Ahmed Hanachi. The investigation resulted in the arrests of a brother, Anis Hanachi, in Switzerland as well as another brother in Italy. Police found that Anis arrived in Europe through Italy on a migrant boat in 2014. He was deported back to Tunisia but joined ISIS in Syria after that and then came back to Europe.[61] After his brother's train station attack in Marseille, police found Anis under a false name, claiming to be Algerian. The public record is unclear about how he returned, but police caught him riding a bicycle in Ferrara, Italy, near the Adriatic coast after French authorities issued an international arrest warrant. He undoubtedly got into the country under cover of migration. When Italian police found him, he provided a false name, claimed to be Algerian, and was living at the time with a Tunisian.

French Secretary of State for the Interior Laurent Nunez told local media that antiterror police forces thwarted sixty attacks from the beginning of 2014 through the end of 2019.[62] That tally has only risen since then. In January 2020, French antiterrorism police raids in and around Brest netted seven alleged ISIS-pledged jihadists, ages sixteen through thirty-eight. All were suspected of plotting an attack on unspecified targets and were to flee to Iraq and Syria afterward. At the heart of the cell was a thirty-five-year-old Syrian migrant identified as Mohammad, who arrived in France in 2015 and obtained refugee status a few months later.[63] Shortly after the Paris attacks, police on heightened alert arrested Mohammad for having mimicked an automatic weapon firing on a passing police patrol, a case that earned him a three-year suspended prison sentence in 2018.

No matter, with asylum, he left prison free to plot real attacks.[64]

THE HAPPIEST COUNTRIES IN THE WORLD

ISIS has been innovative and determined in its pursuit of attacks in the West. The group has exploited weaknesses in European border security to great effect by capitalizing on the migrant crisis to seed attack operatives into the region… Further, ISIS is continuing its efforts to circumvent European efforts to shore up border security by identifying new routes. Europe's struggle to screen the people crossing its borders highlights the importance of ensuring strong

United States borders so that terrorists cannot enter the United States. As defeated fighters and their families disperse, the United States and our partners must remain vigilant to ensure that terrorists cannot evade our security measures to threaten our people and way of life.

—National Strategy for Counterterrorism of
the United States of America, October 2018.[65]

The sparsely populated Nordic country of Finland, spared jihadist attacks so far off the beaten track, suffered its first one after agreeing to double the number of asylum seekers in 2015, from 15,000 to 30,000, many of them Iraqis. Finnish Prime Minister Juha Sipilä told his people that Finland was obliged to set an example to the rest of Europe on migration and even offered one of his own houses to migrants.[66]

"We should all take a look in the mirror and ask how we can help," the prime minister told an interviewer. As those in favor of multiculturalism marched for the migrants in Finnish cities, Sipilä tweeted that he wanted to "develop Finland as an open, linguistically and culturally international country."[67]

In 2016, and with the Paris and Brussels attacks fresh on the books, Finland took on even more migrants—65,000 asylum applications by year's end.[68] Among them was Abderrahman Bouanane Mechkah, a twenty-two-year-old Moroccan asylum seeker (initially reported as eighteen)[69] who showed up as "part of a record wave of people fleeing poverty and violence and seeking refuge in Western Europe," the New York Times reported.[70]

He lived in a reception center in Turku, a center of Finnish culture and business on the Baltic Sea coast, while he appealed denial of his asylum claim on grounds that Morocco was not a dangerous conflict zone.[71] Mechkah made a video of himself pledging allegiance to ISIS, then went to one of the city's main downtown squares and began his attack. Brandishing a knife and screaming the classic holy war cry "God is great" in Arabic, he mounted a running stabbing spree that mostly targeted women, at one point plunging the knife into a young mother holding her child.

He killed two of them, slashing one woman's neck so deeply it struck some as a near decapitation. As Finns scattered, running and screaming, so did Mechkah to another city square. He continued slashing at women.

Two men who tried to subdue him were stabbed. In all, Mechkah cut and stabbed eight more people, bringing his total tally to ten, the oldest of them sixty-seven. The tally would have been much higher had Mechkah gotten his way.[72] But police closed in on him and opened fire, wounding him in a leg and ending the attack.

Within a year, the usually measured Finnish national security enterprise was scrambling to process more than 1,000 urgent leads and tips about migrants suspected of terrorism and monitoring 350 suspected jihadists, vastly more than before the migrants were accepted. The country's intelligence and the normally 8–5 security agency Supo, which had previously worried itself about eighty Finns who'd joined ISIS in Syria, were now rushing to stave off kinetic attacks. It had just raised the threat level from "low" to "elevated."[73]

Next door in Sweden, 200,000 border-crossing migrants from Muslim-majority countries let in during 2015 could only have aggravated its security problems. Sweden has long prided itself for generosity to refugees as a signature national moral characteristic, building on the famous foundation of altruism in saving the Jews of Denmark during World War II.

On November 5, 2015, just days before the November 13 Paris attacks, Sweden Prime Minister Stefan Löfven tried to shame eastern European governments for what he termed a "selfish approach" for refusing refugee resettlements, calling their attitude "incompatible with humane European values."[74]

"I can understand if you say this crisis is a worry," the prime minister told the *Financial Times* in an interview. "But to say: 'This isn't my problem, we can't accept Muslims'—no, I don't think this is part of our European values, and I can't understand this kind of attitude."

The migrant wave washed in people like the Uzbekistan-born asylum seeker Rakhmat Akilov. On April 7, 2017, he became Sweden's newest face of terror when he hijacked a beer company truck and ploughed its mass through downtown Stockholm's Åhléns department store. It crushed five shoppers to death and injured ten others. Shoppers scrambled in all directions to get away, a "mass panic," one later recalled.[75] One of the dead was an eleven-year-old Swedish girl. Akilov ran away from the mix of blood, glass, and bodies, and was arrested later in a northern Stockholm suburb. While the dead were taken to the morgue, the wounded went to hospitals.

Akilov came into Europe through Poland first, where he applied for asylum, and then moved inland to Sweden in 2014 and applied for asylum. Authorities rejected this petition, perhaps because he already had one pending in Poland. After all the appeals were up in December 2016, Sweden gave him four weeks to leave. Akilov went underground and didn't surface until he hit the gas pedal of the beer truck. He'd lived a secret online life where he interacted on Facebook with known extremists and expressed sympathy for violent jihad and the Islamic State.[76]

Sometimes, counterterrorism was less than proficient, as in the extraordinary case of Moyed el-Zoebi. The twenty-something Syrian migrant arrived in Sweden on September 14, 2015, with his wife and infant son during the border-crossing migration crisis peaking that year.[77] But terrorism trouble, like a dark cloud, followed el-Zoebi to Sweden and then to Denmark. Like many others from Syria seeking to resettle in Europe's most prosperous countries, el-Zoebi arrived with a dark and violent hidden past that would foreshadow a murder plot that became intertwined with accusations of separate fire-bombing against fellow refugees, albeit the wrong kind from his perspective. El-Zoebi would soon demonstrate an extraordinary dedication to the art of killing, in that he was willing to strip the sulfur from no fewer than 17,000 matchsticks to get the explosive material he needed.

After war in Syria broke out, he joined the al-Qaeda affiliate al-Nusra and fought on the frontlines near Aleppo. El-Zoebi evidently brought his war with him into the infidel enemy's camp of Europe, along with like-minded jihadist migrants and tethered online to a mysterious handler back in Syria.[78]

The family applied for asylum in Sweden after arriving in September 2015, and then the online overseer introduced el-Zoebi to another Syrian migrant he'd never met, twenty-one-year-old Diab Khadigah, then living in Germany. The overseer set them in motion to attack Denmark's capital city of Copenhagen in December 2016. El-Zoebi and Khadigah were to detonate five handmade antipersonnel bombs at maybe a foreign embassy there or a foreign tourist attraction, then move in afterward and stab everyone within reach.

In the months before the attack date, the overseer arranged for the plotters to purchase the components, and then meet in Copenhagen, construct the bombs, and attack. The grocery list included two large knives, thousands of matches, batteries, fireworks, and communication radios. In

October 2016, el-Zoebi made it to Copenhagen's main train station and waited for Khadigah. But Khadigah never got there because, after the Paris and Brussels attacks, Denmark reinstituted border controls. Khadigah didn't have his passport, and when Danish guards saw the matches, batteries, and other components, they sent him back to Germany, where he was arrested. El-Zoebi returned to Sweden where, incredibly, authorities arrested him for an unrelated terror attack there. El-Zoebi and another local Syrian asylum seeker were accused of hurling flaming Molotov cocktails into a Shia Muslim community center in Malmö. No one was hurt, though the place suffered significant fire damage. ISIS attributed the community center arson to "a warrior from the caliphate" on grounds that "infidels" used the center, referring to Shia Muslims.[79]

Swedish authorities apparently never knew el-Zoebi had been in the advanced stages of an attack on Copenhagen when they charged him for the firebombing. But a court acquitted el-Zoebi. He sued for damages and was awarded 97,000 Swedish kronor.[80] Another year would pass before el-Zoebi was arrested for a fake passport as he tried to catch a flight from Copenhagen to Athens, Greece, and then Istanbul, no doubt all bought and paid for with settlement money. That was when investigators discovered the Copenhagen plot and extradited el-Zoebi to Denmark, where he was tried and convicted of plotting terrorism for ISIS.[81]

Norway and the Netherlands had their problems with homegrown jihadists before the migrants came. But as soon as the migrants began arriving in 2015, Dutch authorities were forced to acknowledge that "in some cases IS operatives have applied for asylum in European countries," according to the European Union's 2017 Terrorism Situation and Trend Report.[82] By 2018, the Netherlands was reporting that Dutch jihadists captured in Iraq and Syria "would probably attempt to reach the Netherlands (potentially also posing as victims in order to deflect authorities' attention)," according to the European Union's 2017 Terrorism Situation and Trend Report.[83]

The migrant population influx left a lasting sense of insecurity in Sweden, with tips about suspected extremists spiking from 2,000 in 2012 to 6,000 in 2017. In June of that year, the Swedish Security Service's chief, Anders Thornberg, said the presence of Islamic extremists had increased from 200 a decade earlier to "thousands."[84]

GREAT BRITAIN RESISTING THE TIDAL WAVE

Unlike their confederates on the mainland, British political leaders more warily eyed what was happening with the refugees in 2015 and decided they'd hold off on security grounds.[85] Britain's geographic positioning meant it didn't have to accept refugees under rules that required the first EU countries through which refugees passed to take their asylum claims. The position hardened so much after the Paris attacks that the UK decided that it would not only resist accepting any of the millions of migrants and refugees but that it also would hold a referendum to exit the European Union altogether (a process that came to be known as "Brexit") to prevent any from even crossing in as labor under Schengen Zone rules. The attacks across the channel catalyzed the Brexit movement as a means to block migrant-terrorists in mainland Europe from exploiting open-borders labor provisions to attack in the British isles.[86] The referendum quickly passed but, amid time-consuming fights over implementation, the islands remained exposed.

Terrorists came in on a vibrant, cross–English Channel smuggling business, using the UK's sluggish asylum processes to great advantage after arrival.[87] That smuggling activity of migrants mostly from Muslim-majority countries such as Yemen, Iraq, and Syria—by ship, vehicle, and the Eurotunnel train—continued well into 2020 as the British struggled mightily to suppress and interdict the traffic, the concern about terrorist infiltration always front and center.[88] One emblematic smuggling customer was Ahmed Hassan, who hid in the back of a freight truck for a cross-channel tunnel ride into Britain in October 2015.[89]

He told authorities he was Iraqi and sixteen years old and wanted asylum, though he was likely older. Reportedly, Hassan learned from "people of experience" around him to tell authorities he was underage because his chances of staying in Britain were greater. Initially, a social worker accompanying Hassan to his asylum interview was alarmed to hear him say he had spent three months with the Islamic State, "being trained on how to kill," according to media reports.[90] He was allowed to stay if he entered a counter-radicalization program for youths. Immigration authorities placed him in a foster home and enrolled him in school, where he won a student-of-the year award for filmmaking.

He stayed in the deradicalization program, too, all the way through the time it took him to build a time bomb filled with nails, knives, screwdrivers, and drill bits. While his foster parents were away on vacation, Hassan mixed his ingredients into an explosive, and on September 15, 2017, the eighteen-year-old planted the device on a packed, rush-hour tube train at the Parsons Green Underground station in London.

Later, his foster parent Penny Jones testified that "on the surface he was a lovely boy. He wouldn't let Ron mow the lawn, and he would always carry the shopping in from the car. So when it came out he was building a bomb in our home, it was a real shock."[91]

Something went wrong when Hassan's bomb detonated. Instead of exploding outright, it created a fireball inside the closed, densely packed compartment of the train. It burned the skin, hair, and clothing of more than thirty people. Authorities caught him the next day at the Port of Dover ferry, fleeing to the Continent. Later, in court, it emerged that Hassan felt he had a duty to hate Britain because of its role in the military campaign against ISIS during which Hassan's father ostensibly was killed.[92]

Like in other European countries, homegrown jihadists were attacking inside Britain in the months leading up to Parson Greens. These had nothing to do with migration. But now the plots by migrants who had smuggled in exasperated increasingly frantic counterterrorism police. One of them was Farhad Salah, a twenty-four-year-old Iraqi Kurdish migrant who reached Europe in 2014 after fleeing conflict in Kurdish areas of Iraq.[93] He would take advantage of a massive backlog in British asylum cases. Although details of how he managed it are unclear, Salah flew from somewhere in Europe into London's Heathrow airport that year and claimed asylum there.[94]

As his claim ground through the British system for a couple of years, he collected bomb components and gunpowder from fireworks. Salah's plan was to plant a bomb in a remote-controlled vehicle. Desperate to do something for ISIS, Salah wanted to kill the infidels that surrounded him. But police busted him in December 2017 shortly before Salah was to put his driverless vehicle plan into effect.[95]

OF ETHNIC CLEANSING, KIDNAPPING, AND WAR CRIMES

Mass murderers saw a chance for second life in the migrant flood, like twenty-seven-year-old "Hassan F.," who moved among migrants from Turkey and received formal refugee status in Greece. Of course, Hassan did not use his real name when he applied for refugee status in Greece, György Bakondi, a senior advisor to Hungary's prime minister, told me during an interview in March 2019 in his Budapest office. But since authorities had no means to figure out a real name, the Greeks gave Hassan refugee status, which he then parlayed into a new "special refugee passport" that allowed air travel to many European nations under a 2017 EU program matching refugees to employment opportunities, Bakondi told me.[96] Hungary arrested him with a female companion in December 2018 at the Budapest airport—for smuggling her, Bakondi said. Authorities charged him with smuggling, initially, and were preparing to deport him and the woman with time served back to Greece—until Belgium intelligence passed along that Hassan F. was no ordinary refugee human smuggler. They alleged he was actually an ISIS executioner who personally beheaded people, executed captives with pistol shots to heads left intact for that purpose, and oversaw other decapitations in territories the group seized.[97] Hungary charged Hassan, referred to as the "ISIS butcher," with crimes against humanity the week before I arrived in the country to tour Hungary's border fence system in March 2019.

György Bakondi, Architect of Hungary's border fence project and senior advisor to the prime minister. Photo by Todd Bensman in Budapest, March 2019

Hassan allegedly oversaw one decapitation massacre of twenty-five people, including twenty members of the same family in 2016 after they refused to join the terror group, Hungarian prosecutors said.[98] He personally beheaded an imam in a town in the Homs province in May 2015 after ISIS captured the area. And it was by his own hand that Hassan allegedly killed two other unarmed captives, one with a pistol shot to the head.

Ironically reminiscent of a time when Nazi war criminals had themselves smuggled to Argentina and Bolivia, war criminals, human rights abusers, and those with bloody atrocities on their hands found the same escape opportunities *into* Germany in Merkel's migrant policy. At issue is not only that these heinous criminals would escape justice and live in the bosom of modern economies but that they also pose higher risks of murdering their new neighbors.

In my research, I found that at least forty migrants were arrested for past illegal involvement with terrorist organizations before they got to Europe. These kinds of arrests were predicated on atrocities committed in Syria on behalf of terrorist groups, or on other terrorism-related crimes such as kidnappings, beheadings, terror attacks, and ethnic cleansing.

Consider Turkish mass murderer Suphi Alpfidan, for instance. A salaried ISIS operative and planner, he orchestrated a double mass-casualty suicide bombing that killed 107 peaceful protestors attending an Ankara pro-Kurd peace rally outside the capital's main train station. It was billed as the deadliest attack in Turkey's history. An arrest warrant went out after forensic investigation discovered Alpfidan's fingerprints inside the left rear door of a bomber escort vehicle and how he had arranged all the safe houses. His escape plan: pose as a Syrian refugee for the $600 smuggler's boat ride across the Aegean Sea to Greece and then on to Germany with the migrants.

His fake Syrian identity documents fooled the authorities at the Greek border, who registered him as a refugee and gave him temporary Greek identification papers. He then moved into Germany with the fake name embossed in Greek papers by traveling with a group of refugees on buses and trains. German authorities dutifully directed him to a refugee center, where he reconnected with a network of other ISIS emigres hiding in the wide open. After four months, perhaps under the impression that powerful government friends would protect him, Alpfidan returned on his own to Turkey and, at least initially, did win release after a short detention. But then the Turks had a change of heart. They rearrested and convicted the mass murderer who'd almost made his getaway in Europe's warm embrace.[99]

Dozens more were like the four brothers that police in northern Germany arrested, all Syrian nationals, for conducting ethnic cleaning operations for the al-Nusra Front terrorist group. In Syria, they partook of civilian massacres and then plundered the houses of their victims.[100] In 2015, Finland arrested twenty-three-year-old Iraqi twin brothers who had migrated there and asked for asylum two months earlier on the strength of a video from Iraq. It showed the unmasked brothers in the Iraqi city of Tikrit, during the infamous ISIS "Camp Speicher massacre" of Iraqi Air Force cadets as one of them systematically murdered eleven unarmed captives, shooting them one by one while they were lying on the ground.[101] Their victims were among an estimated 1,700 people ISIS operatives killed during those days in one of Iraq's worst atrocities in contemporary times.[102] Finland prosecuted the identical twin brothers for war crimes, though the effort failed later on issues about which identical brother performed the killings.[103] The Finns allowed the brothers to continue living in the country.

SMALL NUMBERS, CATASTROPHIC CASCADING CONSEQUENCES

Some terrorism scholars still feel compelled to equate low numbers of terrorists and casualties to a low threat to societies, especially in their preferred framework of direct bodily harm to individuals. This outlook has been used as a basis for arguing that all humble international migrants deserve benefit of the doubt, rather than undeserved skepticism and securitization.[104]

But this is a fundamental logic fallacy, terrible analysis, and most often used to ostensibly support obvious political agendas.

Properly assessing terrorism risk requires accounting for effects beyond what the United Nations Office on Drugs and Crime identifies as the "trauma of individual victims;" secondary and third orders of victimization include many other collective harms to societies, such as impacts on trade, investment, and counterterrorism, and are central to more properly assessing terrorism threat and risk.[105]

A RAND study commissioned by the European Parliament on the broader consequences of European terrorism similarly noted that terrorism leads to significant economic effects, that European businesses, cities, and nations lost €90 billion (an acknowledged underestimation) from 2013 to 2016 due to terrorism.[106]

"Despite the infrequent nature of terrorist attacks," the RAND report noted three years after the Paris attacks, in 2018, "the range of impacts on EU citizens remains significant."

The extraordinarily high consequences of these attacks and plots in Europe, relative to the small numbers of terrorists who caused them, argue for widespread acknowledgment and study by terrorism academics in the reasonable expectation that only a handful could cause similar damage in the United States.

Altogether, these few in Europe—relative to the millions who had unwittingly provided their camouflage—changed life for millions of Europeans in the same way that nineteen al-Qaeda hijackers changed America for two decades. It is not overstatement to say that the terror attacks, beginning with the Torcey group in 2014 but especially the Paris and Brussels attacks in 2015 and 2016, ended a political status quo that had been locked in place throughout Europe since World War II. The attacks shifted EU governments to their right and changed the way of life for tens of millions of Europeans. Elections in 2017, 2018, and 2019 in almost every European country pushed out establishmentarian liberal parties entirely or forced them to share power with more conservative ones. The elections reflected widespread perceptions, despite liberal protestations that it wasn't true, that repetitive acts of terrorism by the recently arrived asylum seekers were linked to the immigration wave and liberal policies that brought them into the bloc.[107] While anti-immigration sentiment was often simplistically attributed merely to nationalist xenophobia and racial bias, polling more persuasively establishes that terrorist acts rapidly turned broader mainstream public opinion throughout Europe against migration from Muslim-majority countries.

A July 2016 Pew poll, for instance, showed that clear majorities of eight out of ten European countries saw the refugee crisis and threat of terrorism as "very much" related to one another and found that 60 percent of Europeans believed refugees increased the likelihood of terrorism.[108] A European Commission poll found that Europeans viewed immigration and terrorism as the primary challenges facing Europe, ahead even of economic issues.[109] Pew polling for 2018, conducted after many new attacks and plots, showed that majorities in European countries that took in the most (58 percent in

Germany, 71 percent in Italy, and 82 percent in Greece) believed fewer or no immigrants should enter their countries, with a medium for all EU countries at 51 percent.[110] Polling in 2019 of fourteen EU states showed that citizens identified radical Islamism as the single biggest threat to the future of Europe, though not immigration itself, but that every member state still wanted better protection of Europe's borders.[111] A Gothenburg University poll of Swedish voters, conducted after high-profile attacks and police raids in the country, showed 52 percent favored taking fewer refugees into the country, up from 40 percent two years earlier.[112]

ELECTORAL LANDSCAPES TRANSFORMED

The perception about immigration as having ushered in a new age of Islamic terrorism, which had not previously registered as a significant concern, was a driving factor, albeit among others, for historically transformative election outcomes that included, among many other examples:

- Sweden's 2018 national election saw a voting surge for the Sweden Democrats, which campaigned against immigration and the terrorism it imported. A hung parliament emerged, with center-right and center-left blocks that had dominated Swedish politics for decades forced to include the Sweden Democrats in their ruling coalition. By contrast, the country's biggest traditionalist political party, the Social Democrats, suffered its worst election results since 1911.[113]
- Finland's spring 2019 national elections logged unprecedented gains for the conservative Finns Party and center-right National Coalition Party after campaigns that emphasized slowing immigration and terrorism. The Finns Party increased its seat count in parliament from seventeen to thirty-nine and emerged as the second most powerful party in the country for the first time in memory.[114] The National Coalition Party also joined the ruling coalition.
- In Norway, support for the center-left, pro-immigration Labor Party fell to historic lows. By contrast, voters endorsed the anti-immigration agenda of the nationalist Progress Party to the extent that it maintained its place in a coalition government as the third-largest party by emphasizing immigration issues.[115]

- Denmark's center-left Danish Social Democrats upended two decades of status quo in the June 2019 national election and won upset victories based primarily on its hardline stance against immigration and pushing tough policies on asylum seekers, which attracted voters from the right-wing parties it defeated.[116]
- Italy's 2018 national elections brought two antiestablishment parties to power in an upset, the Five Star Movement and the League party. Both won power after an election campaign dominated by promises to drastically reduce illegal immigration and to conduct mass deportations, which installed Prime Minister Matteo Salvini as head of state.[117]

Beyond causing these highly consequential outcomes, the attacks shattered one of Europe's most prized symbols of contemporary civilizational cooperation: the fabled 1995 Schengen Zone Agreement. This landmark vision of a borderless world had eliminated internal borders across twenty-six countries to enable visa-free commerce and movement. For the first time since its inception, the agreement lay scuttled after the discovery that migrant-jihadists used it to plot and move freely among signatory nations.[118] It had not been fully restored by the end of 2020, due in part to the more recent coronavirus pandemic, but also still because of the terrorism threat.

DEATH OF A PRIZED EUROPEAN PACT

Hungary and Austria were the first to effectively leave the Schengen Area when they built walls along their borders.[119] The Hungarian fence, put up too late to halt the initial terrorist migration flow in fall 2015, eventually did just that, shutting down the much-trammeled Balkans Route almost overnight. In a sure sign that Hungary's European neighbors were still unable to fathom that terrorist migrants had hit them after transiting Hungary, the nations most bloodied in the attacks excoriated Hungary and its leaders for ever erecting it, relentlessly name-calling Prime Minister Viktor Orbán as a racist, anti-immigrant fanatic of the Nazi-collaborationist order, rather than lionizing him as their savior. The irony of that criticism is rich in that Hungary's fence was still very much doing its work when I toured it in March 2019. Crickets, chirping birds, and tractor engines had replaced the sounds of mass humanity that had once crossed the border from Croatia and Serbia.

Following the 2016 Brussels attacks, six other Schengen Area countries cited an "exceptional circumstances," last-resort clause to re-implement internal border checks on a temporary basis of six months, subject to renewals, on passports, visas, and luggage after the attacks.[120] Belgium reinstated border controls with France. Germany reinstated controls at its borders with Austria, which did the same at its land borders with Hungary and Slovenia. Sweden reinstituted controls at harbors in the South and West police regions and at the Øresund Bridge. Denmark put restrictions on its ports with ferry connections to Germany and at its land border with Germany. Norway reinstated controls at its ports with ferry connections to Denmark, Germany, and Sweden.[121]

By the end of 2020, those countries and more had continually renewed their border controls in six-month increments, citing causes such as "terrorist threats," "severe threat to public order," "migration and security policy," and "serious threat to public policy and internal security."[122] Following two terror attacks in 2018, for instance, France renewed its border controls, "considering the number of recent and thwarted attacks…that have hit French territory," according to media reports.[123]

CAUSE OF BRITAIN'S MESSY DIVORCE FROM THE EUROPEAN UNION

The 150 or so terrorists who penetrated Europe with the migrants wrought other permanent changes. The Paris and Brussels terror attacks by operatives who traveled among migrants sparked the first momentum for Great Britain to exit the twenty-eight-member EU it joined in 1973 and set a June 2016 referendum on the matter. The mere thought that migrant terrorists might be ushered into Britain sparked the rancorous ten-week national campaign that has come to be known more simply as "Brexit" and has been described as "the most significant event in Europe since the 1989 fall of the Berlin wall," according to one British press report.[124] Although Britain was not part of the Schengen Area free-movement treaty, the new popular British hostility about EU membership centered on rules that permitted the free movement of labor into Britain, which would include all of the migrants legalized across the channel. At the time of the Paris and Brussels attacks, EU members such as Germany were pressuring Britain and other member states to accept ever-larger shares of migrants from Muslim-majority countries, even after they had proven to be exceptionally dangerous.[125]

Make no mistake, the migrant-terror attacks catalyzed Brexit and all the years of sweeping consequences that followed. The immediate aftermath of the Paris attacks saw sharp spikes in public hostility toward immigration and "anxiety over its perceived effects" in the UK, sparking that first early crush of support for Britain to leave the EU, according to an analysis of the question by British scholars Matthew Goodwin and Caitlin Milazzo.[126] The Brussels attacks the following month, then subsequent gun battles and terror attacks involving migrants, quickly built public consensus to set a national referendum for that June of 2016. British voters, newly fearful of the migrant wave's embedded terrorists acting out not far away, voted in favor of the referendum. But that was just the beginning of the pain.

In the years since the unsettled outcome of that first referendum, Brexit caused years of political divisions over its implementation, the resignation of Prime Minister David Cameron, an election that upended British electoral power balances, reduced the power of Prime Minister Theresa May, and led to the election of Boris Johnson.

To be sure, other concerns predating the Paris and Brussels attacks drove Brexit, such as a currency crisis, sovereignty issues, economic recessions, and antiestablishmentarianism.[127] But after the attacks and with each new one, Brexit proponents consistently made the so-called "security dividend" a centerpiece argument throughout the referendum campaign and easily pushed it over the edge.[128] The nonstop cavalcade of migrant-terror attacks continued to stimulate British popular opinion about the immigration flows for years after Paris and Brussels. In April 2018, a Center for Social Investigation poll showed that regaining control over EU immigration remained the top concern of British citizens who had voted to leave.[129]

FAST-TRACKING AN AMERICAN-LED MILITARY CAMPAIGN IN SYRIA

The terror attacks are rarely acknowledged for causing Brexit and its cascading fallouts, but they most certainly did. Neither are the migrant-terrorist attacks recognized for other terrible ripple effects, such as a major American-led military campaign to close the Syrian door through which the terrorist operatives slipped into the migrant flows. Western airstrikes during this action caused some of the war's highest civilian death tolls. Reporting by the *Wall Street Journal* credited the March 2016 suicide attacks in Brussels— by operatives deployed into war refugee flows—for forcing a US-backed military campaign to close a sixty-mile section of the Syria-Turkey border known as the Manbij Gap through which the attackers began their journeys.[130] The newspaper reported that in the weeks leading up to the Brussels attacks, "Western officials expressed increasing alarm about the continued flow of Islamic State extremists across this 60-mile stretch of the Turkey-Syria border." US officials, it said, were concerned because several of the November 2015 Paris attackers had traveled out of the disputed area and "slipped into the migrant trail in Turkey." One US military official told the newspaper that until the Manbij corridor was closed, there would be no way to "cut off the foreign fighters and it will be very difficult to stop them from hiding among the migrants."

The Manbij Offensive began on May 31, 2016, to retake the town and highway over the Turkish border to deny ISIS operatives further access to the gap. The fighting involved US air strikes in support of several thousand Syrian Democratic Forces (SDF) and small numbers of US special forces.[131] The offensive ended after three months when 200 surviving ISIS fighters, using human hostages, negotiated safe passage out of Manbij.[132] I could find no accounting of munitions cost for the offensive. However, media reports described some of the highest civilian casualties of the war from Western airstrikes occurred there, and it should be assumed that fighters on all sides of the conflict suffered deaths and injuries.[133]

MASSIVE EUROPEAN SECURITY EXPENDITURES

Those who would argue that small numbers of terrorist border infiltrators is nothing much to worry about should also be reminded that, in Europe, 100–200 of them also forced costly and sweeping reformations to security and immigration policy throughout the EU. Overwhelming public demand for action to stop new attacks followed every successful or foiled plot during the 2014–2017 period and forced huge, still-accruing expenditures on a wide range of unprecedented new security and anti-immigration measures in the EU countries.[134] Some measures required concessions on privacy and civil liberties values long prized by European populations, yet another terrible cost by so few. All the measures were designed to increase the power of governments to act against suspects, lower thresholds for necessary evidence to use such power, or both.[135] Though not fully assessed as of this writing, the drain on national treasuries was substantial.

Days after the 2015 Paris attacks, Belgium announced eighteen counterterrorism measures and increased funding for them. These included plans to tap the phones of extremist suspects and allow twenty-four-hour house searches whereas such searches previously were limited to daytime business hours after disclosures that the Paris-attacks mastermind had exploited the house-raid rule.[136] European governments obviously spent significant sums on new initiatives such as expanding corps of antiterrorism police, and standing up border patrols and ports of entry processing. For example, Europol recruited 200 counterterrorism investigators for deployment to "a second line of defense" in Greece and Italy to identify camouflaged terrorist movements that had become a top priority for the EU and Member States involved.[137]

By March 2017, even German Prime Minister Merkel had changed her tune.

"We will never resign ourselves to terror," she told a local newspaper after the March terror attack on a soccer team's bus in Dortman. "We know that we, like many other countries, are threatened and are doing everything in our power to ensure security for our citizens."[138]

The Europeans gave ground on prized civil liberties. New laws in Germany after rejected asylum seeker Anis Amri's 2016 Christmas market attack in Berlin, for instance, allowed security forces to put minors under surveillance, use video surveillance from public places in law enforcement investigations, and monitor refugees' cell phone data.[139]

EU parliamentary authorities pushed a raft of measures aimed at boosting the bloc's response to terrorism that included measures long anathema to their members.[140] Europol Chief Rob Wainwright, following a June 2016 London police shooting of an attacking terrorist, called for rapid counterterrorism measures in every EU country and to monitor the online communication of terrorist suspects as well as messenger service communications.[141] Civil libertarians protested such measures as anathema to longstanding continental values.[142] Still, governments continued to pass new security measures, many of them designed to collect and share intelligence that, like the United States prior to 9/11, had been stove-piped within individual policing agencies and rarely shared.

One such measure required an air-passenger database known as the Passenger Name Record system to require that intra-European policing agencies of twenty-six countries share names of terror suspects, as well as people denied entry and wanted felons. Asylum claimants, once inside the union, are able to fly within Europe to include, for instance, the ISIS war criminal arrested when he was flagged in March 2019 in Hungary after traveling on a so-called "refugee passport."[143]

Another measure that drew the ire of civil libertarians required the sharing of "travel ban" lists among EU police agencies of felons and suspects banned by any one country to close a loophole that had allowed them to enter undetected in other countries.[144] Still others involved expanded police powers in Sweden, following the Stockholm shopping center vehicle-ramming attack, to conduct workplace checks for illegal immigrants without probable cause and to levy sharply higher fines for employing illegal immigrants.[145]

Again, costs to governments were generally unavailable at the time of this writing because such spending is not straightforward and most countries do not reveal their security spending on national security grounds, according to a 2018 European Parliament report that attempted to assess costs.[146] But EU counterterrorism budgets escalated significantly in 2016 "in light of increased terror threats in Europe" as illustrated by €4 billion in commitments and three billion in payments for European Commission's Security and Citizenship program.[147] Staffing and funding was clearly necessary for an unprecedented number of new counterterrorism initiatives involving police and judiciaries throughout Europe.

PAYING TO STAUNCH THE MIGRANT FLOW

Sustained public demand for governments to slow, deter, and eventually end the mass migration and its associated terror threat coincided with the pace of attacks and plots by those who entered during it. As noted by the *Wall Street Journal* in 2016, revelations that Paris attackers used the refugee routes to reach their targets "added to fears of terrorism and the security risks from migration, pushing EU leaders to take increasingly tough measures to limit the flow" and eventually that "German officials, after initially playing down the risk of terrorists sneaking into Europe as part of last year's influx of refugees and migrants, have in recent months warned repeatedly about security risks of the migrant flow."[148]

The programs may have come at comprehensively unknown cost, but some are known. One of the primary measures was a €6 billion Germany-spearheaded EU accord with Turkey to accept deported migrants from Europe, particularly those reaching Greece.[149] The idea was that mass deportations would deter others from coming and slow the influx. European nations agreed to pay €6 billion for Turkey to accept and care for returned migrants in refugee camps on Turkish territory. In exchange, Turkish citizens would gain visa-free travel to the EU, and Turkey's application to join the EU would be fast-tracked. The number of migrants trying fell from 1.2 million to just over 580,000 in 2018 as a result of the accord.[150]

Other counter-migration policies resulting from public backlash over associated terror threats included Germany's recognition that several countries in North Africa—Algeria, Morocco, Tunisia, and a portion of Afghanistan—could be added to a list of "safe countries of origin" to which migrants from those nations could be repatriated, at unknown cost, ostensibly in line with various international treaty obligations.[151] Often, repatriations had to be done by air at government expense, to cover great distances. One 2017 investigative media report estimated the EU was spending millions to forcibly airlift thousands of people to home countries, with costs of between €5,800 to €9,000 per person. The European border agency Frontex, which participates in the airlifts, saw its repatriation expenditures rise from €11.4 million in 2016 to €66.5 million in 2017.[152]

Attacks by failed migrant asylum seekers who had evaded lawful deportations, particularly the December 2016 Christmas market attack by Amri, prompted an array of likely expensive new measures designed to track down missing migrants evading deportations to Africa and the Middle East.[153] Police forces were pressed into service tracking down thousands of deportable illegal migrants. One 2018 report said more than half of Germany's deportees were missing, including more than 50 percent of Somalis and 40 percent of Syrians.[154]

One program offered to pay up to €1,200 to migrants who chose to return home voluntarily. In another controversial and costly program, European governments, including Germany, in 2016 struck a $3.75 billion annual accord with Afghanistan to begin accepting the repatriations by air of more than 80,000 Afghans through a process called "assisted voluntary return."[155] Afghans sign an agreement to leave the deporting country in trade for between $500 and $4,500 upon arrival in the home country. Those who refused were forced onto repatriation flights no doubt funded by European governments.[156]

Europeans have struck deals with other governments, such as Sudan, and even extremist militias in Libya and Niger, for them to suppress outgoing migration in exchange for financial aid or other indirect inducements such as equipment.[157] In Italy, the new populist government pledged to deport up to 500,000 illegal migrants despite significant financial implications.[158] Italian Prime Minister Matteo Salvini has closed ports to charity rescue ships loaded with migrants, struck agreements with violent militias in Africa in which payments and various inducements were laundered to them in exchange for suppressing outflows, and withdrawn asylum protection and welfare benefits for most migrants to make them eligible for the mass repatriations.[159]

SPAWNED IN A FAMILIAR POLITICS OF VIRTUE

The Europeans fairly quickly slammed the gates shut on all of this, or tried to after Paris and Brussels, and as the horrors that befell their people dawned in the form of terror attacks without apparent end. After mass deportations to Turkey, electrified Hungarian border fencing, and refugee ship docking denials, the numbers of "detected" refugees and migrants had fallen from several million in 2015 and 2016 to 141,846 by the end of 2019, roughly an old normal. (The same year, however, about 715,000 applied for asylum, suggesting vast numbers are reaching the interior undetected.)[160]

The EU's border control agency Frontex seemed earnest in its 2020 assessment about the main "omnipresent threat" from continental borders:

"Terrorism is not exclusive to Islamist extremists. This said, when it comes to counter-terrorism efforts within the border dimension, it is assessed that the main threat emanates from Islamist extremism," opened section 6.6, Managing and Interdicting Terrorist Mobility.[161]

But in America, the sound of gates slamming was not heard. During the Democratic presidential primary campaign season of 2019, a majority of candidates sounded the familiar refrains of pre-Paris multicultural embrace of mass migration over the southern border, also brushing aside security considerations, as though widespread terrorist border infiltrations had not been occurring in Europe for years already.

Their messages harkened to the same ideological sentiments that Chancellor Merkel and the other European leaders cited in initially throwing open the gates in an audacious gamble with security. Most of the US Democratic candidates in 2019 and 2020 repeatedly promised to decriminalize illegal border entry, end detentions, halt all deportations of non-criminal aliens, provide a path to citizenship for all undocumented migrants inside the United States, and provide them government-run health care.[162]

Those who raised concerns about security and terrorist infiltration were pointedly decried and shouted down as xenophobic racists, familiar refrains.

Such warnings, of course, were put out there, credibly so, by entities that could hardly stand credibly accused as racist xenophobes. West Point's highly regarded Combating Terrorism Center released a study in 2019, for instance, that acknowledged the Islamic State exploited the refugee crisis in 2015 "to smuggle operatives in among the migrants" and went on to declare one of the terrible results:

> "Never before have there been so many jihadi terrorist plots in Europe as in the period between 2014 and 2018. Never before have so many plots gone undetected and resulted in attacks. Never before have so many Europeans been killed in jihadi terror attacks. More people have died from jihadi terrorism in Europe between 2014 and 2018 than in the previous 20 years."[163]

No matter, evidently. In the United States, the prevailing sentiment on the Democratic side of the political spectrum going into the 2020 presidential and national elections remained pre-2015 Germany, France, Italy, and Scandinavia.

During the 2020 presidential campaign, Democratic nominee Joe Biden promised policies that essentially eliminated border controls and provided powerful incentive for mass caravans to resume from Central America. These included, for instance, a 100-day renewable deportation moratorium on illegal immigrants, free US health care, limited detention, generous asylum regulations, and an eventual path to legal residency and citizenship.[164]

What happened in those countries warrants telling in some detail as a counterweight to similar American political forces that will remain a potent influence on US border security and immigration policy for a long time to come. The political force of these attitudes can be expected to turn aspiration into hard policy after the November 2020 elections but also in distant cycles beyond it, always with the prospect hanging in the balance that mass migration will be ushered in—unthinkingly, once again, without security prudence—until, perhaps like in Europe, only bloodshed turns it back.

This need not be so, given the advantage of forewarning provided by the continuous attacks and plots in Europe by terrorists who rode those very same political winds of virtue right over its borders.

CHAPTER TWO

ORIGINS OF AN AMERICAN COVERT BORDER WAR

DHS apprehensions of special interest aliens, or extra-hemispheric migrants, have increased in recent years. This population consists of unauthorized migrants who arrive in the United States from, or are citizens of, several Asian, Middle Eastern, and African countries. While many citizens of these countries migrate for economic reasons or because they are fleeing persecution in their home countries, this group may include migrants who are affiliated with foreign terrorist organizations, intelligence agencies, and organized criminal syndicates.

—DHS Assistant Secretary for International Affairs Alan Bersin, testifying before Congress March 22, 2016.[1]

On June 24, 2016, President Obama's top homeland security appointee, Department of Homeland Security Secretary Jeh Johnson, quietly disseminated an unusual three-page memorandum to his ten top law enforcement chiefs responsible for border security. It was titled "Cross-Border Movement of Special Interest Aliens." This was unusual because the Obama administration had scarcely addressed the issue during any of its previous seven years. But now Europe's terrorism body count, enabled by border infiltrations among refugees and migrants, was in a skyward trajectory.

Each of Johnson's recipients would have recognized the term "special interest aliens" as the formal lexicon for referencing Muslim-majority country immigrants who reached US air, sea, and land borders.* The people on Johnson's distribution line also would have known this flow of immigrants spoke not Spanish but Pashto, Arabic, and Horn of Africa tribal dialects and were coming from the same countries as those then burning down Europe. SIAs were from the Middle East, North Africa, and South Asia.

But just in case memories had slipped, Johnson briefly reminded them, "As we all appreciate, SIAs may consist of those who are potential national security threats to our homeland. Thus, the need for continued vigilance in this particular area."

In demanding their "immediate attention," the memo ambiguously noted an "increased global movement of SIAs" that required an American reprioritization of this traffic. He issued orders for the formation of a "multi-DHS Component SIA Joint Action Group" and production of a "consolidated action plan." This older, sometimes ridiculed terrorist infiltration threat would be moved to the front burner.

Johnson's memo made no mention that frantic European counterterrorism task forces that summer in 2016 were still raiding migrant refugee centers and emerging with handcuffed jihadists who had infiltrated EU borders, that police were engaging in hours-long gun battles with supposed migrants somehow armed with automatic weapons and explosives, and converting cities across the continent into security green zones. A *New York Times* story had just reported that ISIS camouflaged at least twenty-one jihadists among migrants to conduct the still-fresh Paris and Brussels attacks.[2] (In a telephone interview that summer, Johnson confirmed for me that the memo was authentic and spoke for itself. He requested that we otherwise speak off the record, which I will respect.)

The memo outlined plan objectives. Intelligence collection and analysis, Secretary Johnson wrote, would drive efforts to "counter the threats posed by the smuggling of SIAs." Coordinated investigations would "bring

---

*   Over time, different homeland security agencies referred to such migrants as "Aliens from Special Interest Countries" or "Third Country Nationals," and the number of countries on lists has sometimes fluctuated as some were added or removed. For purposes of consistency, this book will use the term Special Interest Aliens.

down organizations involved in the smuggling of SIAs into and within the United States." Border and port of entry operations capacities would "help us identify and interdict SIAs of national security concern who attempt to enter the United States" and "evaluate our border and port of entry security posture to ensure our resources are appropriately aligned to address trends in the migration of SIAs...."

Tellingly, Johnson included DHS's public affairs department on the recipient list. Perhaps in anticipation of political backlash from the Democratic base, Secretary Johnson ordered public affairs staff across DHS to craft messaging that the coming operations were necessary to "protect the United States and our partners against this potential threat."

"The message must be clear," he continued. "DHS will use the full array of its authorities and capabilities, here and abroad in concert with US government and foreign partners, to detect, disrupt and dismantle human smuggling organizations, particularly those who specialize in smuggling migrants into the Western Hemisphere."

Targeting Muslim SIAs in a presidential election year like that one—in a whole-of-government way certain to attract media attention—was a serious political risk Johnson had to have recognized but felt too spooked—by something—to ignore. Amid an election campaign in which the leading Republican, Donald Trump, was decrying Muslim-world immigration, the Democratic base was steeping in the very same ideological marinade as were European leaders when they opened their gates to mass migration from Muslim-majority countries without hedging for obvious security risks. American Democrats, like their liberal European counterparts, regarded (and still do) the notion that jihadists would infiltrate land borders among bedraggled war refugees as an outrageous fantasy of fringe racists, nativist immigration restrictionists, and conspiracy lunatics.

They could not possibly regard Jeh Johnson as any of those things, however.

When it came to legal or illegal immigrants from distant troubled lands, his party's 2016 platform messaged that everyone from anywhere who came in over the southern border should be regarded as "assets to their communities" and "be incorporated completely into our society through legal processes that give meaning to our national motto: *E Pluribus Unum.*"[3]

When initial reports about ISIS terrorists crossing the border turned out to be false, prominent Democrats often leapt to loudly and publicly deny that any such thing ever could or had happened. The compulsion to undermine the claims was necessary for them, lest any find traction justifying restrictions and crackdowns. In April 2015, El Paso Congressman O'Rourke, at the time appealing to his Hispanic base during his run against Republican Senator Ted Cruz, posted on Facebook about the false ISIS-crossing report.

"Stories like these are good at scaring people and getting attention for those who spread them. But they are terrible for the country's image of the border, for El Paso's ability to recruit talent, and for our region's opportunity to capitalize on the benefits of being the largest bi-national community in the world," O'Rourke opined. "El Paso—let's fight back with the facts."[4] (In early 2016, I briefed O'Rourke in his El Paso congressional office on my Naval Postgraduate School thesis about SIA smuggling—apparently not very effectively).

Even by the presidential primary campaign season of 2019–2020, as European counterterrorism police were still busting migrant-jihadists or studying their exploded remains for evidence, the whole slate of US Democrat primary candidates, including O'Rourke, repeatedly promised to decriminalize illegal border entry and remove all hindrance or legal consequence such as deportation. It was Germany, France, and Scandinavia 2015 on steroids.

Still, Johnson and his memo stood in mute testament of a fuller, more complicated story. The memo wasn't the only clue that America's homeland security establishment was ingesting information that people like O'Rourke did not. The FBI's San Diego office was just then holding its "2nd Annual Special Interest Alien Conference," meaning something the year before, in 2015, had prompted the bureau's California border office to elevate the issue. The conference was classified; attendees came from across the spectrum of homeland security agencies who needed to start working on the ascendant border issue.

What was this politically dangerous counterterrorism program that Obama's DHS Secretary proposed to study and revamp at the American southern border and that the FBI suddenly felt required classified conferences?

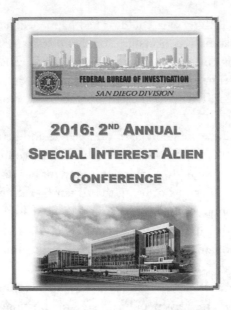

ORIGINS: AMERICA'S LAST UNREVEALED 9/11 COUNTERTERRORISM PROGRAM

Belying the FBI's SIA conferences and Johnson's SIA memo was that the United States already had a semblance of the envisioned counterterrorism enterprise in place. It had been deployed many years earlier as the dust from 9/11 was still settling and developed in iterations over time in two distinct, albeit complementary, parts. Put most simply: One part intended to strain and filter higher-risk migrants for terrorist travelers at the physical land border. The other part was to find them as they traversed Latin America before they could reach the border and to disrupt the smuggling networks that make their transits possible.

The Johnson plan seemed to recognize that current leadership had not been tending these gardens very well at a time when need of them seemed heightened.

This project, with all its seemingly disconnected parts, represents perhaps the last great unrevealed counterterrorism enterprise America built after the attacks. Once journalists and congressional investigations revealed they existed, other projects of the era became famous or infamous, depending on point of view, such as the one involving harsh CIA interrogations of jihadists captured overseas, the so-called "rendition program" of terrorists to countries less attuned to restrictive human rights rules, and, of course, the drone strike assassination project, which remains an ongoing affair as of this writing.

But the one at America's borders and border approaches qualifies as the most unique of the cloak-and-dagger intelligence operations of the 9/11 era because its center field is so very close to home and the stinging domestic politics knowledge of them would stir. This counterterrorism enterprise, had journalists wanted to make something of it, would have punched the most sensitive of the nation's domestic political buttons: immigration from Mexico but also the securitization of non-Latino migrants by religion and nationality as a civil rights problem, their interrogations and America's choices for dealing with those thought to pose a national security risk. There could be no juicier national security story left to tell and have debated.

Disclosing and critically examining secret government programs, especially those having to do with counterterrorism after 9/11, was always a spigot of media pride and Pulitzer Prizes. Yet somehow, even despite what was happening in Europe, no major American media outlet seemed interested in casting a critical, evaluative eye on *this* War-on-Terror enterprise. The neglect persisted despite a profusion of clues over many years of its existence and, as in the case of the Johnson memo, affirmations that apolitical professionals on both sides of the aisle regarded terrorist land border infiltration as a quite real issue.

Nor would journalists write about it when high government officials spoon-fed it to them. Public court prosecutions chummed the waters with evidence of the infiltration threat and what the American homeland security establishment was doing about it. Homeland security leaders spoke out loud of these things in recorded congressional testimony and sometimes public statements delivered directly to reporters.

In one emblematic instance in 2012, a reporter asked President Obama's DHS Secretary Janet Napolitano during a tour of the Arizona border if terrorists might cross it. The Democratic appointee responded with what *should* have been regarded as a delectable lead: "There's a whole category called SIAs—special interest aliens is what it stands for," Napolitano responded. "We watch that very carefully. We have been working—not just with Mexico, but countries of Central America, in terms of following more closely people transiting the airports and the like. And so, again, our efforts there are to try to…take as much pressure off the physical land border as we can."[5]

In a 2005 testimony before the House Appropriations Committee, then-FBI Director Robert Mueller was asked if terrorists had crossed or posed a threat of crossing.[6]

"I would say that there has been an increase of special interest aliens coming across the border in the last several years, and I would also say that some of those individuals coming from those borders have come from countries in which we have known there to be an Al Qaeda presence," he testified. "I know there have been individuals who claim to be Hispanic who are not Hispanic. They may have come from southeast Asia. They may have come from the Middle East."

No one called them liars and, still, all of this fresh bait rotted.

I've often speculated that American journalists have deliberately avoided disclosing this untold American counterterrorism war at the border because of how it marries Mexican immigration to the foreign jihadist threat. To verify the latter (jihadist travel through Mexico) would expose the former (Mexican labor migration) to potentially harsher restriction. Journalists, a great many of them politically liberal, probably don't want to saddle Spanish-speaking migrants with all the trouble that would come with formal acknowledgment that they cloak the infiltration of Islamic terrorists.

Beyond the potential damage to illegal Hispanic migration, another probable reason why this American counterterrorism program has escaped proper journalistic treatment is that acknowledging its existence would blow up a self-perpetuating myth in which many writers have heavily invested: that jihadist migration over the borders is a big fat lie, because no one has ever reported it and the obvious fact that no border-crossing terrorist had conducted an actual attack on US soil. There has always been a way to break this circular logic fallacy.

Consider as a metaphoric example the infamous ancient Roman city of Pompeii, whose inhabitants died buried under the volcanic ash of a Mount Vesuvius explosion in AD 70. While the disintegrated bodies of those killed no longer can be seen eons later, we know they existed and also what they looked like in death because empty cavities remained where their long-gone bodies fell. Plaster fill and excavation revealed the body forms. When it comes to classified information and plots that never materialized because they were prevented, government programming can be regarded as the ash preserving the threat we can't immediately see but which has been there all along. The cavities of unseen terrorist infiltrations, attempts, and prevented attacks will become evident as I somewhat imperfectly fill them as did Pompeii's nineteenth-century archaeologists.

Public interest, controversy, and high stakes seem just as latent in these counterterrorism operations as in others that became the subjects of nonfiction national security books. And yet, this one remains almost entirely unreported beyond my own lonely efforts to stir the sort of open-air accountability that benefits government programs by making them work right.

The mere thought of terrorist border infiltration after the 9/11 attacks helped spawn new national laws to address the problem, which in turn gave rise to its prospective solution: a counterterrorism program combining intelligence collection, federal law enforcement, and immigration control that plays out at home and abroad in far-flung, movie-worthy law enforcement dramas. The fact that homeland security leaders have continually trained their sights on preventing terrorist border infiltration—that Johnson ordered the whole apparatus into the repair shop, and the FBI in San Diego holds annual classified SIA conferences—runs starkly counter to some public perceptions that the infiltration notion occupies fringe conspiracy territory. That America has warred for so long against terrorist infiltration stands instead as testament to the apolitical seriousness with which professional homeland security strategists and practitioners, under Democratic and Republican administrations alike, have long regarded the threat as having established residence among the tapestry of border-threat types.

Fortunately, one reason for the dearth of such terror attacks from that quarter was that phalanxes of homeland security analysts, intelligence officers, and law enforcement personnel had been laboring in the shadows to prevent them. The conundrum is that people they prevented from entering and what those individuals would have wrought often are not countably tangible. But this American effort unrolled after 9/11 took migrant-terrorists offline before they could kill.

A LIFE-CYCLE ARC BEGINS

Targeting travel is at least as powerful a weapon against terrorists as targeting their money. The United States should combine terrorist travel intelligence, operations, and law enforcement in a strategy to intercept terrorists, find terrorist travel facilitators and constrain terrorist mobility.

—*9/11 Commission Report*

Freshly seated in 2001, President Bush quickly demonstrated to friends and critics alike that no one could ever label him as a closed-border xenophobe interested in preserving America's cultural purity. Bush was an immigrant-friendly former Texas governor who took office with a grand bargain in mind to fix the country's mass illegal immigration problem: a temporary worker visa program for Mexicans to supply the American economy's demand for affordable labor. Bush's program would have legally normalized millions of Mexican workers while simultaneously reducing their need to cross the US border clandestinely.

The new president understood the problem from his perspective as governor of a state attuned to agribusiness and its labor needs. American strategic thinking about border security to that date had focused almost entirely on the clandestine ebbs and flows of Mexican laborers and those living in the country illegally, certainly not anything as exotic as terrorist border infiltration. The president saw his plan as such a priority that his first foreign trip, in February 2001, took him to Mexico to discuss reform with his enthusiastic counterpart, President Vicente Fox.[7] Momentum toward a bilateral accord was advancing so nicely by September 5, 2001, that President Fox and his wife came to the White House for the American president's first state dinner and further discussions.

But, as the president would write in his post-office memoir, "then 9/11 hit."[8]

A mere six days after the Fox visit to the White House, everything changed. As President Bush later wrote: "My most serious concern was that terrorists would slip into our country undetected. I put the idea of a temporary worker program on hold and concentrated on border security."

The former president's reference to the temporary worker program for Mexicans and his choice of the term "border security"—rather than the previously favored "immigration reform"—signaled the profound extent to which the outlook for the physical southern land border had pivoted from managing a Spanish-speaking labor force to filtering for exotic jihadist infiltrators among them. So too was the president's impulse to effectively close the southern and northern land borders, for a brief time requiring inspections of all border crossers and vehicles.[9] The initial fear was quite organic and commonsense, that jihadists might well steal over those wide-open borders for a next round of attacks, which were expected as imminent. Right after 9/11, the ascendant approach to border security shifted from blocking illegal entries of those who spoke Spanish to those who spoke the languages of the Middle East, Central and South Asia, and North Africa.

Massive bipartisan public investments in national security and strategies to do just that followed as the months after 9/11 became early years.

Of course, "borders" are far more than lines on a map representing land demarcations of sovereign nations; the term extends to seaports and international airports too. In July 2004, the 9/11 Commission issued a monograph titled *9/11 and Terrorist Travel: Staff Report of the National Commission on Terrorist Attacks Upon the United States*. It provided a painstaking investigative recitation about how the nineteen terrorists who trained in al-Qaeda's Afghanistan redoubts flew by commercial air into the United States, getting to within striking distance of their targets. It was through the airports that all the 9/11 hijackers entered the country, on various kinds of visas (mostly visitor and business) and using a variety of fraud to embed inside the country long enough to plot the attacks. Those findings are, by now, well known and do not require another visitation here. We know that sustained political and legislative attention and resources poured into tightening up all those abused systems for the approved entries of non-immigrants and immigrants alike.

But legislative and homeland security thinking also turned toward physical land borders, namely to the monumental task of bolstering some 4,000 miles of them, north and south, against infiltration. Planners and strategists prioritized the southern border, given the far greater number of people who entered through it and the fact that dozens of porous, easy-to-enter Latin America countries connected to it. A preponderance of primary source material from the thinking of those early days shows the southern border got more attention than the northern border for those reasons and not out of some racist animus toward Hispanic migrants.

Another key distinctive difference between the two borders is not always obvious. It was that entry into Canada from other hemispheres can only happen by air and seaports, meaning only by government-managed visas and advanced approval processes for most. Canada can control the issuances of various kinds of visas and permissions, which lets Canada's immigration services at least know something in advance about entrants from Muslim-majority countries. Applications for visas and refugee resettlement, after all, have to be filed and approved in advance in order for the applicants to fly commercial into a Canadian airport. In Canada, thousands of complete SIA strangers, violent jihadists hiding among them, therefore, would not be able to show up entirely unannounced or uninvited for a clandestine trip into Montana unless they parachuted into the Yukon wilderness with a dog-sled team.

By contrast, the overland pathway through a notoriously indifferent Mexico to the US southern border runs through some two-dozen contiguous, equally porous, and indifferent nations in Latin America, each open to just about anyone from any country of national security concern. To be sure, some migrants could defeat Canada's vetting and screening processes to hide their jihadist predilections and then travel south over the American border, or do so later in their lives after radicalization. Some did before 9/11 sensitized both countries. Among the thwarted plots was the 1997 New York subway-bombing scheme, planned by two Palestinians who had illegally crossed the Canadian border into Washington State for the operation.[10] Then, in 1999, two al-Qaeda operatives crossed from Canada into Washington State with plans to bomb Los Angeles International Airport.[11] Security tightened up between Canada and Mexico after 9/11.

But when judged by the volumes of unscreened total strangers who suddenly show up at a border, the Canadian circumstance after 9/11 contrasted so starkly with the Latin America circumstance that American planners knew they would have to tailor a very different strategy for the southern border.

And so they did. The one deployed to the nation's southern approaches is unlike any enterprise necessary for the US-Canadian border in terms of breadth, expanse, and complexity.

Although a powerful political mandate for land border security arose from the 9/11 attacks, the underlying ideas had been gestating for a while. To simplify a bit, throughout the 1990s, national border control policy centered mainly on managing illegal Mexican migration and drug running. The 9/11 Commission Report found that, prior to the attacks, immigration enforcement agencies actually "were not asked to focus on terrorists" and had no access to terror watch lists.

That thinking started to turn after the 1993 World Trade Center bombing, conducted by various undesirable visa holders and immigrants who had flown commercial into airports.[12] The late '90s millennial attack and New York subways plots already mentioned, plus the US embassy bombings in Africa and USS *Cole* attack deepened the awareness that al-Qaeda was really gunning hard for America. How to keep this new kind of enemy outside the gates, away from enabling legal visa systems, became a subject for government-appointed commissions to study.[13] The commissions published reports that focused on those entry methods but also identified the land borders as vulnerable to terrorist infiltration.[14] Still, even as Congress dedicated increased appropriations to counter spiking Mexican migration and drug trafficking during the 1990s, the rise of al-Qaeda terrorism and commission reports about the land borders did not kick the sleeping American public giant hard enough.

It took the 9/11 attacks to do that. Polling showed the American public, far more fearful than ever before about terror attack, wanted military interventions abroad in countries like Afghanistan, suddenly became far less tolerant of immigration, and demanded sharply increased investments in border security.[15] Although the nineteen hijackers entered by air, intelligence community planners knew they had to shore up land borders too. The 2004 9/11 Commission staff report on terrorist travel, for instance, cited intelligence linking Islamic terrorists to Latin America smuggling networks as well as the 2001 California border crossing of a ranking Hezbollah operative (in the trunk of a car) later convicted of terrorism.[16]

This was going to require the services of immigration enforcement agencies that were already there but in greater numbers and with greater capabilities. The evidence is persuasive that concern about infiltration over the southern border, rather than nativist hatred of Latino migrants, drove the coming paradigm of counterterrorism and immigration. Even ideological opponents of the whole idea of securitizing illegal immigrants for national security purposes acknowledged that it happened exactly for the reason of blocking jihadist infiltration. In his 2008 book *The Closing of the American Border: Terrorism, Immigration, and Security Since 9/11,* Edward Alden acknowledged the attacks left policymakers believing that "the obvious solution to the threat of terrorists crossing US borders was simply to beef up enforcement through tougher scrutiny of border crossers; greater inspection of vehicles; and the use of Border Patrol agents, physical barriers, and sensing devices to safeguard the barren regions between the official border crossings."[17]

Peter Andreas, in his 2012 book *Border Games: Policing the U.S.-Mexico Divide,* also acknowledges that, in a relatively short time, the attacks changed border control "from a low-intensity, low-maintenance, and politically marginal activity to a high-intensity, high-maintenance campaign commanding enormous political attention on both sides of the territorial divide."[18]

Any reading of the national legislation that came out of 9/11 should diminish narratives that the notional threat of terrorist infiltration was some sort of fig leaf for xenophobic action against Hispanics.

On full display then, in the wreckage of 9/11, was the power of The Idea. At one time, the notion of jihadist infiltration demonstrated its power to move legislative mountains and to open wide the national treasury spigot. No wonder the notion so catalyzes those, like Beto O'Rourke or nongovernmental migrant-advocacy organizations, to work furiously to discredit it. These are the voting blocks and leaders who would feel very much at home among pre-2015 Europeans in their desire to encourage mass illegal migration for their various self-interested reasons.

BIRTH OF A COVERT BORDER WAR

The grand bipartisan acts of legislation after 9/11 birthed the two-pronged global counterterrorism strategy at the heart of this book. One was a campaign to identify and interdict the SIAs who reach the physical border and to sift their ranks for potential terrorists or terrorist sympathizers or supporting players. I will refer to this as "the near war," and I describe in Chapter Three how it is prosecuted. The other campaign was to find and disrupt the long-distance smuggling organizations that transported SIAs to that border, which I call "the far war" and describe it at length in Chapter Five.

The foundational legislation was always explicit about what Congress, the president, and the national security establishment at the time wanted. The legislation always insisted that homeland security agencies prevent terrorist travel over the land borders and to disrupt the transnational smugglers who make it possible and all the means by which they do so.

Consider the Homeland Security Act (HSA) of 2002. This was the first among a series of sweeping new laws that transformed homeland security and became the foundation of the new defensive order to prevent future 9/11s. The 2002 HSA described one significant part of the nation's mandate as "preventing the entry of terrorists and terrorist weapons" by threat actors described as "transnational terrorists, transnational criminals and unauthorized migrants."[19]

Another law that laid more bedrock for the coming American counter-infiltration enterprise was the hallmark Intelligence Reform and Terrorism Prevention Act of 2004. This required that new Department of Homeland Security agencies pursue "a cohesive effort to intercept terrorists, find terrorist travel facilitators, and constrain terrorist mobility domestically and internationally."[20] The act created a Human Smuggling and Trafficking Center that would collect intelligence on human smuggling globally, especially about "clandestine terrorist travel" far south of the actual physical border to serve these new objectives.[21] The center remains an ongoing enterprise.

Other foundational laws indicated expectations to get in front of jihadist infiltration over the land borders. The Secure Fence Act of 2006, which authorized construction of hundreds of miles of border barriers along the US-Mexico line, almost preordained for Trump's claims about this many years later. The Secure Fence Act emphatically states that the barrier's purpose is "the prevention of all unlawful entries to the US, including entries by terrorists."[22]

The new statutory mandates left the specifics up to federal agencies as to how they would fulfill them. These came in the form of strategy documents among federal agencies that often mirrored the language of the new statutes. The Central Intelligence Agency's (CIA) 2006 National Strategy to Combat Terrorism described one of its top goals as "denying terrorists entry to the United States" by disrupting their travel "internationally and across and within our borders" and undermining the "illicit networks" and "in-house forgery operations" providing false identification documents that facilitate the travel.[23]

The first of successive Border Patrol strategic plans in 2005, for instance, marked that agency's new priority mission as "establishing substantial probability of apprehending terrorists and their weapons as they attempt to enter illegally between ports of entry."[24] All the strategic plans in the years since similarly earmark the threat of terrorist infiltration as a high-priority objective.

If the notion of terrorist border infiltration after 9/11 drove border security legislation as former President Bush said it would and did—more so than the legacy problems of drug smuggling and Spanish-speaking immigrants—then that also was what drove spending to more than double the number of Border Patrol agents from 9,212 in 2000 to 21,444 ten years later.[25] All spending on technology, planes, vehicles, and boats soared, in fact, to service the new terrorists-at-the-border paradigm. Getting that done became the law of the land, and agency strategic plans reflected that they would carry it out.

The question now turned to how.

For the first time, US national strategists fused counterterrorism and illegal immigration enforcement into a single undifferentiated strategic tool with which to take on anticipated al-Qaeda attempts to breach either US border. On the northern border with Canada, security vetting and intelligence-sharing systems were improved—such as tracking SIAs and watch-listed individuals arriving in Canada by plane and ship. But the far greater challenge, the greatest expense, still was seen as the geographically vexing Latin America routes that delivered a steady flow of total strangers through Mexico to the American frontier.

The position that counterterrorism work was necessary at the border and in the immigration enforcement establishment was mainstreamed. There is no evidence that the Bush administration or forces within Congress were animated by racism. Indeed, President Bush would lead a second effort at immigration reform in 2007 that featured significant accommodations for Mexican citizens. It failed, but internal White House memoranda in the George W. Bush Library in Dallas and consistent public statements by administration officials in the aftermath of 9/11 reveal that national security elbowed away all other priorities. Evidence lends far more credence to the narrative that countering terrorist infiltration over land borders was the administration's driving motivation.[26]

Ryan Bounds, the president's domestic policy advisor on immigration, embossed White House thinking at the time in a memorandum at the close of the president's final term. In the memo titled "Immigration Reform Legacy," Bounds remembered the moment:

> "The prospects for a deal with Mexico were upended by
> the terrorist attacks of September 11, 2001. Although both

Presidents remained supportive…an agreement of the kind under discussion earlier in 2001 was much lower on the list of priorities and no longer viable in any event. Instead, the national focus with respect to immigration issues immediately shifted to tighter borders and more robust enforcement. The Bush administration is committed to ensuring that our immigration policies and practices do not allow terrorists to enter or remain in the United States."[27]

THE NEAR WAR

Already at this time, American immigration enforcement professionals were well aware of a steady cross-border traffic of migrants from Muslim-majority countries where the nation's new terrorist nemeses lived, bred, recruited, and plotted. If homeland security agencies were to beat down the odds of a terrorist strike from over the border, those travelers from higher-risk Muslim-majority lands were the most obvious targets and so were the human smugglers without whom the distances could not be easily navigated.[28] As referenced in Secretary Johnson's memo, such travelers would come to be called special interest aliens, SIAs, as well as by other terms of similar meaning, under the rubric "Other Than Mexican."[29] But identifying a list of countries whose citizens should undergo further security screening took quite some doing. Agencies of the US intelligence community (a kind of designated club currently composed of seventeen agencies) were called in to come up with the lists.[†]

The agencies developed—for the first time—"country of interest" lists based on intelligence assessments about which populations were at higher risk of radicalization or membership in indigenous terrorist organizations,

---

[†] According to INTEL.gov, "How the IC Works," as of August 2020, the seventeen organizations that made up the US Intelligence Community were Air Force Intelligence, Army Intelligence and Security Command, Central Intelligence Agency, Defense Intelligence Agency, Department of Energy Office of Intelligence and Counterintelligence, Department of Homeland Security Office of Intelligence and Analysis, Department of State Bureau of Intelligence and Research, Department of Treasury Office of Intelligence and Analysis, Drug Enforcement Administration Intelligence Program, Federal Bureau of Investigation, Marine Corps Intelligence, National Geospatial Intelligence Agency, National Reconnaissance Office, National Security Agency, Office of Naval Intelligence, Office of the Director of National Intelligence, and US Coast Guard Intelligence.

according to former officials who were familiar with the project. Countries ended up on the lists, for instance, if al-Qaeda and other Islamic terrorist organizations operated in them or found operational support in their territories.[30] Homeland security professionals viewed the compilation of country lists as an important first step because, by the guidance these provided, FBI, ICE, or Border Patrol personnel could know to single out which emigrants to put through additional security checks.

In the earliest days of this, lists went into play as early as June 2002 with a DHS program known as the National Security Entry-Exit Registration System (NSEERS). The program didn't last long but, for its duration, required non-immigrant aliens from twenty-five identified Muslim-majority countries—people who presented "an elevated national security threat"—to register with the government.[31] The idea was to ensure they were legally present and in good standing, and could be fingerprinted, photographed, interviewed, and tracked entering or leaving the country. Initially, men of military age already present in the United States, if they were citizens of the listed countries (plus North Korea), including Iran, Libya, Sudan, and Syria, often reported in local school auditoriums. Finding out who didn't report and checking anyone who did for terrorist ties or their legal status was a pure counterterrorism play using immigration enforcement resources.

But this project also took place in plain media sight, and it drew highly critical coverage. I recall attending one session as a reporter for the *Dallas Morning News* in early 2002. The auditorium brimmed with mostly Pakistanis carrying packets of papers, looking confused, and being ordered to move here and there by local FBI agents. Many were upset, worried, and a little offended. I wrote my story. After civil rights complaints of religious and nationality profiling in other cities, the government in 2003 abandoned the special registration part of NSEERS, despite its having uncovered eleven individuals tied to terrorism and found 13,799 to be out of legal status and ordered deported.[32] In 2011, the Obama administration gutted the rest of NSEERS after "input from community groups and advocacy organizations."[33]

But that early practice of singling out noncitizen aliens from a listed country deemed by American intelligence agencies as a terrorism source did not disappear; it just moved to darker operating spaces.

In fact, country-listing became the nucleus of the American near war to combat terrorist infiltration and survives to this day.

The State Department and elements of the intelligence community defined the term "Specially Designated Countries" to describe those showing a "tendency to promote, produce or protect terrorist organizations or their members."[34] Individuals from those countries, if they showed up at US borders or ports of entry, or even if found anywhere in the United States years after entry, got stamped for enhanced security screening. One of the most universally used terms for them over time was, as already mentioned, special interest aliens. But different agencies under various administrations have used terms of similar meaning, such as "Aliens from Special Interest Countries," "Third Country Nationals," or "Aliens from Specially Designated Countries." The US government has lacked a formal, across-agency definition of SIAs, although meanings for other terms that came into being seem not to differ significantly. DHS/ICE once defined a special interest alien as a "foreign national originating from a country identified as having possible or established links to terrorism."[35]

Once the new national laws demanding counter-infiltration at the land borders passed and the agencies had drafted their strategic plans for implementation, DHS applied the system to SIA flows over the land borders. The plan wasn't complicated and made common sense.

Migrants from the listed high-risk countries of national security concern, once Border Patrol encountered them, got tagged as "SIA," or some of its other variants later. Once so tagged, federal agents—most often the FBI in the early years, but also Border Patrol and ICE intelligence officers—conducted enhanced security vetting on them to help agents determine if they were authentic asylum seekers, war refugees, economic opportunists qualifying for American welcomes and legal due processes, or terrorist infiltrators planning harm after their US arrivals. The rationale was that if common immigrants could reach a land border from terrorist-source countries such as Saudi Arabia, Afghanistan, Pakistan, Yemen, and Somalia, then so too could terrorist travelers from the same countries. One 2006 National Counterterrorism Center intelligence report characterized the thinking this typical way: "Terrorists could try to merge into SIA smuggling pipelines to enter the U.S. clandestinely.... Al Qaeda and other groups sneak across borders in other parts of the world and may try to do so in the US, despite risks of apprehension or residing in the US without proper documentation."[36]

The first known formal SIA interdiction guidance distributed to the field agents traces to a February 2004 Headquarters Office of Border Patrol directive titled "Apprehensions of Aliens from Special Interest Countries." This was superseded by a November 2004 memorandum from US Border Patrol Chief David Aguilar to "All Sector Chief Patrol Agents."[37] It listed the thirty-five "countries of interest" whose citizens would automatically warrant the SIA tag and eight steps for special handling.‡

OBP 50/8b-P

U.S. Department of Homeland Security
Washington, DC 20229

U.S. Customs and Border Protection

NOV 0 1 2004

MEMORANDUM FOR: ALL SECTOR CHIEF PATROL AGENTS

FROM: David V. Aguilar
Chief
U.S. Border Patrol

SUBJECT: Arrests of Aliens From Special Interest Countries

The following 35 countries and the territories of the West Bank and the Gaza Strip have been designated as special interest countries:

Afghanistan	Kuwait	Somalia
Algeria	Lebanon	Sudan
Bahrain	Libya	Syria
Bangladesh	Malaysia	Tajikistan
Djibouti	Mauritania	Thailand
Egypt	Morocco	Tunisia
Eritrea	North Korea	Turkey
Indonesia	Oman	Turkmenistan
Iran	Pakistan	United Arab Emirates
Iraq	Philippines	Uzbekistan
Jordan	Qatar	Yemen
Kazakhstan	Saudi Arabia	Territories of Gaza and West Bank

For any person taken into Border Patrol custody from one of above countries or territories, at a minimum, the following actions will be taken:

These were mostly Muslim-majority countries, but the list also included the Philippines and Thailand. Including some countries with problematic Muslim-minority populations, among them plenty of radicalized jihadists ready for action, made sense at the time and now too. The 9/11 investigations, for instance, determined that al-Qaeda's terrorist mastermind, Khalid Shaikh Mohammed, had hatched various plots while living in the Philippines, including the so-called "Bojinka" plot to blow up twelve US commercial

---

‡ The November 2004 Aguilar memorandum listed the following thirty-five countries and the territories of the West Bank and the Gaza Strip as having been designated Special Interest Countries: Afghanistan, Kuwait, Somalia, Algeria, Lebanon, Sudan, Bahrain, Libya, Syria, Bangladesh, Malaysia, Tajikistan, Djibouti, Mauritania, Thailand, Egypt, Morocco, Tunisia, Eritrea, North Korea, Turkey, Indonesia, Oman, Turkmenistan, Iran, Pakistan, United Arab Emirates, Iraq, Philippines, Uzbekistan, Jordan, Qatar, Yemen, Kazakhstan, Saudi Arabia, Territories of Gaza, and West Bank.

jumbo jets over the Pacific and the 9/11 plot too. The Philippines southern provinces were home to global jihad-oriented terror groups such as Abu Sayyaf, which seized the Philippine city of Marwari in 2017 and had to be expelled with a vicious, protracted government military siege that lasted five months. Thailand too is home to armed jihadists in its southern provinces, notably Malay insurgent groups that were resurgent at the time of 9/11. As well, intelligence community agencies also would have known that the truly horrific October 2002 jihadist suicide bombing of a Bali tourist district, which killed 202 people from twenty-one countries, had been planned in Thailand, a revelation that at the time "highlighted the country's role as an unwitting haven for foreign terrorists," according to the International Crisis Group policy institute.[38]

In any case, frontline Border Patrol agents who encountered SIAs from any of these countries were instructed to take the following eight steps, according to the Aguilar memorandum:

- Contact Sector Communications for initial records checks.
- Contact the National Targeting Center for additional records checks.
- Contact the local JTTF [FBI Joint Terrorism Task Force] for follow-on interviews.
- Contact the Station and/or Sector Intelligence Unit for follow-on interviews.
- Copy or scan any pocket litter for possible intelligence value.
- Generate and submit within one hour a Significant Incident Report to the US Customs and Border Protection Commissioner's Situation Room.
- If intelligence is developed, complete and forward a G-392 Intelligence Report through Border Patrol intelligence channels.
- Enroll all aliens fourteen years of age or older from the above countries or territories who are amenable to removal proceedings into the ENFORCE/IDENT systems and screen them through IAFIS, without exception.

Aguilar, a Bush appointee who was retained by the Obama administration, left office as CBP Commissioner in 2013. In a May 2020 interview with me, Aguilar recalled the genesis of his 2004 directive establishing this near war to defeat terrorist infiltrators.

"The attacks (of 9/11) were very fresh in everybody's mind," he recalled. "We were getting constant intelligence feeds for the potential for follow-up attacks."

The border and immigration enforcement agencies of the time already had ramped up airport and visa security, the means by which the 9/11 hijackers entered, and were working hard on sewing up security at land border ports of entry, Aguilar said.

But everyone in leadership recognized instinctively and from real intelligence community reporting that "the potential for SIAs coming in between" (the ports of entry) among high numbers of Mexican migrants—"the threat in the mix," Aguilar called it when we spoke—posed a major national security threat that would be harder to reduce. Aguilar said his agency came up with the program outlined in his November 2004 memo based on intelligence community agency assessments and recommendations. The IC identified the initial thirty-five countries based on whether they were "promoting, producing and protecting terrorists." The recommendations for how frontline law enforcement should handle apprehended migrants from those countries also came from the IC agencies. Aguilar said the agency went with the list and many of the recommendations.

"It [the eight-step program] was a means to prioritize the focus against the threats that were very real at that time and continue to be very real," Aguilar told me. "These efforts were absolutely critical to understanding the use of approaches by terrorists and terrorist intent."

I asked Aguilar if he would attribute what they put in place as preventing attack.

"Indirectly? Absolutely. Directly? I'm going to leave that one open," he said, citing classification of intelligence generally. "I'll say there was tremendous value to the interviews done and the intelligence gathered."

Aguilar said his program has survived in various forms to the present day under both Republican and Democrat leaderships because "there's very little light between their thinking about what needs to be done on this. The reality is that those in charge all have seen the need and the need to act on it."

The program has changed, ebbing and flowing in terms of which of the original eight screening measures still occur when SIAs are apprehended and with what consistency.

The most commonly named "countries of interest" reprinted
with permission of graphic artist, Joe Stafford.

In 2007, I submitted questions to CBP asking how the system was still working three years later. The answer: not much differently than prescribed in the Aguilar memo. In the response, the agency explained that "when an alien from a special interest country is apprehended, notification is made to the FBI's Joint Terrorism Task Force (JTTF) and CBP's National Targeting center to determine whether the alien has any nexus to terrorism or is of any investigative interest to other agencies." The SIA names and fingerprints were still being run through every conceivable criminal database for warrants or past criminal activity, but then through the higher-tier counter-terrorism databases controlled or accessible by the intelligence community.

If the migrant was found to be of special investigative interest, he or she may be "remanded to the custody of the FBI or Immigration and Customs Enforcement's Office of Investigations pending further investigation," the CBP response to my 2007 questions read.

Items number three and four of the Aguilar memorandum, which called for FBI and CBP intelligence officer "follow-on" interviews, proved especially meaningful to the mission effort because migrants of the thirty-five countries often showed up at the border with no identification and largely unverifiable stories of woe for their asylum applications, which entitles most to bond out into the United States to wait for distant asylum hearings and to work authorization. Time was therefore of the essence, hence the requirement that Border Patrol immediately notify the FBI.

The main purpose of the threat assessment interviews was to fill in at least something on the blank slates of migrants who would otherwise be released almost completely unknown into the nation's interior. The debriefing interviews generated at least an impression of whether they may pose a threat. The interview program put migrants from countries like Afghanistan, Iraq, and Egypt in front of federal officers trained to a high level to ferret out deception, who had access to classified intelligence databases as well as to foreign partners they could call for checks in some of the origin countries.

Retired FBI Special Agent Norman Townsend, who was supervisor of a Joint Terrorism Task Force that conducted hundreds of SIA security threat interviews in the Texas border town of Laredo from 2003 through 2009, recalled agents and task force officers feeling the weight of responsibility in the long and tedious SIA interviews.

"Our main focus was 'if and when the next 9/11 happens, we don't want to learn they came through Laredo,'" Townsend recalled. "If we were responsible for a terrorist getting by us, that's one we're not going to be able to survive."

Before going in for a threat assessment interview, the agents would examine a subject's "pocket trash," meaning cell phones, maybe personal notebooks or papers with email addresses, names of people, and phone number scribblings, whatever a given migrant had on them when Border Patrol picked them up. If the agents had a migrant's name, they ran it along with fingerprints through international intelligence databases to see if they were wanted criminals or on a terrorism watch list.

Going through these steps formed a basis for the questioning, though Townsend explained, "We had a format too, but we could adapt questions to the circumstances. A Muslim male of military age would get more scrutiny."

Once they were face to face with SIAs inside ICE's border detention centers, with vetted interpreters on speaker phones, the FBI task force members plumbed migrant stories of home and the journey. They looked for signs of deception in eye contact and body language. No Laredo-area detainee in Townsend's memory, of course, ever just came out with a big terrorism plot confession, though he concedes that anyone who had trained in counter-interview techniques or had practiced a memorized story could have hidden their true motives and hearts.

If it seemed like the migrant was not likely involved in terrorism or interested in extremist ideologies, agents would ask about terrorists back home or any they may have suspected they met on the journey, Townsend recalled of his service on the border. Absent indications of criminality, deception, or association with terrorist groups, the migrants proved exceptionally valuable in the information they provided about their smugglers. This information was always passed along to ICE counter-smuggling investigators working in the "far war" zones of Latin America to be discussed at greater length in Chapter Five.

Often enough, the migrants identified their smugglers and all their associates by name and descriptions, in photo lineups. They provided cell phone numbers and other information about safe houses, routes, corrupt officials, and other smuggling methods that would prove vital for other US agencies working to dismantle those organizations.

"The chances of you catching a terrorist are slim, okay, but agents and task force officers would spend hours doing these interviews and write up very lengthy reports," Townsend said. "The way I saw it, we were building up an intelligence base that might be, at some point in time, relevant to somebody down the road."

It's unclear whether federal officers have been able to interview all arriving SIAs because, as far as I can ascertain, no government audit of this program has ever been done.

SIZING UP THE THREAT

In the absence of public audits and threat evaluation and the fact that country-of-national-security-concern lists fluctuate fairly wildly over time, it's highly challenging to know how many SIAs reach the border and cross it, meaning how big the problem set is. To independently count SIAs apprehended each year, so that the general contours of the problem can be seen in a public way, remains a tough proposition, though I and a few others have tried hard.

For almost all of the program's existence, DHS has purposefully withheld public reporting about the number of SIAs who cross, and especially the ever shrinking and expanding country lists used by the agency. Homeland security held the lists close to the vest, in part, out of concerns that they would cause diplomatic offense to the nations on it. The precaution was somewhat valid, though the practice came at the expense of letting the American public know about the true multinational makeup of all the migrants crossing the border. Meanwhile, in its annual public reporting of apprehensions by nationality, which would provide the public with a sense of how many migrants from terrorism-spawning nations were crossing the border, DHS has long preferred to let provide one large amalgamated number under an "Other Than Mexican" (OTM) rubric, then only list Chinese, Central Americans, and Indians and not the ones from, say, Yemen, Saudi Arabia, Iraq, and Syria. Putting out details more specific than Central American or Chinese OTMs also risked the sort of domestic political contention and litigation that beset the NSEERS program lists in 2002. Avoiding publication of the countries and SIA numbers was the easier way to avert potential political trouble.

Still, in one attempted 2018 tally of SIAs, the Libertarian Cato Institute analyzed apprehension data of migrants from sixty-three countries of national security concern, far more than Aguilar's thirty-five. The organization explained that it chose the sixty-three countries because DHS agencies had listed them at various times over the years. From 2007 to 2017, Border Patrol apprehended 45,006 SIAs from any of the countries between ports of entry, Cato found. However, in addition to a very inflated countries list, Cato did not tally the "inadmissibles," meaning SIAs who openly self-presented at ports of entry rather than to clandestinely come in between them. The inadmissibles would have significantly hiked Cato's 45,000 number.[39]

I decided to go a more conservative route, by filing Freedom of Information Act (FOIA) requests with CBP for a much shorter list of government SIA encounters from thirty-seven countries of national security interest that CBP most often listed for the most years between 2008–2019. The encounter numbers reflect two sets of data I thought were applicable: apprehensions *between* ports of entry, meaning people caught in the brush soon after illegal crossings, and the "inadmissibles" who turned themselves in at an official port of entry, often at the end of pedestrian bridges and to claim political asylum. My reasoning was that regardless of how they finally entered—sneaking over the border or presenting themselves at the ports of entry—all still made the journey using combinations of smugglers and document fraud, and American officers physically "encountered" all of them at the border in one way or the other.

My FOIA return showed a total number of government encounters with SIAs of 22,000 between 2008–2019 at the southern border. Topping the charts in my FOIA data were Bangladeshis (5,703), Eritreans (3,774), Somalis (3,029), Pakistanis (1,653), Uzbekistanis (1,353), Turks (888), Iraqis (867), and Syrians (761). The majority are usually encountered in Texas each year, with California a close second.

But all of the data—whether mine or Cato's, whether based on thirty-seven or sixty-three countries—show the same troubling trend line: upward. The encounters in my data tripled and Cato's quadrupled from 2007 forward. Cato's numbers, for instance, show that SIAs from all of the sixty-three countries rose from the 2,000 per year range for 2007, 2008, and 2009 to the 8,000 a year range in 2016 and 2017.

My data, based on only the thirty-seven countries, shows CBP encounters with SIAs at the southern border rising from 1,026 in 2008 to 3,003 in 2019. (A 2019 DHS "Myth/Fact" sheet confirmed my 3,000 SIA encounters the previous year.)[40]

Pieces of official government reporting provide confirmation that the numbers have steadily climbed through the years, and where they show up the most. A joint DHS-California fusion center intelligence report showed that CBP apprehended 729 SIAs from twenty-four designated nations across the southwest border during fiscal year 2007 and 944 in fiscal year 2008.[41] The numbers kept climbing. A confidential Texas Department of Public Safety intelligence report leaked in 2015, citing CBP data, disclosed

439 encounters with SIAs in only Texas during the first nine months of 2014, a 15 percent increase over the previous year.[42]

Encounters with SIA migrants on the northern US-Canadian border also indicate a continuing proliferation threat from that country, although, as already mentioned, most of these migrants likely would already be somewhat vetted before arrival at international airports. Again, SIAs coming from Canada present a very different kind of security issue that would require appropriately different countermeasures than the elaborate smuggling-hunting and intelligence collection operations deployed for the southern border.

The threat from Canada remains an issue outside the scope of this book, as the covert border war was tailored to the unique geopolitical circumstances of southern approaches and not about very different programs for the northern ones, but is certainly worth separate study and analysis. Still, for any value of disclosure, a return of data from a separate FOIA request showed that US border authorities encountered 22,789 SIAs who crossed between and at Canadian border ports of entry from 2008–2018, increasing from 1,523 in 2013 to 2,294 in 2018. Iranians seemed to be encountered most often on the northern border, with 4,673 of them documented, followed by Filipinos (3,639), Pakistanis (2,111), Iraqis (1,532), Saudis (1,019), and Syrians (898).

The rising SIA encounter numbers on the southern border are problematic because they strain the near-war vetting and intelligence collection systems that Aguilar put in place in 2004. As the numbers rise, so too does the race-against-time urgency to complete the database checks and face-to-face debriefing interviews before the migrants bond out and go free, as they so often did in the European theater. Worryingly, CBP told me in response to my 2007 FOIA that "absent national security, public safety concerns or mandatory detention requirements, ICE may have no available detention space to physically detain an alien pending administrative proceedings, requiring CBP Border Patrol to release an alien on their own recognizance."

Bed space ebbs and flows with various crises, benefiting SIAs at homeland security cost when space is scarce and allowing for normal vetting when space is adequate.

All available evidence shows that mass-migration events have buffeted this near-war program and severely exposed the nation at times. But I also know from my time with Texas DPS that the program of flagging and screening SIAs with combinations of interviewing and investigation has survived intact into 2020, just as publicly unnoticed as it was in 2004.

Why have these programs survived as long as they have? The answer is, in part, because homeland security officials knew from reading the intelligence reporting that they had no choice but to keep them intact; terrorists harbor their own brand of the American Dream. Beyond the long, empty land borders, to them, there are shining beacons of opportunity—to kill.

TERRORIST ASPIRATIONS TO CROSS

> *The reality could not be more clear: jihadists are coming home, and they are piggy-backing on the refugee flows to avoid detection. We saw this in November with the Paris attacks... and in February when German authorities arrested two terror suspects for allegedly plotting an attack in Berlin. Intelligence officials have notified me that possible terror suspects in Syria have already tried to enter our country as refugees.*

—Rep. Mike McCaul (R-TX), Chairman of the US House Homeland Security Committee in an opinion column dated March 9, 2016.[43]

In 2015, FBI agents arrested several Somali members of a Minnesota terror cell as they were staging in San Diego for a southern crossing *into* Mexico. All wanted to join ISIS in Syria but couldn't simply fly out of their local international airport; they were on the US No Fly List, so the plan was to first travel into Mexico and fly out of there or some other airport in Latin America.[44] But it eventually emerged through court filings that at least one of the young American Somalis had thought long and hard about how to make the Mexican border pay other dividends for their beloved ISIS.

Guled Ali Omar, one of the defendants, was recorded during the investigation saying that "once the defendants have found a means of reaching Syria by going through Mexico, the defendants will be able to tell ISIL of the route so that ISIL can send fighters into the United States via that route to mount attacks."[45]

This is, of course, one of many pieces of anecdotal evidence that the US southern border has long occupied space in the aspirational imaginings of Islamic terrorists as a soft underbelly point of access for the coveted interior attack.

Streams of intelligence reporting about terrorist interest in the US-Mexico border have forced elements of the US homeland security establishment to focus on it. Of course, al-Qaeda was just as interested in entering the country in the traditional ways, on visas by passenger plane into US airports. But those entry methods got much harder as the Americans tightened up security screening for those processes and built systems to check air passengers. The US-Mexico border has no doubt come to look like a real option as time has worn on. This makes sense. As America tightened visa and air-travel security, the chances of discovery and capture increased. Islamist operatives and leaders spoke more often of using the land border.

As early as 2005, for instance, DHS Deputy Secretary James Loy testified before the US Senate Select Committee on Intelligence that "recent information from ongoing investigations, detentions and emerging threat streams strongly suggests that Al Qaeda has considered using the Southwest Border to infiltrate the United States. Several Al Qaeda leaders believe operatives can pay their way into the country through Mexico and also believe illegal entry is more advantageous than legal entry for operational security reasons."[46]

A 2007 National Counterterrorism Center report noted the same dawning of an attitude among terrorist leaders that the land borders were starting to look pretty good.

"The Intelligence Community continues to receive information indicating Al Qaeda planners view border infiltrations as a possible, though secondary alternative to entering legally with official documents," the NCTC report said. "Al Qaeda and other groups sneak across borders in other parts of the world and may try to do so in the US, despite the risks of apprehension or residing in the US without proper documentation."[47]

In the 2011 raid that killed Osama bin Laden, Navy SEALs captured a trove of al-Qaeda documents from his compound. Some of the letters and notes from bin Laden's personal papers and computer files showed that he instructed his deputies to recruit an operative with a valid Mexican passport who could cross illegally into the United States, according to a 2012 *Los Angeles Times* report that cited a former intelligence official who had seen the documents.[48] The *Times* also cited a declassified 2003 CIA report titled *Al-Qaeda Remains Intent on Defeating U.S. Immigration Inspections*, which asserted that the terrorist group maintained an "ongoing interest to enter the United States over land borders with Mexico and Canada."

Later, other groups showed they too were well aware of the southern border's increasing value as having fewer impediments than increasingly policed airport-to-airport travel.

In 2014, I ordered my unit at Texas DPS to monitor known ISIS social media accounts for a one-week period that August. In a three-page bulletin titled "ISIS Interest on the U.S. Southwest Border," we conveyed that thirty-two Twitter and Facebook posts by ISIS operatives reflected "an increased interest in the notion that they could clandestinely infiltrate the southwest border of the US, for terror attacks."[49] (The bulletin I ordered and edited unfortunately found its way to the press.) Unbeknownst to anyone in my group at that time was that ISIS was just then sending teams of assassins into Europe over its borders, posing as war refugees, but had not yet struck widely.

The Texas DPS bulletin detailed numerous specific "calls for border infiltration," including one by a militant confirmed to be in Mosul, Iraq, who administered an ISIS propaganda training group and beckoned the "Islamic State to send a special force to America across the border with Mexico" because "the US-Mexican border is now open to large numbers of people crossing." It detailed another message sent out on Twitter that said ISIS fighters had already entered the U.S. over the border, warning that as a result, "Americans is in for ruin [*sic*]."

Whether any of this chatter reflected real activity, or might inspire someone, duty requires that homeland security practitioners take such reports seriously until other information justifies standing down. That being the case, our bulletin created an appropriate stir, circulating in the upper echelons of the US Homeland Security establishment and briefed in the White House situation room.[50]

DHS Undersecretary for Intelligence and Analysis Francis X. Taylor felt duty-bound to inform senators who asked about our bulletin and what DHS was doing to deter terrorist border infiltration. Responding to a question from Arizona Senator John McCain, Taylor replied that he was aware that there had been "Twitter, social media exchanges among ISIL adherents across the globe speaking about that as a possibility."

He correctly assured the Senate committee that Homeland Security was not ignoring this threat problem.

"Certainly, any infiltration across our border would be a threat," Taylor said. "I'm satisfied we have the intelligence and the capability on our border that would prevent that activity."[51]

McCain was not satisfied with Taylor's assurances. "The fact is there are thousands of people who are coming across our border, who are undetected, who are not identified. And for you to sit there and tell me that we…now have the proper protections of our southwestern border, particularly in light of the urgings over Facebook and Twitter for people to come across the southwestern border, is of great concern to the citizens of my state."

Over the years, credible reports about terrorist interest in the border and awareness of an unsecured access gate have stalked the homeland security agencies responsible for guarding it.

In May 2019, for instance, a captured ISIS operative still in Syria told American researchers of the nonpartisan International Center for the Study of Violent Extremism that ISIS had recruited him and others to penetrate the US southern border by infiltrating migration routes through Latin America and Mexico.

The captured fighter, Abu Henricki, who held dual Canadian and Trinidad and Tobago citizenship, told researchers the ISIS external operations division had approached him and several other Trinidadians in 2016 to develop an infiltration plan in league with a sympathizer then living in New Jersey. The US-based sympathizer would help smuggle the group over the border with false passports for eventual attacks on unspecified financial system targets inside the United States to create economic chaos. Abu Henricki said he refused the assignment and had no idea whether others had been sent in his stead, although he thought some of those chosen had been killed in action first.[52]

Not long after the Center published a story about this in the online *Homeland Security Today* in June 2019, I called its author, Anne Speckhard, one of the researchers who had interviewed Abu Henricki in Syria. Speckhard and her team had by then interviewed more than 160 ISIS terrorists in captivity in the war-wrecked Middle East country. Speckhard described herself as not exactly a conservative Republican and certainly had never counted herself among those who believed the southern border was vulnerable to terrorist infiltration. But Speckhard told me she'd been so alarmed by his credibility and story that she acted in an unprecedented way: she called the FBI and provided the full videotaped interview. She also published the *Homeland Security Today* story to drive home the point that someone needed to do something.

"We were surprised by this and concerned as Americans," she told me. "After reflecting on the case, that they (ISIS) would try this no longer seems incredible to me. Our ethic is to report the facts, not pander to either political party. Our intent was not to support any political agenda. We don't want this to be used for fearmongering."

Aspiration alone did not give longevity to America's counterterrorism project on the land border, of course. Real movie-worthy chaos and drama involving actual jihadists did, each and every year of its existence.

CHAPTER THREE

JIHADISTS RATTLING THE GATES: THE NEAR WAR

Flying in is a path. Taking a ship in is a path. Coming up through the Mexican border is a path. Now, are they doing it in great numbers? No. Because we're finding them, and we're identifying them, and we've got watch lists, and we're keeping them at bay. There are numerous situations where people are alive today because we caught them. We catch them or we prevent them because we've got the sources and methods that lets us identify them and do something about it.

—Director of National Intelligence Mike McConnell, 2007 interview with the *El Paso Times*, when asked if terrorists had crossed the US southern border.[1]

In late 2018, as the Trump administration was fielding press demands for "proof" of his claims about dangerous Middle East migrants at the border, Rep. Trey Gowdy (R-SC), as chairman of the House Committee on Oversight and Government Reform, issued an unusual demand for investigation that went oddly unnoticed given the swirl around the president's claims of a terrorist infiltration threat. In a letter, Gowdy's committee asked DHS's Office of the Inspector General to investigate how exactly a Somali migrant had been able to smuggle up to the California border through Mexico, gain legal freedom inside the United States, and then, in September

2017, go on to conduct a double-vehicle ramming attack in Edmonton, Alberta while carrying an ISIS flag.[2]

The migrant was Abdulahi Hasan Sharif, and he holds dubious distinction as the first border-crossing SIA to have conducted a terror attack in North America. Sharif had himself smuggled from Africa to Brazil-Panama-Guatemala-Mexico and then to the California border in July 2011. He somehow got through immigration processing and to freedom long enough to achieve international protection in Canada.[3] Within thirty-six months of resettling as a refugee, a coworker reported to Canadian counterterrorism investigators that Sharif held to a "genocidal belief" system and wanted to kill polytheists, a notorious Islamist extremist trope about Shia Muslims.[4] The informant later told Canadian media that Sharif had already embraced the beliefs of jihadist groups like ISIS from "years before" and often "ranted" on about them.[5] The coworker said Sharif especially had it in for people who believed in multiple gods. "He said they need to die. That sort of thing."

But there was no evidence to charge Sharif with anything, and Canadian authorities let him go.[6] Sharif finally struck his generous Canadian hosts on September 24, 2017, in what appeared to be a well-planned jihadist attack. Taking along a black ISIS flag, Sharif cruised a white Chevy Malibu toward a Canadian Football League game outside Commonwealth Stadium in Edmonton and rammed a police officer. He got out with a knife he'd brought, along with the ISIS flag, and tried repeatedly to stab the officer, who fended off the attack. Sharif fled, apparently to a U-Haul cube truck he had rented for the occasion. With that, he ran over four people before leading police on a wild vehicle chase that only ended when the truck overturned. In 2019, an Edmonton jury convicted him on five counts of attempted murder.[7]

In his letter to DHS Office of Inspector General, Gowdy wrote that his committee was "deeply concerned the vulnerabilities existing in 2011 which allowed this individual to enter, be released, and transit through the US may still exist today despite demonstrated efforts by the Department to close important policy and procedural gaps in identifying and managing high risk aliens.[8]

"More than one year has passed since the attack, and it appears there has been no comprehensive study of the incident. Therefore, the Committee requests the Office of the Inspector General investigate the circumstances that allowed Sharif to enter the United States, then Canada, and carry out the attack."

The American media, which at that very moment was haranguing President Trump to back up his claim that the southern border was vulnerable to terrorist infiltration, did not notice the case even though the border-crossing Somali jihadist was heading for trial on five counts of attempted murder and had drawn Canadian media investigation. So far out of sight and mind was the Edmonton attack inside the United States that even the president didn't know to mention the attacker's California border crossing, though the *Edmonton Sun*'s justice reporter Jonny Wakefield had at least locally published an elaborate investigation documenting Sharif's movements.[9]

The committee remains the only organ of American government to formally acknowledge North America's first border-crossing terror attack. Gowdy's letter probably had its origins in a column penned by Center for Immigration Studies' Resident Fellow in Law and Policy, Andrew R. Arthur. He cited the *Edmonton Sun*'s reporting and my reporting of the *Sun*'s reporting in calling for government investigative action on grounds that, without government investigative powers, "even the most intrepid reporter" would be unable to discover the "exact mechanics" of how Sharif was handled once he arrived at both borders.[10]

The committee's demands seemed reasonable. It wanted to know what DHS policies, guidance, and communications were in place to vet SIAs at the border, how many had been apprehended in the last eight years, and the extent to which SIAs were involved in asylum fraud.

But by the end of 2020—two years after the letter was penned—no OIG response was in evidence. Nor is it likely there will ever be one. Not only did DHS OIG apparently ignore the written request but so too did an American media supposedly starving for proof of a terrorist border infiltration threat. The big questions and knowledge of the "exact mechanics" about this laboratory case study of a terrorist crossing of the US southern border remain unanswered, the case unknown to the general public and unplumbed for lessons learned.

It is hardly the only one.

As the Trump administration was fending off demands for evidence of jihadist border crossings, I could not help but wonder why the president did not order the declassification of a trove of materials I knew would have sated the questioners and informed a nation hungry for knowledge but was being told the whole notion was theoretical and imagined. I knew the American counterterrorism programs set up after 9/11 *had* caught jihadists crossing the border and on their way to it, that apprehensions *had* prevented many attacks, and that the Sharif case amounted to a rare one that got through.

In early 2020, I asked James Dinkins, former director of ICE Homeland Security Investigations under President Obama until 2014, if he shared my view that a largely secret American counterterrorism program at and beyond the land border had prevented attacks on US soil to date.

"Absolutely, absolutely," Dinkins responded. "I definitely think that there are people who have been interdicted. A lot of dangerous threats were prevented from coming into the US because of the great screening that's been conducted."[11]

In disclosing this to me, Dinkins was in good company. A decade or so earlier, Bush-era National Intelligence Director Mike McConnell told reporters during a visit to the Texas border city of El Paso the same thing, that homeland security agencies had caught terrorists at the border and saved lives in unheralded events.

"There are numerous situations where people are alive today because we caught them [terrorists]," McConnell told the *El Paso Times* during a wide-ranging interview in August 2007. A reporter asked why the American public didn't hear about them. McConnell admitted, "The vast majority you don't hear about" because that might compromise "sources and methods" used to intercept them.

"Remember, let me give you a way to think about this," he continued during the *El Paso Times* interview. "If you've got an issue, you have three potential outcomes, only three. A diplomatic success, an operational success or an intelligence failure. Because all those diplomatic successes and operations successes where there's intelligence contribution, it's not an intelligence success; it's just part of the process. But if there's an intelligence failure…"

A reporter interjected: "*Then*, you hear about it." McConnell, probably nodding, picked up from there.

"So, are terrorists coming across the Southwest border? Not in great numbers. There are some. And would they use it as a path, given it was available to them? In time they will."

Things that don't go boom on US soil are hard to tally. Dinkins cited a frustration common among homeland security officials who work on the terrorist infiltration threat.

"I think it's dangerous to come to the conclusion that there's no risk just because something hasn't happened. It's a fallacy to think that [absence of attack] is your measure, the same way you wouldn't think that bank security wasn't successful because a patron hasn't robbed them."

A veteran DHS officer who spent years chasing SIAs and terrorists in the Americas said those men and women who have worked in the counterterrorism enterprise are responsible for an achievement that will likely go unheralded by history.

"I believe it's kept us safe," the retired officer told me, after I had to draw him out on the question.

"It's kept another terrorist attack from happening."

ACTION AT THE GATES

SIAs cross the border from Mexico in one of two ways after their incredible long-distance smuggling journeys to get as far as our Rio Grande. The SIA migrants often use localized "coyote" smugglers on the Mexican bank to help them cross over by rubber rafts or a swim. The other common entry method is to simply walk over a pedestrian bridge to a well-staffed official port of entry and ask for asylum. Frankly, the majority turn out to be economic migrants with no hint of terrorism connections or interest. But often enough, those doing this work found needles in the haystack.

My counterterrorism intelligence job with the Texas state police—the Texas Department of Public Safety—often required me to determine truth from fiction when word came that terrorists had crossed our border. If it was a media report alleging that ISIS terrorists were raiding across the river, our governor and state legislators would beat down the DPS door wanting to know if it was true. Finding out always fell to me and my team.

Some could be quickly shelved as ridiculous, like a media report asserting that terrorists were set to spring forth from an ISIS training camp in a very specific part of the Mexican border city of Juarez, which adjoins El Paso. I'd typically check with the FBI, CIA, US Southern Command's intelligence group in Miami, and National Counterterrorism Center in DC, who had eyes on the ground by satellite or drone and access to informants in Mexico and Mexican troops and intelligence officers who could be sent to scout around. Sometime after I had ruled out that particular media report, while visiting the multistory El Paso FBI office building overlooking Juarez, I found myself talking over that media report with a group of counterterrorism task force agents who also had to check it out. A giant pair of binoculars stood upright on the windowsill of the third-floor conference room overlooking Juarez as we chatted about *how* the agents had found the report to be discreditable. One of the agents pointed out the window by the giant binoculars and chuckled, "Dude, we can *see* where they said the terrorist training camp is, the dumbasses. It's right *not* there."

As Europe's recent experience with systematic border infiltration shows, terrorists don't cross with guns blazing and suicide belts exploding. They don't arrive with mark-of-Cain terrorism tattoos on foreheads or having been already convicted in courts of law. Nothing about this near war is that simplistic because SIAs with connections to jihadist groups seek to mask those affiliations and histories as best they possibly can from federal agents who are trying just as hard to uncover them.

As one longtime DHS veteran of this covert border war explained it, "The reality is that there's no blood test that tells you if someone's a terrorist. There's just not some way you can take a test that someone's a radicalized terrorist. You have to have derogatory information that you can tie them to."

The officer was referring to intelligence information, upon which the entire enterprise rests. The way things actually work is that terrorism-related intelligence reporting, tips, and leads come in about real-live SIAs. When terrorism-related intelligence does arrive, it triggers responses akin to a homeland security five-alarm fire. It sparks intense investigative activity. It can draw in officials at the highest levels of the American government and homeland security establishment. Eventually, the investigation results come in, get analyzed, and results in decisions about what to do with the migrant. The outcomes of such investigations range from discreditable to red-alert terrorist confirmations.

From my Texas border vantage point, I knew how these responses looked and felt because I was often part of them or was aware of them. My professional stake in the matter came from the fact that our own annual Texas DPS intelligence assessments showed two-thirds of the arriving SIAs—Somalis, Syrians, Iraqis, Pakistanis, Afghans, and Iranians, among many others on the country-of-interest lists—crossed the Rio Grande border into Texas Department of Public Safety jurisdictions where our troopers patrolled.[12] We and our state leaders felt a need to know if dangerous jihadists were crossing. My team produced regular intelligence analyses for all of our law enforcement partners about SIAs and suspected terrorists among the SIAs. After learning that many SIAs were bonding out on asylum claims before federal officials could interview them, I arranged with ICE for me and my team to conduct interviews with the SIAs inside the detention centers before they could bond out. I interviewed untold dozens of SIAs myself, providing the intelligence reports to ICE, the FBI, and several intelligence community agencies.

Because we were dialed in to the broader covert war, raw or partially investigated intelligence reports about SIA terrorist connections would land on my desk like flaming missiles about half a dozen times a year between 2009 and the time I left state service in 2018. And if I was not directly involved, I was a collector of all the reporting about such incidents.

What did that look like? A typical one sometime around 2016 landed when federal colleagues called to let me know a high-interest Somali had just been caught at the Mexico-California border. As usual, with no identity documents, another Somali had given a name and claimed US asylum. But this one's real identity was soon discovered and set off the full five-alarm response. Because along with his real name came a detailed intelligence file about him from a trusted allied country in Europe.

When any SIA flagged trouble like this, ICE intelligence, the FBI, and representatives of intelligence agencies such as the military's Defense Intelligence Agency (DIA) rumbled to life like fire trucks speeding off to a reported blaze. They made a beeline to whichever detention center had the migrant to begin interviews and investigations that could go global fast and often reached the White House. The federal officers of the different agencies would analyze the pocket trash, dump cell phone data, rerun the databases, and start checking the stories by considerable means available to them, to include the intelligence of many cooperating allied governments. The idea was always to advance, validate, or discredit the initial bad word about the migrant. In about 2015, CBP created Tactical Terrorist Response Teams of investigators dedicated to interviewing and investigating suspected terrorists who crossed, and other bad guys, as well. They hovered near the busier ports of entry and immersed themselves in intelligence while they waited for their bat phones to ring.[13] They were very much in the mix too. I once spent time with the El Paso team in 2017 in a nondescript office at the bridge, listening to one close-call story after another where the CBP guys zeroed in on probable terrorists for days on end, piecing together their histories and cutting through the lies.

This particular Somali detained at the California border, it turns out, was a virulent Islamic jihadist committed to violence against the hated United States. It was the real deal. He had been living in the allied country and fled after an extended counterterrorism investigation led to the arrest of members of his cell for plotting a major terror attack there. Agents with the FBI, DIA, and other agencies descended on the ICE detention facility where the Somali was being held and interviewed him at least for several days. Having received debriefings about the situation as the feds worked it, I knew this case, as others before it, had escalated to agency headquarters leaderships in Washington, DC. The officers on the ground checked his testimony against databases and intelligence files, pushing to box him up in lies and hoping to wring a confession as to his intentions. Importantly, they dug at the Somali SIA about whether any associates had come in or were on the way and if he had any inside the United States. The reporting on this one was briefed to the White House.

The federals had the Somali transferred to a Texas detention facility for reasons unknown to me. Then, he was sent to a third detention facility in the Virginia area near Washington, as I knew sometimes happened with migrants of high-grade security concern, where other intelligence officers would have access. From there, the Somali was deported to an unknown country.

Attack averted? Probably. To those of us working in the space, cases like that one fairly regularly validated the threat of potential attack from the porous borderlands and of the need for unrelenting attention to the work. In any given year, there was plenty of that work to go around, not all of it as fruitful but just as necessary to eliminate nagging possibilities.

One illustrative case came in from a Texas DPS informant who let us know that three Pakistani al-Qaeda operatives moving through Mexico were about to cross the Texas border. Sure enough, within a few days, Border Patrol picked up three Pakistanis who'd just come over the river and called it in to us.

The usual alarms sounded. Red flags zipped all the way up the pole to the governor's office, who wanted a full assessment. A DIA intelligence officer and I hopped in a truck the next day and dashed down to the border detention center in Pearsall where the Pakistanis were detained. We were proud to have beaten the FBI there. For two days, we grilled two of the Pakistanis, a Pashtun-speaking interpreter on the speaker phone, while the FBI got the third one and then reworked our two after the DIA officer and I finished. The final report: Pakistani terrorists may have been en route, but these three guys surely weren't them. The knowledge was needed. Having it allowed the hunt to go on elsewhere along the border for the reputed terrorists, with every Pakistani SIA during that time enduring grueling interviews by agents from multiple agencies. That's how it had to work.

The terrorism intelligence tips that set off these tempests came from all manner of sources—an informant, another country's intelligence services, a number in the suspect's phone that matched the number of a known terrorist somewhere else. It may come in well-developed and credible already, or fairly raw and unconfirmed. Sometimes, negative terrorism intelligence came inadvertently from the migrants themselves.

In 2014, a Somali national who'd walked over a pedestrian bridge in Texas and asked for asylum said things about himself that all but guaranteed visitation by three-letter agencies. This Somali entrant told US immigration officials that two months prior to his border entry to claim asylum he had completed al-Shabaab training for a suicide attack in Mogadishu but instead went to African Union troops who were able to thwart the planned terrorist operation. He disclosed that he had trained with thirteen other Somalis for ten weeks to use suicide belts, AK-47s, and grenades.[14] While there would have been almost no way American investigators could have found out any of this in a phone call to Somalia or even in a standard detention-center interview, admitted involvement in any designated terror group did his American dream no good, despite assertions about a change of heart. Had he ever planned to attack in America, its prevention is another that would gratify us but would also go neither confirmed nor counted beyond us.

Sometimes, the tip came out of an active investigation. In 2011, for instance, information teased out of an SIA smuggling investigation in Virginia sent FBI agents on a desperate nationwide hunt for dozens of reputed Somali terrorists who the agents learned, long after the fact, had gotten into the country over the southern border. The feds were investigating Islamic convert and Virginia native Anthony Joseph Tracy for running a business in Kenya that fraudulently provided Kenyan passports and Cuban visas to more than 270 Somalis.[15] During the investigation, Tracy admitted to the FBI that the terrorist organization al-Shabaab asked him to provide the documents to its operatives, and he failed a polygraph test in insisting he'd declined the terrorist group's entreaty. In court, investigators produced an email from Tracy to an associate in which he admitted, "I helped a lot of Somalis, and most are good, but there are some who are bad, and I leave them to Allah."[16]

That was too much to ignore. The FBI had no choice but to scramble to find Tracy's "bad" Somali customers on grounds that, as one lead investigator testified during case proceedings, "we have no idea who these individuals are that he assisted. These individuals pose—possibly pose—a risk of national security to the country."[17] A couple of years later, an FBI analyst familiar with the operation told me the names of the Somalis were too vague or common for agents to track them all down.

Likewise, the 2018 smuggling prosecution of a Pakistani SIA smuggler named Sharafat Ali Khan revealed that terrorists were smuggled in over the border among his clientele. The December 2018 ICE press release about Khan's deportation noted that "several of the individuals smuggled by Khan's organization had suspected ties to terrorist organizations."[18] In line with the rules surrounding this sort of thing, ICE provided no further details about this brief acknowledgment.

But the *Washington Times* read sensitive Khan case material obtained by former Congressman Duncan Hunter (R-CA), which provided a rare public peek behind that curtain where credible intelligence lay hidden. Hunter, a consummate illegal immigration hawk when he held office, once tried to float an ISIS infiltration that later proved to be patently untrue. In an October 2014 televised interview with Greta Van Susteren of Fox News, the congressman claimed that "At least 10 ISIS fighters have been caught coming across the Mexican border in Texas" and that there were "dozens more that did not get caught."[19] In vetting that claim for my Texas DPS leadership, I had to report it to be unfounded.

But per the rule of thumb when it comes to terrorist infiltration reporting—that behind every bogus infiltration claim hides real ones—applied in Hunter's quest for information about the Khan smuggling case. His office evidently shared the information received from homeland security agencies.

The *Washington Times* reported that one of the smuggler Khan's "several" migrants with ties to terrorist organizations was an Afghan SIA who had crawled under a fence near Nogales, Arizona, with five Pakistanis and Palestinians and had made his way with the group to a ranch fifteen miles inland, had been "involved in a plot to conduct an attack in the U.S. or Canada and had family ties to members of the Taliban."[20]

The Afghan was already on American terrorism watch lists when he crawled over the border—for his family ties to the Taliban—but he also was on the more exclusive No Fly List, an indication of an assessed high danger.

Once again, something that never went boom was neither widely noticed nor tallied.

Except perhaps by US District Judge Reggie B. Walton at Khan's 2018 sentencing, when he admonished the convicted smuggler about those he smuggled into America: "You don't know whether they're seeking a better life or whether they're trying to get in here to engage in terrorism. People could have died, people could have gotten injured, families could have lost loved ones."[21]

ON AMERICA'S TERROR WATCH LISTS

These SIA cases come in as no-brainers for five-alarm response treatment because presence on the watch lists presents a higher order of threat. It signals that American intelligence officers with the military or CIA, somewhere in a dangerous world far downstream, had already done homework and found derogatory information credible enough to reach the higher "reasonable suspicion" or "articulable evidence" standard for adding people to the lists.[22]

The number of SIAs who showed up already on US terror watch lists is classified. So-called "Known or Suspected Terrorists," or KSTs, would be those on the Terrorist Screening Database list (TSDB), the Terrorist Identities DataMart Environment list (TIDE), and the No Fly List.[23] After my departure from government, intelligence community sources agreed to let me report an indication of how frequently KSTs are caught at the southern land border. Between 2012 and 2017, American homeland security discovered that more than one hundred SIAs caught at the American southern border, or by cooperating governments en route, were already on one or more of those terrorism watch lists.

About twenty a year when averaged during those years. The breakdown between how many were caught while still traveling through Latin America and those who made it to the physical US-Mexico border is unclear. Few public sources enable us to see how many were apprehended after 2017, or where, except that watch-listed migrants have continued to show up at the border and also on their way while still south of it, as I will detail extensively in a later chapter.

In the first half of 2018, for instance, CBP reported encountering six SIAs at ports of entry whose names were on the federal list of suspected terrorists, according to data the agency supplied to NBC News.[24] Oddly, NBC reported the number as *"only* six," (author's emphasis added), as though these were so few as to barely warrant grudging mention in a news report, let alone to drive informed immigration policy. But reporters and partisan researchers are neither paid nor trained to think like homeland security professionals, among whom any single one of six, or twenty very high-risk SIA arrivals is simply unacceptable. Each watch-listed migrant who showed up raised collective blood pressures and required total, intense attention for days, weeks, and even months.

In 2020, a DHS whistleblower named Brian Murphy, once head of intelligence for the agency, filed a complaint against top Trump homeland security appointees alleging that they had demanded he overstate the number of watch-listed SIAs who reached the border. Whatever the complaint's value to political partisans, Murphy's claim disclosed that, in 2019, three watch-listed SIAs reached the US-Mexico border.[25] Of course, he did not address how many were apprehended before reaching the border, as I'll show many often are. But nine known or suspected terrorists who got through the various cordons to reach the physical US-Mexico border in 2018-2019 constituted major homeland security emergencies that warranted intense management. These kinds of numbers also confirm my own experiences, albeit minus what I also knew was happening farther south in Mexico and Latin America.

Of course, the presence of a migrant's name on a terrorism watch list does not automatically confirm hardened terrorist status or reach the same confidence threshold as would a terrorism conviction at trial. In this world, the pros are forced to take what they can get, then make the best decisions they can as lives hang in the balance. The criteria for the FBI or an intelligence agency officer to watch-list someone could range from that person's direct or indirect association with real hardened terrorists, or that they surfaced in an active terrorism investigation, to the belief that they *were* the hardened terrorist. Most worrisome were the ones coming from war zones where Americans were especially hated, possibly nursing vengeance grudges.

But the presence of an arriving SIA on one of these lists, or on others kept by the Europeans, will always spark angst and deployment of the three-letter agency guys for further investigation.

DHS and FBI officers in California kept a great many late nights in June 2010, when no less than nine East Africans on US terrorism watch lists showed up at the port of entry in San Ysidro, California, five in a single day.[26] They were Eritreans, Somalis, and Ethiopians who had been living in Sudan, a US-designated State Sponsor of Terrorism. Some reputedly were connected to al-Shabaab.

Other watch-listed SIAs made their own ways over the border from terrorism-riven nations like Pakistan, Somalia, and Yemen. It emerged from the prosecution of one SIA smuggler (a Mexico-based Jordanian) that "some" of at least six Yemenis he had smuggled over the border were on the American terror watch list.[27] They had been smuggled into Texas wearing brightly colored reflective vests and hard hats of construction workers. That anyone from Yemen had reached the border and would enter in such purposeful disguises, without identification, was problematic because, at the time, al-Qaeda in the Arabian Peninsula controlled large swaths of the country in a civil war. Federal authorities would never talk about these costumed Yemenis on the watch list. But the fact that some were on US watch lists suggested which side of the war they were on.

What became of these construction-worker Yemenis and how serious a threat they posed was only narrowly known, in typical fashion, though sources close to the investigation told me only three of the six Yemenis were still inside the United States and had helped with the prosecution. The suggestion was that the watch-listed ones were either deported or lost. US Attorney John Bash of the San Antonio–based Western District of Texas tried as best he could to indicate how his case underscored the terrorist infiltration threat.

"This case vividly illustrates how border security is a key component of national security," he said in a press release. "We simply must know the identities of every individual crossing our southern border, particularly those who are nationals of countries where terrorist organizations operate freely."[28]

They were hardly the only Yemenis who crossed the border in recent years who were on terror watch lists. In a separate October 2017 instance, four Yemenis were apprehended near Del Rio, Texas, who were all on the US terror watch list. Intelligence community sources told me a running theory about the four was that they came to test border strengths and weaknesses. Clearly, dangerous smuggling routes developed in recent years from Yemen to Mexico. In 2018, several Yemenis were caught in "panga" motorboats zipping over the marine border off the shores of Tijuana and San Diego, knowledgeable sources told me. In May 2020, three Yemenis crossed the Texas border among a group of fifteen Bangladeshis.[29]

In an interesting twist of diplomatic logistics, not all watch-listed SIAs were caught on the American side of the border. After detaining one Pakistani, Mexico found such egregious terrorism intelligence that its intelligence service officers delivered the Pakistani directly to the Americans on an international pedestrian bridge, a story my intelligence community sources relayed to me at the time. Intelligence information picked up in Mexico matched his name and likeness as a violent member in good standing of the Pakistani Taliban, a US-designated terrorist group.

He was hardly the only such suspected migrant terrorist the Mexicans handed off to the Americans on an international pedestrian bridge. In October 2017, the Americans knew from intelligence and surveillance in Central America that a Somali colleague of a known high-grade al-Shabaab terrorist was making his way through Mexico. The Mexicans caught the watch-listed Somali and walked him up to the US border for a handoff, intelligence community sources told me.

It's one thing to catch bad guys but quite another to deny them freedom inside America so they can do no harm. So what does homeland security do with these terrorist suspects after catching them?

For the short answer, consider the case of Somali migrant Maulid Jama, who came in over the border in late 2017 and was in a vehicle making a break for the nation's interior when Laredo police flashed the vehicle down in south Laredo. My intelligence community sources told me the vehicle carrying Jama led Laredo police on a wild chase that ended in a crash. The cops arrested Jama and took him to an ICE detention facility, where agents did their SIA interview-databases thing. They soon discovered that Jama had worked as a pirate in Somalia. It wasn't just the pirate job that disqualified him for enjoying any time inside the United States so much that this fact was compounded by clear and convincing intelligence information that Jama also was a hard-core member of the al-Shabaab terrorist group. He had not traveled to the border alone, either, but was part of a group of al-Shabaab fighters who had made the journey, the intelligence community sources say.

The United States did not prosecute or imprison Jama for any of this. That would require months of unnecessary evidence collection and the huge expense of a trial. The cheap, easy, and legal way to dispatch with any possible threat was to deport him back to Somalia. And that's just what the government did.

THE BETTER-SAFE-THAN-SORRY OPTION

Think also about how many restrictions we have on air travel, how many lists and scrutiny people have to go through to get a visa to get into this country, especially if they're coming from a place like Yemen, which has a significant terrorist presence. You don't have to go through any of that process. You just have to fly to Ecuador and walk across the border. This is a huge loophole in our national security system. We need to know every single person who's coming into this country, what their identity is, whether they fly in, whether they take a boat in, whether they walk in, drive in…we need to know who they are. And to have a system where you have tens of thousands or hundreds of thousands of people a year walking into the country [is] a massive loophole.

—US Attorney for the Western District of
Texas John Bash, April 29, 2019, press conference
announcing sentencing of SIA smuggler of Yemenis.[30]

What the homeland security establishment does with terrorism-flagged SIAs usually takes place in offices, not courtrooms or before judges. As we saw with the self-professed Somali suicide bomber caught in California, deportation is most often the default move for SIAs deemed to have unacceptable terrorism baggage.

This is part of a better-safe-than-sorry gambit that happens far outside normal public realm due processes, prized because it cleanly and legally short-circuits any immediate threat as well as distant future problems indicated by what was learned about the SIA. Quiet deportations confer one other benefit: unlike noisy public terrorism trials where government evidence must be produced, deportations allow for the secret means and methods used to collect foreign intelligence to remain secret so that nefarious actors are unable to murder informants or adapt their behaviors.

Homeland security decision-makers who consider final investigative reports about terrorism-flagged SIAs and recommend their fates do not enjoy the luxury of choosing a course of action based on some judicial process like a jury trial, where allegations are vetted through rigorous adversarial legal processes. Nor are those officials who make these decisions legally required to lay formal terrorism charges against noncitizens who have illegally entered the country, their terrorism offenses having occurred in other countries where any burden of proof would likely be hard to meet.

Preemptive deportation decisions do need to be made on the basis of the good information, best judgment, and perhaps occasionally in league with immigration judges considering whether to allow asylum claims to proceed, which almost all SIAs stake. Who renders such judgments and how are among the most opaque aspects of the near border war. Deportation simply removes them from the calculus, including the expensive, high-bar trudge of a federal prosecution of some sort. It appears over and over as a way to ensure dangerous actors are removed from the battlefield with the least fuss and muss. This clear-the-decks deportation option can be credited with helping prevent terror attacks while also preserving the veil of secrecy thought to protect current and next operations.

One case that came the closest to breaking the silence code initially popped into the open like a flare from a gun in July 2004, when the media breathlessly reported the illegal crossing into Texas of Pakistani national Farida Goolam Ahmed. I was a reporter in Dallas at the time and remember consuming every morsel of news about the case. Airport officials from the Rio Grande Valley border town of McAllen, Texas, arrested Ahmed while she carried clothing still wet from swimming the Rio Grande and a passport mutilated to hide her airport arrival in Mexico City. She drew intense national media attention, which immediately faded to complete black after official government declarations that she was *not* connected in any way to terrorism.

Except that she very much was, as I confirmed later.

The initial flurry of national reporting that summer included a *New York Times* dispatch that tied Ahmed to an al-Qaeda plot to transport non-Arab operatives over the Mexican border for multiple vehicle-borne bomb attacks against large corporate facilities in New York City.[31] After meeting with senior FBI officials, the New York Police Department issued warnings to building managers and corporate security personnel to step up their security against car bombs rigged with chemical agents. The newspaper quoted an anonymous law enforcement official in the city as saying "the information is considered credible" and that the warnings "appeared to be linked to the arrest on July 19 in Texas of Farida Goolam Mohamed Ahmed after she entered the United States from Mexico by crossing the Rio Grande and crawling through the brush." [32]

Then the story completely disappeared, but I did not forget it. A few years later, when I was hired as an investigative reporter for Hearst Newspapers closer to the border in San Antonio, the very first thing I did was start digging on the story again. I found a US Border and Transportation Security intelligence summary dated December 9, 2004, four months after the *Times* report, that stated, contrary to government assertions, that Ahmed had indeed been "linked to specific terrorist activities."[33]

Knowing the heat was no longer on three years later, in 2007, I phoned the Houston-based federal prosecutor who had handled the case, Abe Martinez, chief of the Southern District of Texas national security section in the US Attorney's Houston office. I asked if Ahmed or anyone she smuggled might have been involved in terrorism.

"Were they linked to any terrorism organizations? I would have to say yes," Martinez flatly told me.[34] He wouldn't say more or why the government had felt so compelled to risk the public lie back in 2004 that she wasn't. As I continued my excavations elsewhere, an FBI official with direct knowledge of the investigation finally told me that Ahmed's husband was a confirmed member of the Muttahida Qaumi Movement (MQM), a Pakistan political movement and party whose various iterations and factions have long conducted terroristic political violence.[35] The US government regarded MQM itself as a "Tier III" terrorist organization and has routinely denied members' immigration applications for "terrorist activities."[36]

Court transcripts and government investigative materials provided to me later seemed to support the *Times* reporting that Ahmed was linked to an al-Qaeda plot to smuggle in operatives over the border for attacks in New York City. They identified Ahmed as a South Africa–based human smuggler for MQM who my law enforcement sources—who had direct knowledge—said operated an MQM safe house in Johannesburg, South Africa, sheltering associated terrorists of other groups who were "on the run." One fugitive she and her husband sheltered participated in a 1995 ambush murder of two US consulate employees in Karachi, Pakistan.[37] As a smuggler, Ahmed regularly transported Pakistanis and others associated with MQM over the US-Mexico border and also into Canada and Australia.[38]

The US government chose deportation for Ahmed, a better-safe-than-sorry remedy that not only removed her physically but also would have safeguarded how the US government collected any intelligence about her or the New York plot investigation. A deal was cut. After taking Ahmed's guilty plea for illegal entry (a federal misdemeanor carrying up to six months in prison), the government gave her "time served" and quickly deported her back to South Africa, court records show.

A fair argument is that deportation was the wrong choice for someone as mobile as Ahmed and some of the others too. With her smuggling and travel experience, Ahmed could well be right back herself or simply continue smuggling more Pakistani murderers and terrorist fugitives into the US from afar.

That is a risk. There is some merit in the argument that deportation, rather than prosecution and imprisonment inside the United States, leaves dangerous and determined national enemies free to try again. Something like that actually happened in the 2011 case of Tunisian terrorism provocateur and radical cleric Said Jaziri.

In 2007, Canada deported Jaziri for lying about a lengthy criminal history to gain legal permanent residency seven years earlier.[39] Jaziri was leading the largest North African mosque in Montreal, Quebec, by the time Canada discovered his prevarications. What Jaziri lied about on his refugee application was that, before he immigrated to Canada, France had deported him after convictions for involvement in an attack on a less-devout person for closing down a prayer room, as well as illegal entry. Jaziri had immigrated to

France after a conviction in his native Tunisia for membership in the illegal and violent Islamist political group Hizb Ennahda.

Other criminal history included assault and destruction of property and illegal entry into France and possessing a fraudulent passport in Brussels. After he fooled Canada into granting him refugee status on an obviously unvetted persecution story, Jaziri drew disastrous attention to himself for espousing extreme anti-Western rhetoric and advocating for Sharia law.[40] After his true past was uncovered and refugee status revoked, Jaziri hid in his mosque for weeks and then waged a two-year legal battle to stay that failed.

But Canada's deportation of him in 2007 didn't deter Jaziri from coming back. On January 11, 2011, Border Patrol agents on a road south of San Diego, California, discovered him in the trunk of a professional smuggler's black BMW sedan they'd pulled over on Old Highway 80 near the main entrance to the Golden Acorn Casino. A Mexican national was in the trunk with him. Jaziri had spent $5,000 to return from Tunisia, aided on the last leg by an organization in Tijuana.[41] In an interview with federal investigators, Jaziri said he had flown from Tunisia to Spain, then to Guatemala, El Salvador, Belize, and Chetumal, Mexico. In Chetumal, he took a bus to Tijuana and found a local coyote to smuggle him over and then to someone who could drive him into the country's interior. The plan, Jaziri told American investigators, was "to go to a safe place anywhere in the United States."[42]

The US deported Jaziri in exchange for his testimony against the BMW's driver, a middle-aged white man who needed quick cash, and this time, apparently, it stuck.[43] By 2019, he was serving as a member of Tunisia's Assembly of the Representatives of the People.[44]

Still, the idea behind deportation as resolution is that it's not so easy for most suspected terrorists to return from countries on the other side of the globe. Yet another Somali detained at a Mexico-California port of entry in May 2011 came up in US intelligence databases as a member of the al-Shabaab terrorist organization who had previously been denied a US immigration visa while he was still overseas, according to records I have reviewed. He'd been traveling with a group of seven other Somalis in Mexico, all of whom were suspected of having ties to al-Shabaab and of posing a threat to the United States. The Mexicans let the Americans know the whole terrorist gang was coming (more on that operational relationship in Chapter Six), but only this one migrant was found as far as I knew.

Undeterred by the US consulate officer's rejection of his refugee reset-tlement claim abroad, the Somali simply had himself smuggled to the California border instead, where he knew he'd have better luck with an asy-lum claim.[45] The feds ran him through the paces and found out that not only was he on the terror watch list and the No Fly List but also so were his mother, father, and four siblings, some of whom this asylum seeker, had he succeeded with a claim, would undoubtedly have brought in later under family reunification immigration programs.[46] The Somali's asylum claim, of course, ran into "interference," and he was deported to Kenya instead, unlikely to leave his extended terror-watch-listed family again, knowing he couldn't bring them along. I never found out what became of seven Somali traveling companions.

Short of full-court convictions, a rare confession, or a lucky investiga-tive strike, intelligence information like this often presents the only chance to save lives that might be lost later. A watch-listed migrant like Jama the pirate-terrorist had to be viewed as high-risk for the United States, the cleanest available cure being deportation.

Likewise, with yet another Somali SIA unrelated to any others in this chapter. In 2015, Border Patrol captured Mauad Dahir after he crossed the Mexico-Arizona border. Somehow, US agents didn't get to Dahir in an Eloy, Arizona, facility for nearly three months, an almost fatal screw-up, the intel-ligence community source told me. They were lucky he didn't bond out first. When investigators finally put him through the paces of interviews, database checks, and a cell-phone data dump, they learned that Dahir was in regu-lar communication with hard-core al-Shabaab operatives still in Africa and that he too was a fighter for the group. Was he plotting a specific attack, or might he one day be called upon to do so? Better safe than sorry. Deporting Dahir took almost a full year because of various paperwork snafus and legal circumstances, but he was sent back to Africa, the source told me.[47]

Deportation likewise would have been necessary for Pakistani nationals Muhammad Azeem and Mukhtar Ahmad, who got caught in December 2015 just north of Tijuana after traveling from their home town and district of Gujrat through Latin American and Mexico.[48] Once in Border Patrol cus-tody, they would have been flagged as SIAs, of course, triggering terrorism intelligence database checks.

Those showed Ahmad was on the American terrorist watch list as "an associate of a known or suspected terrorist," according to media reports generated when California's Representative Hunter demanded more information about the encounters in a letter to DHS Secretary Johnson. It came out that Azeem was a positive match for other "derogatory information" in a different terrorism database.[49] Little else in the public record indicates what that was or what became of them, but it is highly unlikely they escaped deportation.

MISSING IN ACTION

There are discomfiting indications that others are slipping the Border Patrol gauntlets and getting to the interior, easily the most worrisome class of SIA since they have time to do damage. A 2009 Government Accountability Office audit of Border Patrol inland checkpoints found one anecdotal tell: 530 SIAs were discovered the previous year at highway checkpoints twenty miles inland aboard vehicles, having gotten by Border Patrol, including "three identified as linked to terrorism," the report stated.[50] It stands to reason that unknown numbers of SIAs and watch-listed terrorist suspects among them probably bypass Border Patrol *and* the inland road checkpoints undetected and are not counted for years until they are caught in the interior.

In 2001, for instance, Lebanese national Mahmoud Kourani was smuggled across the Mexican border and into the US in the trunk of a car and settled in Dearborn, Michigan.[51] Not until several years later, in 2004, did the FBI discover that Kourani was a "fighter, recruiter and fund-raiser" for Hezbollah, sent from Lebanon to operate in the United States. Court records said Kourani had received "specialized training in radical Shiite fundamentalism, weaponry, spy craft and counterintelligence in Lebanon and Iran." Prosecutors said his brother, Haidar, was chief of military security for the group in southern Lebanon. Kourani was prosecuted and convicted of material support for terrorism, served fifty-four months in federal prison on a terrorism conviction, and then was deported.

But that's not always the outcome as we have seen repeatedly with missing Somali, Bangladeshi, and Pakistani terrorist suspects. A 2004 investigation into the Lebanon-Tijuana smuggling ring that brought Kourani over the California border in a car trunk found it had also transported a worker for the US-designated terrorist entity that was Hezbollah's satellite television network, Al Manar.[52] This was more problematic than first glance would have anyone believe because Hezbollah used the station to cover the movement of terrorist operatives, according to the US Treasury Department.[53] The US State Department also added the station to its Terrorist Exclusion List in 2004. There's no evidence that the Al Manar terrorist was ever found. And like Tracy's missing "bad" Somali document customers, others have gone missing too.

In June 2010, in another instance, one of two Bangladeshis caught illegally crossing near Naco, Arizona, admitted to US Border Patrol interviewers that both had worked in the General Assembly for the US-designated terrorist group Harkat-ul-Jihad-al-Islami Bangladesh (HuJI-B), a radical terrorist group that has drawn inspiration and direct assistance from Osama bin Laden's International Islamic Front. The US State Department designated HuJI-B a global terrorist organization on February 15, 2008. Too late to realize the mistake in disclosing their connection to HuJI-B, they tried to recant. One of the two detainees was deported back to Bangladesh, but the other somehow made bond on an asylum claim and disappeared.[54]

CROSSERS OF OTHER NATIONAL SECURITY CONCERNS

Some SIAs coming over the border were not jihadists at all but of high national security interest to the American intelligence world. They were espionage threats. Looking through an ICE list of SIAs who hadn't been interviewed yet one day, I was surprised to find an Iranian. The usual agencies sent representatives to interview every Iranian who turned up on the US side, in part to ferret out whether they might be an intelligence officer posing as a migrant, not so much a terrorist.

Soon into my interview, this Iranian revealed a stunning story: he'd been a member of the Grand Ayatollah's elite personal bodyguard unit. He'd been swept up in an internal purge of traitors in the rarified cadre and ended up in a gulag. He was let out, imprisoned again, and then ran for the US border the second he was freed again. Or so he said. My final report set off a battle among three-letter intelligence agencies to be first to lay claim to him. (The FBI won the fight by opening a preliminary terrorism investigation on him and waving off the other agencies.)

Author interviewing an Iranian migrant in Costa Rica, December 2018

Another Iranian, this one caught after crossing the Texas border among twenty-one Mexican nationals in the spring of 2012, was so successfully evasive with his ICE and CBP interviewers at the Port Isabel detention center that agents who interviewed him told me he had clearly undergone counter-interrogation training.

While doing field research in a migrant camp in Acuna, Mexico, on the Rio Grande banks in 2019, I came across a Russian emblematic of the need for American homeland security agencies to vet migrants' backgrounds. Through a phone translator application, the Russian would only give his name as "Vladimir" and his home as the city of Yuzhno-Sakhalinsk on Russia's Sakhalin Island, which is just north of Japan. In responding to a question about why Vladimir left home and chose the US southern border as his entrance point, he would only answer on a cell phone translation application: "problems with police." He would not elaborate other than to suggest that whatever happened felt like persecution to him.

"I had to leave," Vladimir typed of his mysterious law enforcement issue. He told me it had been easy and inexpensive to travel on his own this far, without smuggling assistance or breaking any laws, that many Russians were making the trip, and that they all kept in touch on social media. A flight from Moscow to Havana, Cuba, on a cheap visitor's visa, then a flight to Monterrey, Mexico; all Russians can easily arrange visas to Mexico online.

Assuming Vladimir made it into the United States, it would have been incumbent on US agents to determine whether he deserved sanctuary on the asylum claim he planned to lodge or posed an espionage threat or even a run-of-the-mill dangerous criminal threat.

Migrants cross posing other high-end kinds of security threats as well. In Newark, New Jersey, federal prosecutors busted an Afghan interpreter who once served US military forces for smuggling at least two other Afghans over the Texas border, where they applied for asylum.[55] Mujeeb Rahman Saify was accused of smuggling the Afghans over in 2016 because neither could qualify for special immigrant visas being given out to Afghans for their helpful military service.[56]

According to an unsealed federal complaint, the military had fired one of the smuggled Afghans as a "security risk based on his association with a foreign intelligence service." That would be the reason the SIA couldn't qualify for the special visa. Now he was inside the United States, having illegally crossed the southern border, and would have remained had there been no investigation. Court filings provide no further details about the nature of the "security risk," though it would appear to be related to espionage or intelligence support to a foreign terrorist organization.

Other SIA members of US-designated terrorist organizations could not be regarded as posing a direct threat to the United States but demonstrate a diversity of unwelcome guests. For instance, I recall a case in about early 2018, when three Turks crossed the border into Texas and created the usual stir. Federal investigators rushed to the detention center and eventually learned they were members of the Kurdistan Workers' Party, or PKK, a Kurdish separatist group that often bombed targets in Turkey. The US had designated the PKK as a terrorist organization as a diplomatic favor to NATO ally Turkey, so technically this wasn't a good thing. They all would have been deported as suspected terrorists in the technical sense. But truth be known, hackles fell after we learned the trio were PKK since that organization was uninterested in attacking the American homeland.

Likewise, after 2009, quite a few migrants who identified as belonging to Sri Lanka's Tamil ethnic minority began reaching the US border, after the central government militarily destroyed their separatist forces, known as the Liberation Tigers of Tamil Eelam, and more colloquially as the Tamil Tigers, following decades of vicious war. The US had designated the Tamil Tigers as a foreign terrorist organization, in part, because of its widespread use of suicide bombings in Sri Lanka and in India, both US allies like Turkey. In 2007, prior to the Tamil Tigers defeat, Border Patrol apprehended only four Sri Lankans at the southern border. That number leapt to 173 after the war in 2010, to 214 in 2011, and hit 465 in 2019, according to Border Patrol apprehension statistics.

Sri Lankan migrants traveling through Costa Rica, December 2018. Photo by Todd Bensman

Several of the Tamils who came over the Mexico-US border were discovered to have belonged to the Tigers. In March 2012, for instance, one who crossed from Mexico into Texas let slip that they were Tamil Tigers on their way to join family and associates in Canada.[57] In February 2017, a Border Patrol agent arrested Tamil Tiger Vijayakumar Thuraissigiam after he crossed from Mexico, leading to an extended legal battle over his asylum claim.[58] There were others.

Again, privately, homeland security authorities have told me they did not get too exercised when Tamil Tigers showed up at the border because the organization had never expressed aspirations to attack the US homeland or American interests abroad. But the organization was designated as a foreign terrorist organization. Its operatives had been prosecuted in the United States and Canada for fundraising and weapons procurement schemes, such as two New York operatives indicted in 2012 for trying to acquire surface-to-air missiles, AK-47 rifles, and submarine design information.[59]

And I once read an intelligence assessment that worried its members were attempting to reconstitute the organization by bringing its leadership into North America and starting up illegal schemes to rearm.

Homeland security leaders, however, did start to worry more about this human traffic after coordinated jihadist bombings in April 2019 killed more than 300 Sri Lankan Christians celebrating Easter in their churches. The bombings were attributed to operatives once affiliated with the island-nation's Salafi-jihadist National Throwed Jamath group and claimed by ISIS. After ICE busted the prolific Sri Lankan-Canadian smuggler Sri Kajamukam "Mohan" Chelliah in July 2020, American homeland security officials overseeing the case indicated high awareness of a national security aspect of the investigation.

"Transnational Criminal Organizations use human smuggling as a means for profit while at the same time threatening the security of the United States," ICE-HSI Miami's Special Agent in Charge Anthony Salisbury said in the indictment statement. Likewise, Acting Assistant Attorney General Brian C. Rabbitt noted that smugglers like Chelliah "jeopardize our national security."[60]

A MOST COMMON OCCURRENCE

Occasionally, SIAs judged to be dangerous terrorists are not secretly deported in counterterrorism moves. They get prosecuted for other crimes as an expedient means to get them off the street.

One of the most notable of these was the case of Somalia natives Abdullahi Omar Fidse and Deka Abdalla Sheikh, who would both later be prosecuted for asylum fraud and sentenced under a terrorism enhancement for obstructing an FBI terrorism investigation.[61] But their story underscores a common method that SIAs use to enter and potentially embed themselves in the United States: filing for asylum.

Their story, available now in court records, began on June 24, 2008, when Fidse and Sheikh walked across the pedestrian bridge from Reynosa, Mexico, to the port of entry in Hidalgo, Texas, and requested political asylum from an American immigration officer. They'd paid Ethiopian smugglers $4,000 each to get them from Africa to the bridge on counterfeit passports and Mexican visas.

The pair told authorities they had only met during the trek to Texas but had fled Somalia and needed American sanctuary for the same reason: the terrorist group al-Shabaab had killed their family members. The story worked for Sheikh; she was quickly awarded asylum and took up permanent residence in Fitchburg, Wisconsin, on a path to American citizenship. While still in Texas detention, however, Fidse confided to two fellow Somalis— who turned out to be paid FBI informants—that he actually came to conduct an unspecified "operation" for al-Shabaab.[62]

Fidse said he cried when a US airstrike killed al-Shabaab leader Aden Hashi Ayrow and that "the infidels must suffer the consequences." To one of the FBI informants, as a recording device rolled tape, Fidse discussed the Quranic imperative to "terrorize the infidels" and stated, "We are terrorists."[63]

Fidse elaborated as the informants secretly recorded him. He described details of an aborted plot to attack the US ambassador in Kenya, drawing out the assassination plans on paper and describing how mines would have been used to "blow up" the US Marines in the protective detail.[64] Fidse said he loved al-Qaeda leader Osama bin Laden and believed all good Muslims must commit two acts of jihad a year. He confided that he had gotten military training at a camp run by an Afghanistan war veteran and had extensive knowledge of heavy weapons, including shoulder-fired rockets, machine guns, AK-47 assault rifles, and explosives.[65]

He wasn't just boasting to look the tough guy in his detention block; investigators found a number in Fidse's cell phone memory card belonging to a well-known al-Shabaab terrorist who would be implicated two years later in a Uganda soccer stadium bombing that killed more than seventy spectators. Prosecutors pushed for and initially received a rare "terrorism enhancement" adding a decade to Fidse's sentence for asylum fraud, though this was later overturned on appeal (though on arcane legal grounds rather than for lack of evidence). Sheikh, who'd already received asylum and was living in Wisconsin, was arrested and charged with federal crimes. In 2012, Sheikh and Fidse pleaded guilty to asylum fraud and lying to the FBI about his terrorism. After completing their time in 2018, ICE put them on deportation flights to Somalia.[66]

The fact that Sheikh had already received US political asylum within three months of her arrival with her terrorist husband—and was comfortably resettled in Wisconsin—underlines one of the most dangerous and tenacious gaps in America's imperfect border cordon. In the anecdotes described here, readers will see that almost all of the actors flagged as probable terrorists had applied for political asylum as soon as they reached the border. Just as in Europe, the mere act of filing an asylum claim triggers a legal process that allows for releases from detention and the right to live and work in freedom for months and years. For jihadists like Canada's Edmonton attacker Sharif, the system spells opportunity to embed and prepare for violence when it suits.

The Fidse and Sheikh cases demonstrate that a terrorist traveler's very best and most reliable friend is the United States asylum system as it now stands.

CHAPTER FOUR

THE ASYLUM CALAMITY

There is nothing more important to a terrorist than getting where he needs to go and being able to stay there long enough to carry out his or her instructions. We call this 'embedding.'

—Janice Kephart, an author of *9/11 and Terrorist Travel: Staff Report of the National Commission on Terrorist Attacks Upon the United States,* testifying before the US Senate, March 14, 2005.[67]

Mohammad Ahmad Dhakane and his young wife walked together over the international pedestrian bridge from Matamoros, Mexico, to the Brownsville, Texas, Port of Entry on March 28, 2008. Dhakane introduced himself and Leyla Osman Agal as Somalis to the Customs and Border Protection entry inspections officer; like many Somalis from their government-less country, they had no passports or identification.

But Dhakane, who was twenty-five at the time and knew American law, came with a few magic words that would usher him and Leyla into the United States and then a release to live, work, and pursue citizenship.

"We want asylum," Dhakane declared in English.

And they were in.

CBP transported the couple to the ICE detention facility in Pearsall, Texas—the protocol when undocumented petitioners walk up to a border crossing and ask for asylum. Within a few days, an asylum officer with

United States Citizenship and Immigration Service (USCIS) telephoned to perform a perfunctory half-hour or forty-five-minute interview to hear Dhakane's tale of persecution that would allow him to proceed with a US asylum application. This initial screening, known as a "credible fear" interview, is a legal prerequisite.

An applicant's entire life hangs in the balance when an asylum officer assesses a persecution story. The officers' jobs are to judge whether an immigrant facing deportation had a "significant possibility" of persecution on one of five grounds embedded in US asylum law: race, religion, nationality, membership in a particular social group, or political opinion.[68] The consequence of reaching critical mass could not be more clear or stark. The officers hold truly great power in their pens.

If the interviewing officer figures the persecution story does not squarely enough hit any of the five categories, or comes off as somewhere south of credible, the result is a mark in the "NO" box, which leads to an appeal to an immigration judge and, if unsuccessful, to a one-way deportation ticket. But a shower of gifts befalls the claimant whose officer checks the "YES" box on the inquiry form. Immigrants with the "YES" check don't get deported; they typically get to file an asylum claim, bond out of the detention center, and start new lives in America. They get access to public welfare. They can get legal work authorization and the right to live freely inside the United States for as long as it takes a federal immigration judge to hear the full case. Asylum case backlogs in the immigration court stretch that wait into years.

Dhakane offered a particularly riveting, hair-raising persecution story. It was downright gruesome in the litany of atrocities he claimed he had suffered at the hands of Somalia's ubiquitous Islamic extremists. The story also came off as very credible, given its detailed, layered richness. It not only fit many of the five qualified categories of persecution; it exceeded critical mass. YES, it was decided; Dhakane's fear was credible. He definitely got to stay for his shot.

According to a copy of his formal asylum application, Dhakane had committed one of the most unforgiveable of sins in Somalia: as a university student in 2002, he converted to Christianity, "partly from seeing the violence that Islamic extremists were carrying out…in the name of the Islamic religion."[69] That put him afoul of a US-designated Somali terrorist organization, the precursor to al-Shabaab known as al-Ittihad al-Islamiya (AIAI), or the Islamic Courts Union.

The armed Islamic group, linked to the 1998 al-Qaeda bombings of US embassies in Kenya and Tanzania, held territory in parts of Mogadishu, where Dhakane's family lived. On August 9, 2006—the exact date still seared in Dhakane's apparently excellent memory—a nine-member AIAI militia led by a man with a pistol stormed his small underground church in Somalia, called the Voice of New Life. With uncanny detail, Dhakane recalled the twenty additional armed fighters waiting outside in two trucks with mounted machine guns. They handcuffed Dhakane, several other congregants, and the pastor and drove them to the Hararyaale Islamic Court in the Ifka Halane neighborhood of Mogadishu.

Their holding cell "had a strong smell of urine," he recalled. With a cadre of executioners at his command, an AIAI sheik demanded the captive Christians renounce their religion and revert to Islam or face a terrible execution and end up burning in hell. Steadfast in their dedication to Christ, none would do it. The AIAI guards beat them every day with gun butts. Then came a stick-beating regimen ordered by the sheikh. The guards would encircle each condemned Christian, then beat them with sticks and spit on them while calling them names, as Dhakane recalled, "like Abdi-Gaal, which means a person who does not believe in God."

Then the killings began. All were forced to watch. The masked executioner put a bag over the pastor's head, tied his hands behind a pillar with a chain, and stabbed him exactly twice. But somehow after the second stab, the pastor broke free and tried to run. The executioner chased him down and "stabbed him repeatedly until he was dead," Dhakane recalled. "When I saw my pastor being killed, I vomited," Dhakane wrote in the sworn statement. "I felt like I did not want to live anymore." The survivors had to watch as the Islamic court hanged another parishioner—"Aanogeel," his name was.

Dhakane said he finally relented after reading the biblical story of Abraham where "Abraham says that Sarah is his sister even though she is actually his wife in order to keep the Egyptians from killing him. I decided to tell the Islamic Court that I was not a Christian."

After his reversion and release "with new clothes and a Koran"—on November 9, 2006, Dhakane recalled with precision—Islamic stalkers and haters still threated him over his continued secret Christianity. A month after his release, Dhakane "found out from a neighbor of [his] uncle's" that AIAI had just murdered his father at a restaurant "in the Bar Ubah neighborhood." He rushed and found his father's still body lying on the ground. The dead restaurant owner lay there too, killed by a stray bullet in the same AIAI attack. (Dhakane's father had supported a political party AIAI didn't like, reportedly.)

But there was even more mortal danger gathering on the horizon. Dhakane and his "wife," Leyla, had never been able to marry because they belonged to rival clans that forbade intermarriage, he explained. That ban was enforced on pain of death. Now, in early 2008, there could be no more hiding their forbidden Romeo-Juliet relationship, because she was pregnant. It was no longer just their lives at stake but now "our child would face mistreatment and harm from powerful clans who injure and kill those of mixed majority and minority clan parentage."

They had to flee the country now for the sake of an innocent unborn Christian child. He bought some fraudulent identity documents and flew with his wife to Dubai before embarking on a month-long journey through Latin America to the American border and sanctuary. Or so he said.

THE TRUTH ABOUT AMERICAN POLITICAL ASYLUM

Dhakane's persecution story was a pack of lies. This was revealed not through the asylum process but by a serendipitous external anomaly; an undercover Somali FBI informant inside the Texas detention center had gained Dhakane's confidence. Were it not for this informant, Dhakane would most likely have been lawfully released into the United States with his secrets and intentions, which very likely weren't beneficent. He was no victim of AIAI's reign of terror; Dhakane was a full-throated, trusted, senior terrorist group insider, trained as a guerrilla fighter in all the usual armaments.[70] He likely derived the granular details of his bogus asylum story from atrocities *he himself* had perpetrated on others.

More than a decade later, his story stands as an emblematic indictment of deep unresolved vulnerabilities baked into the American asylum system that terrorists, when they do finally attack, will have exploited absent permanent reforms. For those reasons, his story justifies comprehensive treatment here.

For the previous two years, Dhakane hadn't been in Somalia or Dubai; he was making a living in Brazil as a human smuggler after AIAI leadership "sent (him) from the war." That's how Dhakane came to learn how to game the US asylum system, with its shallow, perfunctory, "credible fear" interview process never designed to discern truth from fabrication. Dhakane the smuggler sent 300 Somalis and other East Africans to the US southern border with fraudulent persecution stories concocted to exploit the asylum system's many flaws, chief among them a blindness about counterterrorism security.

Dhakane revealed to the FBI in San Antonio that he had smuggled at least five AIAI members whom he thought were indoctrinated in violent jihadist theology and were dangerous. Two went to other western countries but three made it over the US border, Dhakane having coached them to defeat the asylum process.[71] One of the AIAI Somali operatives, who favored the nickname "Al Qaeda," got into California. Dhakane said he did not know their individual plans but, from long conversations in hotel rooms along the way, knew "all of these individuals are ready to die for the cause" and also that they "would fight against the U.S. if the jihad moved from overseas to the United States."[72]

Dhakane told agents that, "based on his conversations with his smuggling clients and his extensive familiarity with United States asylum law, he knew that none of the individuals he smuggled had a valid claim to be in the United States."[73] The revelations set off a desperate FBI hunt for the Somali asylees.[74] This same frantic search would happen again a couple of years later when another FBI investigation of the American document-fraud jihadist Joseph Anthony Tracy revealed that many of his Somali clients had been "bad." An FBI intelligence analyst with direct knowledge of the search told me the names Dhakane or Tracy supplied were too common among Somalis to allow the agency to locate many of the reputed jihadists.

But at least the FBI had Dhakane, a terrorist prize in his own right, neither the Christian nor saint he'd claimed during his credible fear interview.

He was not only a trained AIAI fighter well-schooled in gaming America's asylum processes, but also a trusted member of an organizational elite back in Somalia. He was entrusted to procure weapons for the group, like a $100,000 battle wagon that was subsequently blown up, killing all aboard.[75] An uncle occupied a senior position of authority with AIAI. Another senior leader was so enamored with Dhakane that he offered a daughter's hand in marriage to him. From 1997 through 2003,

Dhakane served as AIAI's "hwaladar," or transferor of funds outside normal banking systems. He wittingly used the al Barakat financial entity for two years after the US Treasury Department designated it as a banned terrorist finance organization.[76]

And his wife, Leyla? She revealed she was an underage, paying smuggling customer who had been kidnapped, raped, and impregnated in Brazil by Dhakane, who then forced her to accompany him to the US border.

PAPERWORK FIRST, BOMBS LATER

The Dhakane case offers a rare unadulterated view into just how easily border-infiltrating terrorist operatives, other SIAs, and their international smugglers exploit vulnerabilities in America's naive asylum system to get into the country legally and stay for years. Keep in mind, too, that border walls may well be effective in slowing drug trafficking and deterring illegal entry of all but the fittest athletes among them who can climb high and drop far. And many SIAs do cross between ports of entry and claim asylum after they are caught. But walls are not applicable to SIAs and terrorists for the simple reason that they can cross, just like Dhakane did, at any established port of entry, claim they want asylum to anyone wearing a uniform, and achieve the same result. Walls don't prevent asylum abuse.

Once inside the country on such a claim at the port of entry, Dhakane's successful credible fear interview shows how the asylum process bestows benefit-of-the-doubt on unknowable strangers with plausible, heartbreaking stories—and is almost engineered to miss the darkest of pasts portending a higher probability of future misdeeds. And the case showcases the asylum system's fundamental inability to see the fraud greasing the skids for any good yarn-telling jihadist who would choose to waltz over an open pedestrian bridge.

Recall how in Europe, migrant-terrorists routinely exploited similar built-in security flaws to breach EU border defenses and to plot and attack under protective legal status. When terrorists cross borders, they are not packing nuclear and bio-weapons in rucksacks, nor firearms and bombs. They don't declare themselves and open fire on Border Patrol. They apply for asylum the same way the legitimate poor huddled masses do.

My study of Europe's migrant-terrorist border infiltrations between 2015 and 2018 found that, among the fifty-five cases that could be tracked, Europe's asylum processes ferreted out few, if any, infiltrating terrorists, or war criminals whose hands were drenched in blood. Prior to the migrant crisis of 2014–2018, Europe's recommended wait time for asylum was already a dangerous six months. During the crisis, the average time from asylum claim to attack or near-miss arrests in Europe in five dozen terrorism cases was eleven months—even better for plot incubation and bomb-building in cities of choice filled with multitudes of targets to consider and surveil.[77]

But even the EU's pre-crisis wait time of six months offered plenty of time for plotting and attacking, including seventeen cases where jihadist migrants did so in under three months. European police arrested at least twenty-two migrant-terrorists while they were still living in their asylum center shelters.

For instance, German police arrested Syrian asylum seeker and midlevel ISIS commander Leeth Abdalhameed within two weeks of his arrival. Abdalhameed applied for asylum under a false name and avoided providing his fingerprints. He was only arrested after a fellow refugee informed police of his past work as a midlevel commander who smuggled money, medicine, and ammunition for the terrorist group in Syria.[78] Germany approved the asylum claim of Syrian ISIS migrant Jaber al-Bakr in five months. Then, as a result of roommates diming him out, police arrested al-Bakr in the advanced stages of planning an ISIS-connected bomb attack using 1.5 kilograms of explosives found in his apartment.[79]

Terrorist plotters and murderers lied to European asylum officers about their nationalities and ages to make the most of the adjudicator's inability to see anything below the surface. In their made-up personal stories, they omitted their murdering sprees with ISIS. Asylum officers in Europe were almost never able to detect the extremism hidden within, the predilection for violence, or the ongoing relationships with terrorists still abroad.

One emblematic case among a great many worth mentioning involved thirty-six-year-old Tunisian Haikel Saydani. He was the master planner behind a March 2015 Islamist mass-casualty attack on the National Bardo Museum of Art in downtown Tunis, where twenty-one mostly foreign tourists from nearby cruise ships were slaughtered in hails of bullets. In that attack, a dozen assailants in military uniforms, believed to be members of al-Qaeda in the Islamic Maghreb, accosted buses emptying their tourist passengers into the museum. The gunmen slaughtered nine right there and murdered ten hostages during a four-hour gun battle with Tunisian security forces. Some five months later, with an international Tunisian arrest warrant against him in August 2015, Haikel made his way undetected into Germany at the height of the migrant flow, possibly by migrant boat from Libya. He would have had to request asylum under an assumed name to avoid detection of the international arrest warrant.

For nearly eighteen months, he was free as an asylum petitioner to build up a network of supporters with the aim of carrying out terrorist attacks in Germany and across Europe. He most likely worked with an ISIS external operations group in Libya.[80] Haikel was linked to another attack in Tunisia in 2016 while still hiding in Germany. Finally, in February 2017, 1,100 German police in full combat gear raided fifty-six homes, businesses, and mosques in Frankfurt. Haikel was swept up in it, a kind of operation that had become typical in Germany by then as the number of terrorist suspects soared into the hundreds.

Another migrant-terrorist who benefitted from an asylum free pass initially arrived in mainland Europe and sneaked across the English Channel into Britain in February 2014 to claim asylum. Eritrean national Munir Hassan Mohammed got in to stay legally using a persecution story. The British eventually turned down his claim and ordered him deported, but with appeals available to him and lengthy backlogs of cases—as those who apply in the United States—Mohammed had at least two years inside the country to do as he pleased, which was to plan jihad.[81] Through a Muslim dating website, Mohammed met British subject Rowaida El-Hassan, a pharmacist knowledgeable in chemicals. Steeped in ISIS literature, the couple went about manufacturing the deadly poison ricin to load into the bomb for a Christmas Day 2016 attack. They were getting close enough to have tested the ricin on hamsters in the weeks before Christmas when British antiterrorism police arrested them.

BBC News admitted it could not figure out why the deportation took so long but, in one report, said that "what's clear is he sat and waited. And as he waited, he began to plot."[82]

The problem is that, even in the best of times, the severely dysfunctional US asylum system would easily accommodate migrant-jihadists like Dhakane, Fidse, Sheikh, and others like the Pakistanis and Yemenis described in Chapter Three. The asylum system would discover none in just the same way as Europe's asylum system uncovered none. The weaknesses permeate the US asylum process to this day, in good times and especially in bad. After all, three million migrants all at once swamped Europe's asylum system in 2014, but US immigration court backlogs have long suffered under massive backlogs, pushing wait times for those who are not detained to one or two years. The United States asylum system is often flooded by mass migration crisis-level episodes, pushing wait times much longer.

At the heart of the backlog and interminable wait times are the almost axiomatic, universal credible fear approvals, required by senior political bureaucrats in the agency who have essentially removed the authority of asylum officers whose duty it is to make those judgments. One veteran USCIS asylum supervisor once described the high credible fear approval rates to me in this colorfully metaphorical way: "If the applicant says he was rescued from his attackers by a spaceship full of little green men, who are we (credible fear interviewers) to say that there are not other life forms in the universe?"

Indeed, the vast majority of credible fear interview screenings, above 90 percent, were approved as positive for endless years, until the Trump administration managed to reverse that trend in the last year of his 2017–2021 term.[83] For a better comparison with Europe, consider that the 2018–2019 mass migration crisis of Central Americans had, by October 2019, swelled an already notorious asylum case backlog to more than one million. During that crisis, almost everyone who came through the border either received an automatic credible fear approval or none at all, producing wait times extending to an average of four years.[84]

Overwhelming numbers of positive credible fear approvals fed the asylum backlogs and wait times and will again one day if Trump policies are returned to prior norms.

Oddly, during the 2015–2016 national election campaigns, Republican attention zeroed in intently and solely on whether the United States should resettle Syrian war refugees after their terror attacks in Europe. More than thirty Republican governors declared they would accept none! But these declarations and political discussions entirely overlooked that a border route work-around was always available to those denied refugee resettlement via the overseas United Nations High Commissioner for Refugees

(UNHCR) application processes. In those processes, some security vetting actually occurs, however imperfectly. But not the asylum process at the land borders. The big national debate, with Trump front and center, somehow failed to process in the fact that Syrians denied UNHCR resettlement were coming in over the southern border and simply claiming political asylum—and getting in at high percentages. Trump, Republican governors, and their compadres in Congress could certainly turn off the legal spigots, and Trump could sign executive orders imposing travel restrictions (which he did with the inaccurately termed "Muslim Ban.")

But none of those measures addressed the asylum-at-the-land-border option, which always remained an unfettered alternative for Syrians, anyone from the "travel-ban" nations, and anyone from countries of national security concern. That the border-asylum work-around was neither raised nor addressed during months of hot-tempered national debate and political campaigning stands as a profound testament to how the SIA infiltration issue has so persistently failed to permeate the public debate.

Known instances of this back channel's heavy usage are almost ubiquitous. During the early years of the Syrian civil war, the Obama administration curtailed the number of tourist visas it was willing to dole out to Syrians as the numbers of refugees swelled in neighboring countries. So Syrians did the border end-run, obtaining Mexican tourist visas and then walking over the southern border to claim political asylum. According to a *Wall Street Journal* analysis, the tactic worked flawlessly for Syrians like one the newspaper featured named "Mohammad." After he was denied a US tourist visa in Lebanon, he got a Mexican tourist visa, flew to Mexico City and then Tijuana.[85] He crossed the US border illegally and declared asylum to a customs official. The US granted Mohammad asylum, making him eligible to apply for permanent US residency.

In 2013, the US approved 94 percent of Syrians' credible fear requests and 100 percent of every claim in the first quarter of 2014, the newspaper reported, even though some "worry it may offer too easy a path to US residence for potential terrorists, given al-Qaeda's rising presence in Syria."

Among those who could be counted as having worried out loud about that was US House Homeland Security Committee Chairman Mike McCaul (R-TX). But McCaul, asked to comment about a group Syrian women and children who turned themselves in to customs officials in Laredo, Texas, saw a distinction between them and other Syrians who might fit a more obvious higher-risk profile.

"These are refugees, a Syrian refugee family that went to the Laredo port of entry, my state, and basically turned themselves in for political asylum," he said of those families right after the Paris attacks. "They were not infiltrating to conduct terrorist operations."

Women, of course, do conduct terrorist operations around the world, and even Syrian mothers should undergo enhanced vetting at the border. By contrast, in referencing young Syrian men just arrested in Honduras, McCaul told MSNBC: "Some of these military age males could present a threat to the United States. All we're asking for is proper vetting."[86]

The dirty little secret is that any nationality or visa category a president might choose to restrict always had the viable end-run option readily at their disposal. Because of its large, restive Muslim minority, India has sometimes occupied a spot on US countries of interest lists. For years, India's citizens have crashed the southern border in large numbers, more than 32,000 between 2009 and 2019, according to CBP apprehension data. During 2018, Border Patrol apprehended just under 9,000 and in 2019, 7,675.

There was good reason. They were claiming asylum and getting in at high percentages because legal visas for Indians were capped and couldn't be had.

In a July 2020 National Public Radio report about the phenomenon of Indians crossing the border, reporter Lauren Frayer helpfully described what appears to be systematic, mass asylum fraud that revolved mainly around their making up fake persecution stories to get their "YES" checks on the paperwork.[87]

A "burgeoning crop of unregulated travel agents—human smugglers" were charging the Indian migrants tens of thousands of dollars per person, routing them through as many as a dozen countries to the US border, and "often supply the migrants with fake backstories to help them try to win asylum," Frayer reported, citing not only the migrants themselves but also the smugglers and police investigators. Most of the Indian migrants faced no real "credible fear" of persecution and regarded themselves as economic migrants looking for jobs to support better lifestyles.

One Sikh migrant, Sevak Singh, described to Frayer how he decided to lie to US asylum officers that he had been persecuted based on his religion. He told the NPR reporter he had never been persecuted in India and recalled how, along the migration trail, "fellow Sikhs would rehearse fake backstories about Sikh separatism and persecution. The stories were untrue, NPR reported.

Sikh Indian migrants on their way to the US border. Photo by Todd Bensman in Costa Rica, December 2018

AMERICAN ASYLUM'S PEDESTAL IN THE SMUGGLING BUSINESS MODEL

The FBI discovered Dhakane, not the US immigration system, just as European counterterrorism police—and not the European immigration systems—had uncovered its terrorists. The asylum process is poorly geared to ferret out national security threats, and those who administer it often don't even pretend to try. This should change.

Even the post-9/11 SIA security screens failed to catch Dhakane (or, evidently, any of the AIAI terrorists he smuggled in).

As part of normal SIA security practices already in place for several years in 2008, FBI and ICE agents would have interviewed Dhakane (as best they would any SIA) and also run terrorism database checks that would have found nothing. They wouldn't, of course, because the anarchic state of Somalia had completely failed in 1991, leaving the country with no government to collect verifiable criminal and terrorism intelligence records, let alone to issue birth and death certificates, marriage licenses, driver's licenses, or passports. Many Muslim-majority countries are in similar straits, to varying degrees. Dhakane must have felt very assured knowing the agents would back-check his story against a void. If failed statehood is an impediment to American intelligence collection, so are diplomatic estrangements. American investigators can't very well pick up the phone and call, say the US-embargoed, US-designated State Sponsor of Terror nation of Iran, to have them run a quick background check on Iranians caught at the southern border (and quite a few are). There's no one at all to pick up the phone in a place like Libya.

As in Europe's system, the men and women who administer US asylum processes, from credible fear interviews to immigration court hearings, simply are not geared to investigate and verify the stories told to them; lies are just as impossible to suss out as truths are to verify. Gambling that only good ones get through is the standard. Empirically verifying any given claimant's story in distant ungoverned spaces is next to impossible.

A February 2011 Texas Department of Public Safety Intelligence Analysis of the Dhakane case, released by WikiLeaks, succinctly summarized the problem.[88]

> "As Dhakane's personal experience demonstrates, the political asylum process is vulnerable to abuse by individuals associated with terrorist organizations who seek to hide those associations. Because Somalia has no government, it is often described as a failed state, its citizens either travel with no identification or forged ones. These circumstances render US authorities unable to easily verify claims or check backgrounds against terrorist watch lists, forcing the release of inadequately vetted individuals into the general public."

The SIAs, their smugglers, and terrorists like Dhakane count on that for business continuity.

For SIAs from homes thousands of miles away, like Afghanistan and Syria, their first chance across is often their only chance. Whereas Mexicans who can go home and come back relatively easily don't usually succeed in claims for political asylum on the basis of racial, religious, or political persecution,[89] SIAs almost always seek political asylum and come from countries with plenty of real problems to cite.

Most SIAs can only come up with the $30,000 to $50,000 smugglers charge to get to the United States one time in their lives, and terrorists the Americans catch and deport once already know they're identified, on everybody's radar, cover blown. First-timers can afford that risk only if they are sure the journey is going to end with asylum and its lavish benefits, including legal permanent residence and a path to eventual citizenship. If asylum is denied to an SIA, word of which smuggler failed to coach the soon-to-be-deportee will quickly spread to homelands—a business killer.

That's why SIA smugglers have incorporated fraud coaching into their essential service, very much like National Public Radio's Frayer reported about the unending train of Indian nationals making their way through Mexico. Fake persecution stories, good ones, are a valuable commodity.

Court records from American prosecutions of SIA smuggling organizations demonstrate that these are the bread and butter of SIA smuggling businesses. Smugglers simply must possess a sophisticated understanding of American asylum rules. These de facto immigration attorneys often know which claims are trending in and trending out, the length of detention times, and what words never to say out loud.

Mexico City–based Nepalese smuggler Rakhi Gauchan, who smuggled scores of Pakistanis, Bangladeshis, and Indians over the Texas border until her 2013 arrest, exemplifies the type. According to an HSI complaint, Gauchan instructed most of her smuggling clients to falsely claim asylum either when they presented themselves at a US port of entry or were caught after entering illegally between ports, for example by fording the Rio Grande.

A confidential informant in the Gauchan organization reported that the smuggler provided her clients with tailored fraudulent stories that had recently worked. For instance, they were instructed to tell immigration officials that they belonged to political parties that had only recently become persecuted, regardless of their actual affiliation.[90]

Gauchan's knowledge extended to useful arcane legal details of the US asylum process. For instance, upon learning that one Pakistani client had previously been rejected by Italy, she prepared him for the US border by coaching him never to tell US immigration about that Italian denial and to change the story he had used in Italy enough so that it would pass muster with the Americans who heard it. She knew that denial of an application in one Western country was an automatic disqualifier for US asylum.

Abdulahi Hasan Sharif, the Somali terrorist discussed earlier who came in over the Mexico-California border before his double-vehicle ramming attack in Edmonton, Alberta, demonstrated such intricate knowledge of US asylum processes that he knew he could best get into the United States by *not* applying. Recall that the twenty-four-year-old Sharif crossed from Tijuana, Mexico, to the port of entry in San Ysidro, California, on July 12, 2011, with Canada very likely his final true destination, where Somalis he knew had settled.[91] I know from interviewing a great many Somalis in ICE detention that the word-of-mouth grapevine among Somali emigres sings all day, every day with fast, comprehensive information about migration conditions, what's working and what's not.

From my piecing together what is known about his 2017 attack and smuggling journey, I surmise that Sharif undoubtedly knew he'd be able to exploit a US-Canadian agreement that prevented either country from accepting asylum seekers who had already applied in one of the countries. So filing a US asylum claim would have blocked his entrance into his true destination, Canada.

Sharif knew of another way. In 2011 and 2012, all Somalis were well aware that United States law and practice prevented deportations to that country because, a) there was no government in Somalia to receive deportees (a legal necessity for the US), and b) a 2001 US Supreme Court decision forbade indefinite immigration detention in the United States and required that no detainee be held longer than 180 days unless charged with a crime.[92]

Sure enough, within days of his California entry, in the absence of an asylum claim by Sharif, San Diego–based US Immigration Judge Carmene "Zsa Zsa" DePaolo ordered him deported to government-less Somalia. Because he couldn't be deported to a country with no government, immigration officials dutifully released him after only a few months, in December 2011. He was under orders to physically report to ICE in California regularly. But that was never going to happen even once. Because as soon as he was physically and legally free, Hasan made a beeline for Canada. He crossed at the port of entry at Fort Erie, Ontario, in January 2012. He staked his refugee protection claim, nailed it, and resettled in poor Edmonton. We know how that eventually turned out.

From post-9/11 America to the present, smuggling methods have adapted to security changes, moving and dancing in time with it, but the asylum system served as a reliable partner to SIA smugglers like Iranian national Muhammed Hussein Assadi, dating all the way back to before 9/11. His proficiency in asylum law and practice was striking.

Until his 2002 arrest, Assadi ran a worldwide, full-service network that moved Arabs through South America on to the United States by passenger jet to do the asylum dance inside international disembarkation areas. In Brazil, he would have the men shave beards and the women dye their hair blonde and don European clothing to look less Middle Eastern.[93] They traveled on stolen European passports doctored with photo substitutions to match their holders. On his instructions, they would destroy the passports midflight and turn themselves in to immigration officers at international disembarkation areas, declining to say where they were really from. Assadi well knew that under administrative procedures at that time, his clients would be provisionally released into what was technically United States territory, where they could pounce with asylum declarations.[94]

Another prolific SIA smuggler who earned his street degree in US asylum law was Eritrean citizen Samuel Abrahaley Fessahazion. The Eritrean had been smuggling East Africans to the US for several years in 2008 when he decided to give up the game and make a go of it himself. His dramatic story of a two-year wandering escape from Eritrea's oppressive authoritarian government worked like a charm. Lacking any way to back-check the story, an immigration judge granted his asylum claim in November 2008. Only much later, after ICE busted him, did it become clear that his persecution story was an elaborate lie crafted to track with actual country conditions and real circumstances. It just hadn't happened to Fessahazion because he'd been too busy making bank in Guatemala helping other Africans craft fairy tales for asylum officers when they smuggled up to and then over the US border.[95]

RED WARNING LIGHTS FLASHING UNSEEN

"Relentless" would best characterize the frequency with which government auditors and researchers have warned that terrorists can exploit the

American asylum system. But despite the official warnings and protestations, no reform ever comes of them. Neither has anyone of the necessary influence or position in the United States seemed to have noticed how jihadists used Europe's asylum processes to facilitate bloody mayhem from the Mediterranean Sea to the English Channel.

Middle Eastern and South Asian immigrants and the American asylum system have long shared a mutual fondness. A 2011 Congressional Research Service report noted that migrants from Muslim-majority countries have consistently ranked among the twenty top nationalities for asylum approvals, even after 9/11. The report noted that terrorists from "countries of special concern," such as Saudi Arabia, Syria, Iran, Pakistan, Egypt, Lebanon, Jordan, Afghanistan, Yemen, and Somalia, often figure they can slide their questionable asylum claims in, more or less unexamined, among the hundreds of thousands of pending cases.[96] But other reporting also has noted a problem with this arrangement.

DHS's 2008–2013 Threat Assessment noted that the agency's "highest level of concern" was that terrorist operatives among asylum seekers would defeat American vetting processes at the border.[97] Specifically, it found:

> "At the highest level of concern, terrorists will attempt to defeat border security measures with the goal of inserting operatives and establishing support networks in the United States. These illicit actors also could pose as refugees or asylum seekers to gain access to the United States. State failure and internal conflicts abroad will continue to generate sizable refugee flows to the United States— notably from countries of special interest for terrorism in the Middle East, Africa, and South Asia—which could provide opportunities for illicit entry."[98]

While it should be obvious why migrants from global trouble spots would so very much appreciate the partnership with such a pliable, giving system, no plausible explanation avails itself as to why the American asylum system gives with such total abandon, constantly abused and manipulated with almost total impunity and despite clear danger.

Consider just this 2008 Government Accountability Office (GAO) report. It published results from a 2006 survey of all the nation's then-256 asylum officers and all 56 supervisors in the nation's eight United States Citizenship and Immigration Services division field offices that process applications.[99] Using understated, deadpan language for such a stunning finding, this report mentioned that, a little earlier, the Asylum Division at USCIS had investigated instances in which the applications of people had already been processed *before* their alleged ties with terrorism were discovered. That earlier review "identified vulnerabilities to terrorism in the U.S. asylum system," including "the lack of checks to identify individuals, the possibility of an applicant's interpreter perpetrating fraud, and vulnerabilities outside of its control."[100]

The GAO report then went on to discuss the new survey of asylum officers. It revealed that nothing had changed despite that ominous red flag. The vast majority of officers felt themselves ill-trained to detect fraud, conduct security checks, or assess the credibility of asylum seekers. They were too few and didn't have enough time.[101] Seventy percent of officers confessed they found it moderately or very difficult to identify document fraud. They couldn't assess credibility in more than half the cases they had adjudicated in the past year. They reported they had insufficient time to prepare or conduct research before their credible fear interviews. Almost all the respondents felt they needed training to improve "interviewing and assessing credibility"; more than half said they had received none.

The same GAO effort surveyed immigration judges. The majority cited verifying fraud and assessing credibility as moderately or very challenging factors in reaching decisions. Not much improvement was reported in 2014, when four Republican members of Congress asked the GAO to investigate the asylum process after a leaked 2009 DHS report showed that as many as 70 percent of all approved claims contained proven or possible fraud.[102]

In fairness, USCIS tried to fix these problems by adding national security investigators but then somehow got hamstrung.

The closest mechanism USCIS ever had for rooting out national security–related threats is a division known as the Fraud Detection and National Security Directorate (FDNS). This group of USCIS officers is supposed to gather evidence and investigate immigration crimes like the fraud committed by people like Dhakane or Fidse. But then the government inexplicably handcuffed these officers. According to an anonymous government author writing on the Center for Immigration Studies website in 2019, internal policy left them without guns and bereft of arrest authority and left them to beg ICE agents to take the cases.[103]

"That left USCIS, the agency that approves or denies every immigration benefit, with no teeth in the form of a law enforcement capability when fraud is detected," the government official wrote. "Despite this important homeland security work, FDNS officers still have no arrest authority and don't carry firearms. In the meantime, ICE is pretty busy with its own workload.

"To keep things in perspective, even the U.S. Post Office has federal agents with arrest authority," the author lamented.

The agency that handles asylum claims is overwhelmed even in normal flow times. Asylum officers tell me the adjudication process becomes dysfunctional during times of crisis, such as the influx of unaccompanied Central American minors in 2014 and the entry of almost one million illegal migrants from Central America again, the majority in family units, that crashed the system in 2019.

Seven years after the 2008 report, another GAO report came out about the American asylum system. This one from 2015, showed how little had changed. In fact, it was downright ugly and more than a little scary.

Among its litany of terrible findings was that asylum officers were still essentially flying blind, making decisions "with little or no documentation to support or refute an applicant's claim."[104] To render decisions on merely an applicant's word constitutes an egregious public trust violation and yet this no doubt happened as a norm, probably hundreds of thousands of times, if not millions.

The GAO report also found that fraud investigations were rare at USCIS, and when they did happen, it was usually *after* the fraud and *after* the asylum case had already been adjudicated, the report found.

USCIS had added some "national security asylum fraud detection officers (FDNS)" a few years earlier, the report noted without mentioning that investigators were handcuffed from doing their own cases with search warrants and subpoenas or even the ability to refer their investigations to federal prosecutors. Those restrictions were imposed in a 2008 Memorandum of Understanding among the agencies and limits the FDNS officers to merely *requesting* that HSI investigate an asylum fraud case.

But even if the national security officers of Citizenship and Immigration Services would have been free to properly do their own law enforcement work, there were only thirty-four of them by 2015 to cover eight field offices nationwide, which processed hundreds of thousands of cases. Some more have been added. But so thinly spread are the FDNS officers, still shackled, that their existence seems a mere token for appearances and might well not exist as a force at all. To boot, by 2015, no one was had even bothered to track the work those officers did. Fraud detection training across the board was still minimal or absent years after the 2008 GAO report and to this day.

Perhaps most outrageous was GAO's 2015 finding that federal prosecutors declined asylum fraud referrals at very high rates, when they got them at all from ICE HSI—which was rarely—and just as infrequently pursued criminal penalties or even disciplinary action for private attorneys who had helped clients commit it. This problem has its roots in the fact that FDNS officers aren't allowed to do their jobs and, in any case, are so few and far between as to define the term "tokenism." In these circumstances, it was no wonder the 2015 GAO report found that half of the eight asylum offices had referred either one fraud case to US Attorney's offices from 2010–2014 or none at all. One office reported that not a single referral had been accepted in the prior two years. Another reported that its US attorney had accepted no asylum fraud referrals since 2010.

In 2020, USCIS asylum officers I know in two of the districts told me they had no improvements to report. One veteran USCIS officer relayed to me an infuriating story of failed efforts as late as the fall of 2020 to free the FDNS corps from its binds by renegotiating the 2008 memorandum of understanding that put them in place.

"There is an effort; it's just held up in bureaucracy," this USCIS officer told me in September 2020. "USCIS is handcuffed, and HSI in most areas refuse to investigate any immigration fraud and especially asylum fraud, which most have no understanding of."

In the meantime, SIA smugglers remain nimble, held back by no bureaucracy and are no doubt appreciative of the American ineptitudes. Government accountability reports have repeatedly detailed the fraud that SIAs, their smugglers, and terrorist infiltrators know will get them in through the door almost every time and that the exit door, for them, is practically rusted shut. Even in the wake of the carnage in Europe in recent years, there appears to be little political appetite in the US for digesting the evidence that our asylum system is the very definition of a national security danger.

For people like Somalia natives Fidse and Sheikh, the knowledge that they would sail through it on a magic carpet of lies must have given them the security they needed to invest thousands of dollars to have themselves smuggled—with their terrible secrets—to the Texas border.[105] As I described in the previous chapter, they claimed in their asylum petitions to have fled the terrorist group al-Shabaab after it killed their family members. The persecution stories, crafted to meet the usual credible fear standard to start the asylum process, worked like a charm for Sheikh. Fidse no doubt would have joined Sheikh in Wisconsin had he not told an undercover FBI informant in the detention center that he was an al-Shabaab member who had come to the United States to conduct an unspecified terrorist operation.[106] He had trained as a guerrilla fighter, fought with the group, maintained contact with al-Shabaab operatives, and still strongly adhered to the group's abhorrent death-cult ideology.

Sheikh almost achieved her American dream with Fidse's expert coaching, part of which was that she pretended not to even know Fidse. In reality, they were married, and she knew all about the mortal threat Fidse posed.

PASSING UNOPPOSED THROUGH THE TRUMP YEARS

Nothing about the US asylum system has improved under Democrats or Republicans with respect to SIA wide-open access to the asylum system, not even during the years of the 2017–2020 Trump administration, when more was done to reduce the magnetic force of American asylum than at any time in decades.

Somehow, the SIA category of illegal migrants was able to evade all of the Trump administration's avowedly hawkish-on-border-security attempts to deter the system's mass abuse. Some of the Trump initiatives to batten down the asylum system would have proven remarkably effective as deterrents to SIA travel. But none were ever universally applied, and none can be expected to be applied during Democratic control, a circumstance I can only attribute to the continuing secrecy and lack of comprehension about this kind of long-haul migration.

The Trump administration did prove it could make an impact with Indians. With increasing numbers flooding over the border, in April 2019, the administration ordered new India-specific training to asylum officers responsible for making credible-fear decisions.[107] In the six months prior to that training, credible fear yeses were granted to 89 percent of Indian nationals. After the new training, the rate dropped to 17 percent through 2020. For the first time, ICE began flying hundreds of rejected claimants back to India. But the training was never extended to any of the SIA nationalities even though the India experiment had proven so effective.

One of the greatest of missed opportunities to dampen SIA flow was President Trump's so-called Migrant Protection Protocols. This was the so-called "Wait in Mexico" policy, where Central Americans claiming asylum en masse were pushed back into Mexico to await their asylum hearings there, rather than to disappear forever inside the United States pending their long case adjudications. The 2019 policy design was mainly conceived to deter the mass migration of Central American family units, which were then flooding in unimpeded. But again, the policy exempted SIAs, who could come through as they always had and gain release pending distant asylum hearings.

The reason is that Trump administration only pressured Mexico to accept Central Americans (and later Brazilians). But the administration somehow forgot to have Mexico also agree to take back Syrians, Iraqis, Afghans, and the other SIA nationalities. It's unclear whether the Trump administration even thought to ask.

The result was that SIAs from countries of national security concern continued to arrive and work the American asylum system without the slightest interruption, while the Central Americans with whom they might have arrived were sent back over the border into Mexico.[108] Inclusion in MPP would almost certainly have disincentivized SIAs contemplating a US border trip while still in their home nations.

Yet MPP was not the only glaringly missed Trump policy opportunity to dampen SIA migration.

The administration implemented so-called Safe Third Country agreements with nations like Guatemala. The idea was that migrants truly in desperate need of asylum from imminent deadly persecution at home would be made ineligible to apply for US asylum at the border if they already passed through other safe countries. After clearing legal challenges, the Trump administration in 2019 began shipping Salvadorans and Hondurans to Guatemala, their first designated safe country beyond their own dangerous one.[109]

But again, SIAs, who may pass through a dozen different safe countries, were exempted and apparently never even considered for this program, according to senior and lower-ranking DHS officials in early 2020. I asked one USCIS officer in a border asylum office if SIAs were being pushed back to Mexico or returned to distant other safe third countries.

"Nope," the official confirmed of SIAs and other migrants from Africa or Asia. "We wave 'em all through, every last one of them."

In 2020, the Trump administration began the process of adapting a similar regulation known as the Third Country Transit Asylum Bar (IFR), which would require all asylum seekers to have first applied in one of the first "safe" countries through which they transited on their way to the United States, on pain of not being allowed to apply for US asylum.[110]

Of course, many SIAs may well pass through a dozen different countries on their way to the US border. Somalis, for instance, may pass through Kenya, Zambia, South Africa, Brazil, Ecuador, Peru, and so on. But loopholes and practicality favor the SIAs.

For one thing, SIAs can be expected to simply shift to a different claim under the Convention Against Torture (CAT). SIAs would merely have to lodge a CAT claim and they'll be let in that way. And, practically speaking, many origin countries are recalcitrant about accepting American deportees, and so the US could not deport such migrants. And since Supreme Court rulings don't allow for indefinite detentions of noncitizen migrants for longer than 180 days, all such SIAs would be released inside the United States eventually.

Beyond the seemingly endless loopholes and logistical problems is the American Democratic Party, whose candidates consistently and repeatedly promise to undo all that the Trump administration has tried. Nothing that Trump has tried is permanent. All is subject to reversal, eventual relaxation, and selective enforcement.

Some permanent remedies are available, as will be described in Chapter Nine. But unfortunately, it may take a European-style crisis to finally move the needle on US asylum loopholes that beckon jihadists and all manner of other criminals with a tall tale to tell.

CHAPTER FIVE

"WHEN THE GRINGOS CAME": THE FAR WAR

The region is also home to networks that specialize in smuggling illegal immigrants from places like Afghanistan, Pakistan, Yemen, Syria, and Iraq, all places where terrorist organizations like al-Shabbab, ISIS, al-Qaeda and their affiliates operate. Now migrant smuggling is not uncommon. What makes these networks different is the type of people who enlist their services to attempt to enter the U.S. homeland undetected. Some of these people have ties to terrorism and some have intentions to conduct attacks in the homeland.

—Rear Admiral Brian Hendrickson, US Southern Command, congressional testimony on May 23, 2018.[1]

In the early years after 9/11, when the Americans were still figuring out how to guard the nation's open southern flank, an Afghan traveler caught in Mexico caused such terrorism alarm that he ended up at Guantanamo Bay, Cuba, in the notorious American military prison camp reserved for the most hardened of terrorist prisoners. There, in 2003, the US military authorities deemed Feda Ahmed, who admitted he was on his way to cross the American border, "an enemy combatant…based on information possessed by the United States that indicates that the detainee is associated with al-Qaida."[2]

The partial story of Feda Ahmed, a designated al-Qaeda enemy combatant who almost succeeded in reaching the American border, is revealed in declassified records and military tribunal hearing transcripts the government was forced to release after an *Associated Press* Freedom of Information lawsuit in May 2005.[3] But the documents reflecting the 2002 capture of Ahmed in Mexico and subsequent imprisonment at Guatanamo Bay, almost unbelievably attracted no media reportage even as it has resided on a *New York Times* database for years. Not even the Department of Defense's final 2004 intelligence assessment about Feda Ahmed seemed to interest the reporters at the newspaper holding the documents, the wire service that litigated in federal court to get it, or any other reporter who might have read the declassified materials later:

"Detainee is a suspected al-Qaeda terrorist captured in Mexico attempting to reach the US border."[4]

According to the material, Feda told his American interrogators after his Mexico arrest that, shortly after the US invasion of Afghanistan in 2001, his father in Kandahar paid $25,000 to a smuggler named "Khaled" to get him over the American border. Khaled was apparently part of the international smuggling network run out of Quito, Ecuador by the Jordanian-Palestinian Maher Jarad, who worked closely with smugglers for the US-designated terrorist groups Hezbollah and al-Gama'a al-Islamiyya of Egypt. Jarad had been sending his Middle East clients from Ecuador to Mexico aboard merchant ships, then overland to the US border. In February 2002, Ahmed and an apparent subordinate in the Jarad network, an Afghan identified as "Ahmed Jan," whom US investigators said also was directly linked to Hezbollah and al-Gama'a al-Islamiyya, flew together to Ecuador on forged travel documents, including passports. In Ecuador, Jarad put the pair on a ship headed to Mexico's Chetumal port, through the Panama Canal. But after 9/11, the Americans were determined to shut down that ocean smuggling route. With the Mexican Navy, the American Coast Guard and Immigration and Naturalization Service set up the joint "Operation Southern Watch" (alternatively known as Operation Southern Focus) to disrupt Jarad's SIA-shipping scheme. In March 2002, the Mexicans arrested Ahmed and Jan, according to the declassified material.[5]

Mexico hung on to both men for three months, no doubt while American intelligence officers interrogated them, then deported at least Feda back to Afghanistan's capital, Kabul. The Afghan government put him in prison for another ten months, and then, for unknown reasons, handed him over to the US authorities, who shipped him to Guantanamo Bay on May 9, 2003.[6]

The reasons for imprisoning Ahmed at Guantanamo Bay are listed in the documents: "To provide specific information on terrorist networks, financing, facilitators, recruiters, and travel in Afghanistan, Pakistan, and Mexico."[7] But he was also deemed to be associated with al-Qaeda.

At one point, Ahmed told the Tribunal president at the prison that he was going to the United States through Mexico because "I was going to find a job to make some money." But American interrogators caught Ahmed lying about everything, his trip, his family, his travels, whether he could read and write, what languages he spoke, and his work. All the lying was "not indicative of someone simply trying to enter the US," a 2004 intelligence assessment of Ahmed concluded.[8] It seemed clear to the Americans that Ahmed was trained in counter-interrogation techniques. He failed a polygraph when he answered no to the question of whether he had ever received combat training and if he was "trying to sneak into America, to hurt Americans."[9]

The Americans tagged Ahmed as a "moderate" threat to the US, a designation that was downgraded over time to "low," at which point he was transferred back to Afghanistan on April 18, 2005.[10]

That early post-9/11 instance of a suspected terrorist attempt to reach the US southern border occurred in the nascent stages of an American effort that would evolve into distinct but related counterterrorism operations and spread throughout the Americas.

As described in Chapters Two and Three, America shored up its physical land borders after 9/11 in a "near war" to filter against expected Islamic jihadist terror infiltrations of the sort that have bedeviled Europe. New laws requiring the prevention of terrorist infiltrations at the land borders led to expanding Border Patrol and extending walls along the Mexican line. As we have seen, the FBI, DHS agencies, and sometimes military and CIA intelligence officers (and for a time my Texas Department of Public Safety team) have conducted enhanced security vetting investigations and face-to-face threat assessment interviews with SIAs who get apprehended. Most of the suspected jihadists are deported in a better-safe-than-sorry gambit. These efforts almost certainly prevented jihadist attacks from the southern border.

But in one of America's most expansive and audacious other unknown counterterrorism projects, the United States mounted what I call a "far war" to ensnare jihadist migrants *before* they reach the homeland border. Even before the Feda Ahmed case, homeland security sent officers and intelligence personnel to stand watch and to track and neutralize the few-and-far-between jihadist travelers, almost always by causing deportations. In the years since, hundreds have been added to expand and improve the programs. American homeland security leaderships established tripwire systems to do this detection work in partnership with regional governments willing to be trained, equipped, and prepared to act in certain ways when the time comes to nab, hold, and deport suspected traveling terrorists like Ahmed. The other American endeavor was to bust the terrorist-sympathizing SIA smugglers, like Maher Jerod, who made the long-haul jihadist journeys possible.

"For the first bunch of years we started doing this, we didn't see much," my DHS veteran of this far-war told me. "But as we got better and better, getting better with the processes, we started seeing them."

Feda Ahmed the client and Maher Jerod the smuggler stand as some of the first enemy casualties in the early days of this American far war, representative of its targets. Those two have much company now.

SETTING TRIPWIRES FOR JIHADISTS

Acting on a US Homeland Security Investigations "Wanted Alert" in June 2019, Nicaragua arrested four suspected ISIS jihadists who had just crossed their border on a journey north to the United States.[11] The US Department of Homeland Security blasted the bulletin to Central American governments and Mexico, identifying two of the Iraqis and one of the Egyptians and urged their captures so that they could be questioned. A fourth man, an Egyptian, had been traveling with the three when the Nicaraguans detained them. A collective sigh of relief passed quietly among those staffing an American intelligence apparatus that had been set up throughout the region many years earlier.

My intelligence community sources later told me the alert came from a Brazilian tipster close to the human smuggler who transported the Middle Easterners from Turkey, which in the summer of 2019 was awash in ISIS refugees fleeing their recently destroyed "caliphate." Nicaragua's leftist

Sandinista government, diplomatically estranged from the United States but maybe holding even less love for ISIS terrorists, sent the Iraqis and Egyptian ISIS suspects back to Costa Rica where American involvement was more welcome. The American officers—already stationed in the immediate region—went in. At US insistence, Costa Rica deported the foursome back to their respective home countries, any dark pasts or future plots right along with them, according to my sources.

Operations like this—tripwire networks of American and foreign law enforcement and intelligence groups that track and hunt suspected traveling jihadists—form a cornerstone of the enterprise. It grew directly from the scary days right after 9/11 when Feda Ahmed was caught with his terrorist companion and sent to Cuba.

Chasing down suspected jihadists in the jungle often starts with a bit of derogatory intelligence and a bulletin that goes out to all the participating governments of Latin America. These can look and feel like high-wire television dramas where those involved feel the stakes of failure could not be higher. In one such high-wire search-and-deport operation that went down in 2004, the FBI issued a "border-wide alert" asking Mexican and Central American officials to be on the lookout for Adnan Gulshair El Shukrijumah. The wanted man was a twenty-nine-year-old Saudi pilot suspected of serving Osama bin Laden as leader of al-Qaeda's external operations group who disappeared from his Florida home some months before the 9/11 attacks.[12] After the attacks, US Attorney General John Ashcroft singled out Shukrijumah as one of seven especially dangerous international terror figures wanted by the American government and put a $5 million bounty on his head.

State Department cables not declassified until 2016 confirmed why the FBI had asked American allies to the south for urgent help tracking him down.[13] After the attacks, a proven government informant (and relative of a Mexico-based human smuggler of Arabs) told the US consulate in Juarez that the al-Qaeda terrorist leader was hiding with two other Arab militants in a border city across from Douglas, Arizona. The informant "was not absolutely positive." But no matter, the FBI was taking no chances that such a dangerous terrorist directly connected to the 9/11 attacks might come back across. Mexico began arresting SIAs from Muslim-majority countries as a result, in "a growing Mexican crackdown," according to an *Associated Press* account of the operation.

If that was indeed him on the other side of Douglas, Arizona, Shukrijumah slipped the noose. He was never found in Mexico, if he was ever there at all, despite the continent-wide manhunt. We know that now because, in 2014, Pakistan Army Special Forces killed him in Waziristan following a long gun battle.[14]

But this was typical of many operations like it throughout the Americas—the triggering of multinational alert searches for suspected jihadists, asking pre-sensitized governments to hunt, capture and hold them, allowing Americans to interrogate them in foreign detention centers, and sometimes deporting the captured ones to faraway home countries. And while that particular effort came up empty, plenty of others over the years came up full. This jihadist-migrant alert system to the south helps explain why fewer jihadist-minded travelers—Known or Suspected Terrorists—show up to be counted at the actual American border. And that's the point.

Secrecy restrictions cloud how often migrant-terrorists have turned up at the end of this sluice, but the pickings have proven decent in Panama, a bottleneck country through which SIAs must pass to exit South America and enter Central America. The passage is considered so strategic that in 2018, the American government organized an "SIA Joint Task Force" in Panama City where ICE and CBP teams stationed in the US Embassy work hand-in-glove with Panama's intelligence (Consejo), military police, navy, and immigration services. In its short time, the task force "supported several CT-related [counterterrorism] investigations," the State Department's 2020 Country Report on Terrorism gave up.[15]

But operations long predated the formalized SIA task force collaborative. In July 2020, for instance, the director of Panama's Senafront border agency told a group of Arizona State University journalism students that since 2011 the agency has logged "more than 49 alerts on people from different countries linked to terrorist groups."[16] Some of these discoveries likely had origins in the fingerprints and retinal eye scans taken in recent years from thousands of migrants traveling through Panama and provided to American intelligence analysts as part of a collection program.

Intelligence analysis work does not often happen in real time, and so plenty of watch-listed suspects whose biometrics didn't immediately flag a problem were still found upstream in other countries after the usual alerts-and-warnings system was activated. In a rare November 2019 press announcement, Mexico's National Migration Institute disclosed that between 2014 and 2019, the agency determined that nineteen migrants passing through had ties to foreign terrorist groups.[17] The Mexican agency identified them as Somalis, Pakistanis, Bangladeshis, Ethiopians, and Yemenis.

American intelligence and law enforcement officers stationed in Mexico almost certainly would have been involved in each of the nineteen cases, either in supplying intelligence checks, conducting eyeball-to-eyeball interviews inside Mexico, or recommending what Mexico should do with these migrants based on assessments of the intelligence about each, which are unknown to me. Mexico deported all nineteen, its ministry said, which would be in line with American practice and wishes. With the deportee went whatever intentions they might have wanted to carry over the American border. And of course, none would have been counted as terrorists who reached the border because they obviously never made it that far.

Another one who never made it that far, because of the tripwire setup, was a suspected Somali al-Shabaab terrorist identified in a 2015 DHS lookout alert as Mohammed "Moha" Ali. DHS distributed the warning widely through Mexico and Central America, with his photo, as he had traveled to Cuba and was on the loose somewhere in Mexico preparing to cross the US border.[18] Ali was interdicted in Mexico and returned to an African country, according to records I have reviewed.

"WE ARE THE FILTER"

In December 2018, I made my way to one of Costa Rica's migrant camps thirty miles north of the Panamanian border in El Golfito, where just the previous year, at the main aluminum structure, federal police arrested another suspected Somali terrorist. His name was Ibrahim Qoordheen, and he was well on his way to the US southern border until he got caught in this American skein.[19] As a result, we'll never know what he might have planned had he arrived.

Like many of the migrants coming out of the Darien jungle from South America, Qoordheen took advantage of the Panama and Costa Rica "controlled flow" policy in which those countries care for, temporarily legalize, and then transport all migrants northward—out of their own countries—along government rest camps like in El Golfito and another one on the Costa Rica-Nicaragua border, outside of which smugglers line up to resume journeys. Unable to dissuade Panama or Costa Rica from doing the smuggler's work of transporting migrants to the US border under their so-called "controlled-flow" policy, the Americans tried to exploit it for intelligence instead. They gave Panama and Costa Rica immigration officers equipment to collect the fingerprints, retinal scans, and triangulated facial recognition photographs of every migrant they took in. All the data went straight to the Americans, who checked and sifted for matches to terrorism intelligence.

Inside the El Golfito migrant camp in Costa Rica, where several terrorist suspects were detained for the Americans. Photo by Todd Bensman

An alert analyst in the American embassy in Panama City saw that Qoordheen and six other Somalis had come into the country together and registered with the Panamanians for their easy rides to Nicaragua. The fake name Qoordheen originally provided didn't match anything, but his fingerprints were red-hot. A preexisting intelligence file associated with those prints identified him and several of his missing traveling companions as intertwined with a violent al-Shabaab cell and smuggling network in Zambia, two US intelligence officials told me.

It was too late to have him and his fellow travelers arrested in Panama; they'd already boarded the air-conditioned commercial buses and were spread out somewhere along the long trail north. But using collaborative arrangements long in place, the Americans sent out their alerts and had plenty of trip wires already set, from Panama to Mexico.

The following year when I visited the El Golfito camp, a Costa Rican immigration officer stationed there, Freddy Valverde Campos, told me he was on duty when the Americans called asking if the Somali was registered. Campos explained to me that he and his officers were always "in close contact with the Americans" on such matters. Yes, Qoordheen was there. Hearing that, the Americans asked Campos to hold him until they could arrive. In an interview room that Campos showed to me, a small team of Americans interrogated Qoordheen at length. The Somali, as expected, gave up nothing. They had the Costa Ricans arrest the Somali then, based on other intelligence in hand. Taking a better-safe-than-sorry approach, the Americans requested that Costa Rica deport Qoordheen back to Zambia, which they did, according to two American law enforcement sources.

Significantly, Campos also told me, as we stood in the camp chatting, the Qoordheen matter was no isolated incident. Several other terrorist suspects had been arrested before Qoordheen and also deported. There was a routine—normalized jihadist apprehensions and interrogations in the jungle. American intelligence officers often showed up there to interview Iraqis, Iranians, and Pakistanis who had been flagged for terrorism or espionage threats. Sometimes the Americans just call the El Golfito migrant camp and have the local immigration officers conduct the interviews—and forward the intelligence reports to the US embassy where the Americans work. That's how the other suspected terrorists were caught there, Campos said.

"We have deported other people from Costa Rica for terrorism," he confided to me as we stood outside the room where the Americans interviewed Qoordheen. "If they suspect there is a person traveling to the United States for terrorism, they need to know where they are and to know who they are."

"We are the filter," Campos said. "Most are good, but some are bad."

The American tripwire system went into overdrive after Qoordheen. The problem was that five Somalis had been traveling with Qoordheen and couldn't be found, sources familiar with the cases told me. The Americans sent Wanted Alerts to Guatemala, El Salvador, and Mexico. The Mexicans caught one of the traveling associates, Abdi-Wahab Mursal, not long after, an American intelligence official told me. Like Qoordheen, Mursal was also on the US terrorism watch list. Rather than have him deported, the Americans requested a handoff at an international bridge in Texas, which happened on October 11, 2017. Mursal remained in custody for nearly a year before he was deported to Mogadishu. But it's unclear how many of the others were ever found, if any.

The American public knows almost nothing of these distant activities. The publicly available annual 2017 US State Department Country Reports on Terrorism, released in September 2018, did provide a confirming peek at the American counterterrorism partnership with Panama. It said one program objective there now was "to detain and repatriate individuals for whom there were elevated suspicions of links to terrorism."[20]

In the spring of 2020, the Arizona State University student journalists traveled to Panama and returned with largely sympathetic coverage of extra-continental migrants. Prior to their trip, the students reached out to me for tips and leads about where to go. I was happy to sensitize them about the national security aspect of the migrant flow through Panama on the chance that they might stumble across something interesting to me. Sure enough, the students found a group of Yemenis held in a Panamanian migrant camp in Darien Province I'd told them about at the village of La Penita. The students reported that the Yemeni men had been held there for more than fifty days, without explanation, while all other migrants were allowed to pass through after only a few days.[21]

One of the Yemenis, identified as Marwan Mohammed Alud, told the student that Panamanian police took his passport and cell phone after collecting their fingerprints and retinal scans. The student journalists photographed Alud and his detained group and quoted him complaining of "racial profiling." But when the students dutifully asked a DHS official at the US embassy what this was all about, an official acknowledged full awareness of Yemenis deep in the Darien jungle and said the men were not being held just because they were from Yemen.

"There is an ongoing investigation regarding that group," the US official told the students.

The American official also let the students know that "we have had several known and suspected terrorists flying through the region, and they've been denied entry into Panama."

I'm aware of several other cases of suspected terrorists similarly stopped in their tracks by allied governments and what that must look like on the ground. While I was visiting Panama in December 2018, an American official described a recent time when a Pakistani was flagged as a terrorism problem. The migrant had a long history with a terrorist organization that my source wouldn't name. The Panamanians kept the migrant in local custody at the behest of the Americans for almost a full year while they investigated. The investigation turned up no specific terrorism plot, but because of his confirmed history as a terrorist, the Pakistani was deported by plane anyway to easily eliminate any risk, the officer told me. Better safe than sorry.

Another illustrative case involved six Pakistanis who entered Panama from Colombia in August 2016 on their way to the American border and were pulled off the route, then deported home. The deportations of the six were publicly reported but not the reasons why, so it attracted almost no notice. But Juan Carlos Vargas, political editor for *La Prensa* newspaper in Panama City, told me his paper knew the Pakistanis had been arrested on American suspicions that they were associated with al-Qaeda and after they were seen taking photos of sensitive sites around the city, including the Panama Canal.[22]

"The government closed out all information about that news," the journalist told me in his newspaper's comfortable lobby, adding that this wasn't the only such case. "Other [terrorism suspect] cases were shut down too."

The tripwire system is not limited to Central America but ranges far to its south; the SIA smuggling hub of Brazil has been long favored as an initial landing and staging country for migrants readying to travel north. Brazil has hosted one of ICE-HSI's largest overseas contingents, alongside Customs and Border Protection officers and FBI agents. The relationship ramped up after the 2018 election of the mercurial President Jair Bolsanaro, who was only too happy to bust Muslim terrorists, perhaps mindful of the discovery of local ISIS network that was plotting to attack the South American country's 2016 Olympic games. In 2019, CBP and Brazil's federal police opened a pilot program in the country's airports to identify high-risk "travelers with links to terrorism…and alien smuggling" coming and going, American prosecutors noted after its first SIA smuggler bust that year.[23] Brazil even agreed to send its own permanent liaison officer to CBP's National Targeting Center in the United States to work on counter-smuggling and terrorism issues in Brazil.

The American hunt for terrorists was fairly humming in Brazil in 2019—long overdue—when the FBI pushed out a bulletin seeking infor-

mation about Mohamed Ahmed Elsayed Ahmed Ibrahim, an Egyptian suspected al-Qaeda operative living in Brazil and considered armed and dangerous. [24] The public notice—the first of its kind for that region—stated that
Ibrahim was being sought for questioning about his alleged involvement in
plotting attacks against the United States, an investigation that was ongoing
at the time of this writing.[25] A *New York Times* reporter was able to phone
Ibrahim in Sao Paulo and quote him swearing he was merely a happily-mar-
ried furniture mover who was not involved with the terrorist group.[26] But
the *Times* obviously had no access to the intelligence possessed by FBI agents
eager to do their own questioning. A State Department statement, perhaps
hinting at the specific intelligence, said the Americans were particularly concerned about Ibrahim's presence in Brazil because of "the ability of transnational criminal organizations and foreign terrorist organizations such as
al-Qaeda to move money, weapons, goods, and people illegally across international borders, wherever those borders might be."[27] Of course, not mentioned by the *Times* was that it had briefly glimpsed one part of America's
much broader covert "far war" to secure the southern land border.

AMERICA'S SPECIAL RELATIONSHIP WITH MEXICO

In January 2020, I happened to be reporting in the southern Mexican state
of Chiapas, interviewing Mexican military and immigration officers, when
HSI sent out another terrorist migrant alert: be on the lookout for a female
suicide bomber and four accompanying men "of Middle Eastern descent"
headed through Mexico and to the US border.[28] I knew the trip wire system
described earlier had gone live once again.

The Border Patrol intelligence alert, which had been based on intelligence the CIA had briefed the agency with and wasn't intended to be made
public, said the United States had gotten information from a Guatemalan
that the five had gone through Guatemala and Belize and were currently
in the next state over from me, in Veracruz, Mexico. I knew that American
alerts like this, based on intelligence information of unknown credibility,
went out fairly regularly among American partners like Mexico. But usually,
I was nowhere near ground zero of the chase like now.

I also knew the Americans were in excellent position to find the five
reputed terrorists. Since at least late 2015, not coincidentally at the time

of the Paris attacks and under the Obama administration, US agents were sent in force to Tapachula. By August 2016, the American group had vetted more than 640 SIAs inside southern Mexican detention centers, according to *Reuters News* reporting.[29] *Reuters* was given access to internal DHS documents showing that CBP officers were training their Mexican counterparts in the tedious art of SIA interviewing and to use US criminal databases to investigate SIA detainees.

"U.S. concerns about potential security risks from migrants using the unusual and circuitous southern route have been growing in recent years, following a string of Islamic-State-inspired attacks in the West and the surge in Syrian refugees fleeing that country's civil war," *Reuters* reported, neatly tying the knot between Europe's tragedy with border-infiltrating terrorists and American fear of the same.

While sitting on a bench outside my Tapachula hotel, I contacted a US intelligence source on my cell phone. I was some thirty miles from the Guatemala border, which just then was crowded with thousands of African, Haitian, Arab, and Bangladeshi migrants, as well as Central American migrants. The previous day I had interviewed a Pakistani migrant on a central downtown Tapachula street.

My source explained to me that the Mexicans were marshaling to find the five. I knew the country stood a uniquely high chance of finding them too at that historic moment in time, assuming, of course, that the terrorist travelers actually existed.

For one thing, under pressure from President Trump, who at the time was demanding that Mexico end the mass migration crisis of Central Americans where I was on *its* southern border, Mexico had deployed more than 6,000 national guard troops at more than fifty roadblocks throughout its southern states to block once-free northward travel.

It was an unprecedented operation for the Mexicans, aimed at persuading Central Americans to stay home—and a temporary one. But SIAs were getting caught up in the Mexican dragnet for the first time in modern history too, a precedent that should be remembered when it is ever needed for *that*. Quite unintentionally, many SIAs found themselves trapped in Tapachula right alongside the Central Americans, forced to apply for Mexican asylum just like the Salvadorans, Hondurans, and Guatemalans. They would be easy to scoop up for interrogation. The terrorists probably wouldn't get far out of town; as I and my party found out one day when we drove out on a dirt road and were suddenly surrounded by state and federal police who pulled guns, then searched our cars and checked our documents.

I knew that if the five terrorists existed, they would have a hard time evading these temporary army roadblocks, the hidden cops on dirt roads, and the American force of ICE and CBP officers connected to the intelligence community prowling the region. Over the next few days, Mexican military and immigration officials at some of the roadblocks confirmed they were under orders to detain all Middle Easterners and bring them to a particular detention center in Tapachula. Additionally, any Middle Eastern migrants known to be holed up in the area were to be picked up and brought in for questioning.

The whole effort turned out to be unnecessary, this time anyway.

A few days later, my own sources soon told me the Americans had grilled the original Guatemalan tipster and had discredited him as an Islamophobic crank. The tension dialed down a good bit while I finished my reporting in the area, although I thought Middle Eastern migrants seemed harder than usual to come by on that trip to Chiapas, my third.

This whole episode in January 2020—an American terrorist traveler alert that spurred Mexico to detain SIAs for interrogation and investigation—underscores a fairly reliable US-Mexico counterterrorism partnership developed after 9/11. As a transit country for mass immigration through it and by its own citizenry, Mexico's record of cooperation in disrupting general illegal immigration is less than stellar because Mexico is conflicted. On the one hand, Mexico's national interests are served by the $25 billion a year in American remittance cash its citizens working illegally in the United States send back to Mexico. That kind of emigration is good, from Mexico's perspective. But when it comes to migrants from the Islamic world, Mexico was and is just as self-interested.

In 2007, Mexico's ambassador to the US at the time, Arturo Sarukhan, explained all this to me with picture-perfect clarity. In a Washington, DC, restaurant over drinks, the ambassador explained that any terror attack that traced its origins to a border crossing would lead to abrupt and radical border restrictions, which could catastrophically disrupt not only normal trade with Mexico's biggest trading partner but also those billions in annual remittances its people send home. (Likewise, the US immigration advocacy and resettlement industry understands this all too well.)

"The day that happens," Sarukhan said of a terrorist infiltrator who attacks from Mexican soil, "this relationship is over as we know it. Everything. So it behooves my country to ensure that that border is not used as a potential staging ground for terrorist penetration or attack to U.S. soil. Mechanisms put in place by agencies on both sides of the border are providing the results."

Thirteen years later, that bit of diplomatic wisdom still held true as the Mexicans and Americans used those same "mechanisms" in their hunt for the five reputed terrorists in Veracruz.

Mexico probably works harder at US terrorism-related security than on its own. The predominantly Catholic country is hardly a target of Islamic terrorists. A 2018 US State Department Country Reports on Terrorism, an annual assessment of how major countries do counterterrorism, noted the dynamic: "Mexico does not view terrorism as a major threat to its security but acknowledges the United States' concerns and cooperates closely...."[30]

Mexican self-interest in keeping the border open to trade and remittance money also helps explain the messaging in that seemingly out-of-the-blue Mexican foreign ministry announcement in July 2019 that, over the previous five years, it had detained and deported nineteen migrants linked to Islamic terrorist organizations. The government provided no details about any of them, naturally, but the numbers seem to comport with other information about Mexico's trip wire system collaboration with the United States on this issue, which dates straight to the 9/11 attacks.

ENTER THE FBI WITH A HANDSHAKE AND AN IDEA

After 9/11, the US government began urging Mexico to suppress SIA traffic that had always moved unmolested through its territory. The State Department's 2006 Country Reports on Terrorism took note of how the Americans still perceived the top Mexico-related threat at the time: "terrorist transit and the smuggling of aliens who may raise terrorism concerns."

"Our bilateral efforts focused squarely on minimizing that threat," the 2006 report stated.

Mexico's cooperation with the Americans branched out as time went on. Mexico, for instance, prosecuted and imprisoned Salim Boughader-Mucharrafille, the Tijuana-based Lebanese smuggler of Hezbollah agents into the United States, *after* he had served his time on a US conviction. The Mexican authorities kept after the terrorist threat, in collaboration with American intelligence. In April 2003, for instance, when five Hezbollah operatives were reported to be preparing for a border crossing, it was naturally the Mexicans who mounted an aggressive manhunt.[31] The operatives, if they existed, were never found.

Besides ICE, other DHS agencies such as US Customs and Border Protection intelligence officers grabbed an oar. So did the military's Southern Command and the United States Special Operations Command—North (SOCNORTH)—their intelligence groups—after 9/11. Over the years, INTERPOL has played a key role in the American far war against jihadist travel.

But at the tip of the spear was the FBI, already in the country. It added forces in Mexico and, not long afterward, began a diplomatically sensitive, hardly known effort in the country.

The Mexicans began allowing FBI agents and other federal intelligence officers, like ICE's HSI, into its detention facilities to interview SIAs, a program that obviously continues to the present time as we see from the media reports about CBP and ICE agents working the Tapachula detention center in 2016 and beyond.

Now-retired FBI Supervisory Special Agent James G. Conway started it. He was sent to the US embassy in Mexico in the months after 9/11 to serve as program manager of the bureau's counterterrorism program in Mexico and jump-started that operation. Conway told me that prior to the attacks, the FBI's Mexico contingent in the Office of the Legal Attaché mainly worked investigations related to organized crime, drug trafficking, and money laundering. Once he got on the ground, he shifted the focus to SIAs and counterterrorism.

"I realized the threat to U.S. national security was not large groups of terror cells just south of the border but the large, global human smuggling operations that existed in Mexico and Latin America for decades that were smuggling people from all over the world through Mexico and on into the United States," recalled Conway, a private security consultant in Houston, years after he retired. "Knowing that it takes only one individual or a small cell to do significant harm, the flood of people crossing the border without any screening or vetting became alarming to me."

Conway created a working group, or "fusion cell," of Mexico-based agents, Border Patrol, the State Department, and a number of "traditional intelligence agencies." At first, the group reached out to Mexican counterparts and put the SIA matter on their radar, asking them to start detaining SIAs and letting the Americans know when profiles matched a list of risk criteria. The Mexicans starting doing some of their own interviews, sending the intelligence on to Conway's FBI group. The Mexicans let the agents in to the detention centers to do other interviews.

The operation was politically sensitive for the Mexicans on the domestic front because of a dark remembered past when bullying Americans too often coopted independent Mexican decision-making. So the FBI interviews inside Mexican detention facilities remained secret lest the Mexican public find out and accuse its government of kowtowing once again to American demands. For perspective, it's worth pointing out that, conversely, the United States probably would never allow Mexican intelligence officials to conduct investigations inside its federal facilities on *its* prisoners and detainees.

When I first disclosed the existence of this program in a 2007 report on SIAs for Hearst News, a senior ICE official at the time told me the Mexicans immediately suspended the whole program in response, embarrassed, and said he wished he had never disclosed it to me. The interview program was slowly reinstituted to varying degrees, to the extent that in 2015–2016, ICE and CBP personnel had been able to interview 640 SIAs in Tapachula and were still in town in 2020 to hunt for the five terrorists mentioned earlier. At one point, the FBI began giving the Mexicans prepared questionnaires in common SIA languages and asking that Mexican authorities have SIAs in their custody fill them out and return the information to the FBI.

"The Mexicans went out on a limb for us on this issue," Conway said.

I first became aware that some sort of sensitive FBI activity was going on in Mexico in 2007, when the first Iraqi border-crosser I met in Brownsville, Boles, described extensive interviews at the hands of Americans inside the Mexican detention facility where he landed after capture. Boles, who had spent time as a war refugee in Damascus, Syria, told me Mexican immigration detained him in Tapachula and then bused him for twenty hours with other Arabs and non-Spanish-speaking travelers to a facility in Mexico City, which was where Conway and his group were stationed at the embassy. One day, Boles was taken to a well-lit interrogation room fitted with a table, some chairs, and a telephone on speaker with a female Arabic interpreter on the other end. To one side, a Mexican agent stood throughout the proceedings, observing but not participating. But the interrogators were absolutely American, Boles told me.

As the hours ticked by, the questions became more specific. The Americans wanted names, places, and dates related to his time in Iraq and Syria as a war refugee. They wanted to know if he had served in the Iraqi military and what weapons training he had received.

They asked Boles point-blank if he was a member of a terrorist organization that ran a training camp in the Syrian port town of Latakia, which press reports had identified as processing foreign fighters on their way to combat American troops in Iraq. Had Boles ever been to Latakia? What did he know about the terrorist organization that ran the camp? The Mexicans hung on to Boles for three more months, possibly to buy the Americans more time to check the story.

The intelligence gained through the Mexican collaboration led to SIA smuggler busts, including the dismantling of one smuggling group in France, and apprehensions of migrants deemed dangerous enough to be deported from Mexico, Conway said.

"The Mexicans provided us with key interview information as well as information from their personal effects and cell phones," Conway recalled. "Much of that intelligence was analyzed and created the basis of investigations against SIA smuggling organizations based in Mexico as well as other parts of the world."

ANATOMY OF A WORKING PARTNERSHIP

The State Department's 2016 Country Reports on Terrorism noted that Mexican authorities carried out "counterterrorism monitoring" in airports and at migration stations through a "constant review" of regular and irregular people flows and by checking names against terrorist watch lists.

"Mexican and U.S. law enforcement agencies coordinate closely regarding persons who raise terrorism concerns," the State Department report said. "This primarily involves individuals encountered at the immigration detention facility in Tapachula, Chiapas, and also at international airports."[32]

Just like I did while working for Texas DPS, Mexican security agencies also tracked down the real story behind persistent and repetitive media reports about supposed terrorist training camps in Mexico. Confirming my own efforts at Texas DPS, the State Department's annual report that year, 2016, concluded that these were "found to be unsubstantiated."[33] Remember, though, that there is value to confirming reports as bogus and also that plenty were not.

To this day, Mexico continues to alert the Americans about any migrant that flags terrorism trouble. As noted in Chapter Three, the country has hand-delivered especially dangerous ones to the Americans on international pedestrian bridges.

Mexico evidently does some better-safe-than-sorry deporting too.

Mexico's collaboration on SIAs has continued on through the years. In 2012, the Panamanians picked up another problematic Pakistani out of the Darien jungle and called the Americans. According to source material I have reviewed, the Pakistani raised flags on three counts. One, he had been living in Quito, Ecuador, and spoke fluent Spanish yet was on the well-known SIA trail through Panama. These factors suggested the Pakistani worked in the smuggling business and might have been transporting other Pakistanis. Two, he claimed he had left Karachi, Pakistan, after things went sour during his work as a supposedly low-level grunt worker for the highly violent US-designated Tier Three terrorist organization, the Muttahida Qaumi Movement (MQM), and also the much-blooded "Gang War Group" of Pakistan. He claimed that he merely worked for the group as a lowly painter whose service amounted to tacking up MQM placards in public spaces and handing out MQM flags at events.

Third, he was on the US terror watch list. In the counterterrorism intelligence world, all this information adds up to a five-alarm fire.

The Panamanians brought the Pakistani to the American embassy to be interviewed for several hours. The terrorist suspect described recruitment and extortion attempts by MQM that he purportedly resisted and had to flee by going to Ecuador, Latin America's Grand Central Station of global human smuggling. He claimed to have opened up a disco there but that thugs following from Pakistan soon followed, he said, and so he fled to Panama.

The American interrogators probably did not buy any of this. I wouldn't. But, inexplicably—whether part of a deliberate strategy to track him going north or simply due to a really bad screw-up, the Pakistani was inexplicably released. He fled north toward the US border. The Americans set the usual trip wires with all the partners to get him back.

One day a couple of months later, sure enough, the Mexicans called. They had the man in custody, in Tapachula. The Mexicans required the Pakistani to fill out their American-prepared questionnaire about travel tactics and terrorist connections. Then, they opened the gate to HSI agents attached to the American embassy in Mexico City, who flew down to interview the Pakistani. HSI agents spent hours with him inside the detention facility.

It's unclear, from what I was able to learn about this case, what ultimately happened next. The American concern was that he self-acknowledged extensive contact with MQM militants, but his assertions that he resisted their recruitment of him could not be corroborated. It seems highly unlikely this Pakistani would have been allowed to continue his journey to the US border to claim asylum and was likely deported.

Another case illustrating the US-Mexico counterterrorism collaboration unfolded in the fall of 2014 when a Bangladeshi emailed the Houston Police Department warning that a fellow Bangladeshi, trained and indoctrinated by al-Qaeda in Afghanistan, was right then en route to the US border and intended to conduct a suicide bombing after he got over. The tipster gave the name the Bangladeshi was using, a photo, and an itinerary. The usual American alert went out to Mexico and Central America.

The case landed in the lap of HSI agents on the Texas side, who called their Mexican counterparts. Lo and behold, they got a hit. The Bangladeshi described happened to be in custody in Tapachula, having just come over from Guatemala with seven other Bangladeshis. HSI, FBI, and other American agents flew down to Tapachula immediately to interview the detainee inside the main detention center. Mexican intelligence officials were present as well, per the protocol for preserving at least a semblance of national sovereignty. For hours, the Americans grilled the Bangladeshi using a Bengali interpreter on speaker phone.

When they were finished, they'd caught the Bangladeshi in a series of lies, including whether he maintained social media and email accounts, but never were able to connect him to terrorism. Sneaking around so far from home with bogus passports, lying to federal agents, and having a poison-pen letter written about you doesn't bode well for getting a pass to the US. It's unclear what became of the Bangladeshi, but under the circumstances, the better-safe-than-sorry approach would have been applied to him with a one-way ticket on ICE Air.

The anecdotes described in these pages highlight the kind of cat-and-mouse game that plays out constantly in Latin America in the form of foreign law enforcement investigations, military adventures, outright spying, and partnerships with foreign intelligence services and law enforcement agencies of questionable trustworthiness. The American homeland security establishment set up much more than trip wires. Other artillery was wheeled up to distant front lines after 9/11, this to pummel the smuggling networks that brought in this terrorist prey in the first place. One of the central programs of the American counter-infiltration far war is the hunt for special interest alien smugglers and, as good as any place to start was the human funnel running into and out of Panama.

A PROXY ARMY ARISES: WHEN THE "GRINGOS" CAME

> I think we are beginning to see people coming into this hemisphere who have very, very questionable backgrounds, and our law enforcement agencies are paying close attention to that. We just have to recognize that this theater is a very attractive target and is an attractive pathway that we have to pay attention to.
>
> —Admiral Kurt Tidd, commander of US Southern Command, May 2016, speaking to reporters.[34]

In December 2018, I traveled to Panama to report on sharp increases in SIA traffic through the infamous Darien Gap bottleneck. Dangerous foot trails led through this jungled mountain gap upon which guides and smugglers led immigrants on seven- or ten-day journeys out over the narrow isthmus from South America and into Central America. Not so long before my 2018 visit to Panama, migrants coming out of the Darien jungle wilderness would make their way to an archipelago of seedy motels in Panama City where they could rest on the cheap, have money wired in, get some medical treatment for trench foot and other jungle ailments, and hook up with smugglers to continue the journey. I wanted to see for myself what I might still find there.

Intelligence community friends had identified a number of such motels for me, among them the Hotel Miami in the metropolis's oldest quarter of Casco Antiguo. The motel offered much more than $10-a-night rooms to the seemingly inexhaustible river of Somalis, Syrians, Pakistanis, Palestinians, Iraqis, and Bangladeshis brought to it year in and year out.

But everything had changed by the time I showed up unannounced on the motel's doorstep. Proprietor Mary Valderrama, who ran the place with her husband, Victor Sacipa, all those years, met me at the front reception area. After agreeing to an interview, she had me sit in a shabby living quarters of the establishment. She recalled how the migrants used to show up in droves at their motel broke, "filthy, sick, hungry and without even shoes."

Beyond offering rest and steel bunk-bed cots covered by filthy thin mattresses in dark jail-cell-like rooms, Mary said she and her husband, Victor, provided more important services for clueless migrants who usually only spoke native languages and had never gone so far from homelands as this seemingly distant planet. They arranged for the migrants to have money wired in and housed a kind of brokerage where they and smugglers could pair up. The house was always full. There were other hotels in the Casco Antiguo circuit doing it too. Everyone was getting paid, including the Panamanian police who turned a blind eye for their cut, the couple said.

"We would always ask them [the migrants], 'Why are you coming? And the answer was always 'Obama! He will let us in. We know *he* will let us in.'"

During the heyday of 2015, Victor began worrying about news coming in from overseas that ISIS had captured large swaths of territory in Syria and Iraq. Syrians and Iraqis often stayed at Hotel Miami. ISIS was consolidating its fresh Iraq and Syria land conquests. By 2016, ISIS terrorists who'd posed as war refugees and asylum seekers were bombing and killing all over Europe, as Victor and Mary were acutely aware.

"I began wondering what the gringos would think about Syrians and other Arabs from that neighborhood coming through and staying at Hotel Miami," Victor said.

Victor Sacipa, owner of the Hotel Miami in Panama City,
December 2018. Photo by Todd Bensman

But the money was too good to get out of the smuggling business. It turns out Victor's gut instinct was on the money. Victor recalled how "those gringos" finally did come, right alongside Panamanian police, in a surprise, full battle-rattle raid in 2016.

"They put all our guests up against the wall," Victor recalled, then took him, along with everyone else, to jail. Panama charged Victor and nine others with human smuggling. After the bust, he and Mary recalled interrogators asking all sorts of questions about ISIS and their guests' involvement in terrorism.

By the time I heard all of this, the motel had been out of the smuggling waystation business for nearly two years, and so were all the other stepping-stone motels I swung by that year. The whole network was shut down. In its place, the Panamanian government had erected it's "controlled flow" policy of moving the migrants itself to relieve some of the black market headaches of the motel system. Victor was under house arrest inside his empty motel, his passport still in police custody, and feeling crushed under the legal weight of an ongoing prosecution. This he demonstrated by hauling out a heavy stack of legal papers and slapping it down hard on the table in front of me.

TIP OF THE SPEAR AND RAISING A PROXY COUNTERTERRORISM ARMY IN THE HUNT FOR SIA SMUGGLERS

Already described is a trip wire system strung across Latin America for identifying jihadists moving along the SIA smuggling routes of Latin America, how US agents and their pre-sensitized allies in Latin America red-flag probable jihadists on the move, distribute terrorist-wanted alerts, and detain and investigated them—Yemenis, Somalis, Pakistanis and other nationalities—in remote migrant camps or Mexican detention centers. The tripwire component of the project can sometimes result in peremptory deportations—down there—that are never advertised to the American public.

But the arrests of motel proprietors like Mary and Victor speak to another ubiquitous operational component in America's covert counterterrorism far war: taking out the SIA smugglers and their facilitating infrastructures of safe houses and subordinate helpers. Variations of this campaign date to at least 2002–2003, when all the new homeland security legislation and agency strategic plans placed responsibility for disrupting SIA smuggling in ICE's portfolio, its then-Office of Investigation (reorganized in 2010 as ICE Homeland Security Investigations, HSI). DHS moved its people in force into Latin America as the tip of the spear of a dawning campaign to hunt and bust SIA smugglers who needed places like Hotel Miami and the bit players like Mary and Victor who kept the assembly line profits rolling. They were bridge-builders in a sense, connecting hemispheres. The Americans wanted those bridges blown, preferably faster than new ones could be built.

ICE once described this mission as involving 240 agents in some forty-eight foreign attaché offices to "aggressively pursue, disrupt and dismantle foreign based criminal travel networks—particularly those involved in the movement of aliens from countries of concern." [35] In recent years, HSI has worked these cases alongside the US Department of Justice's Human Rights and Special Prosecutions Section. The agents and prosecutors work within an entity known as the Extraterritorial Criminal Travel Strike Force.[36]

James Dinkins, a retired director of ICE-HSI who was there from the beginning through 2014, described the new operation in those days as creating an "outer ring of deterrence" for a "risk that is greater than perceived." Dinkins told me men and women of the agency eventually fanned out to seventy-eight international offices, including in dozens of Latin American countries through which SIAs typically transited and also to many of the origin countries in the Middle East, Africa, and Asia.

"You could easily devote an army to human smuggling," he said. "But we had to prioritize. We looked at those organizations that would pose the greatest national security threat and those would be the ones moving SIAs. We would prioritize that over some other organization moving people from Latin America just escaping an economic crisis and so forth."

Right away, the Americans tripped over their first hurdle in the strategy: US law enforcement has no legal authority to investigate or arrest people in foreign countries. The solution was to build a covert proxy army in those countries that could and would. But finding trustable law enforcement partners in that part of the world had always proven problematic in the war on drugs, where officers were paid such a pittance that drug money payoffs could easily separate cops from their public oaths to serve and protect. The solution was to fashion men and women into so-called "vetted" units the Americans could trust to as high a degree as possible to work with the Americans and their intelligence systems. To get them there, the local officers had to go through extensive background checking and constant security screening and training. Those who made it out the other end got the elite seal of trustworthiness and the enhanced pay that came with it.

The gringos recruited their new army from local and regional police forces and intelligence services in places like Panama, Costa Rica, Honduras, and Guatemala. Once knighted, these officers were deemed unlikely to corruptly leak sensitive intelligence about investigations and to carry out what needed to be done on their own sovereign territory but, let's face it, mainly for American national security objectives.

Dinkins said the US State Department paved the way for creating vetted units under governments it could influence and assisted funding them in the allied SIA transit countries. The government parlance name for this army of proxy units was "Transnational Criminal Investigative Units (TCIUs)," and after a time of training and heavy security vetting, an infrastructure of hundreds of local law enforcement officers in dozens of countries were working directly with HSI agents, Dinkins said.

Guatemala typified the arrangement—and the difficulties involved. In a Guatemala City restaurant featuring the local cuisine back in 2007, Guatemala's former chief federal prosecutor Gustavo Barreno recalled for me how his lawyers were sucked into American counterterrorism operations. Before 9/11, the few American immigration officers in the country concerned themselves with drug smuggling and sex trafficking, he said. SIA smuggling at the time happened in the wide open on an almost industrial scale, especially by ships plying the Pacific Ocean and Caribbean. Most of the government, police, and border patrol in Guatemala were in the pay of smugglers.

Author with Guatemalan police guarding an international bridge to Mexico against a migrant caravan attempting to cross, January 2020.

The human smuggling industry, he explained to me, "is gigantic…. You have no idea. Everyone is involved—*everyone*. And for Arabs to come into Guatemala, it's really easy—*really* easy."

First, American intelligence alerts started arriving in Barreno's office to be on the lookout for "people with Arabic features," he recalled. Next came a stream of "wanted" posters featuring suspected terrorists. Then a whole bunch of new gringos showed up in force to push major investigations of Arab smugglers. The Americans put him and his prosecutors through intense personal security screenings and then to work.

These first hunt-and-capture operations were given names such as "Operation Southern Focus" (2002) and "Global Thunder" (2003). As mentioned earlier in the case of the Afghan terrorist, Feda Ahmed, who traveled on one of these ships, these early aggressive multinational operations involved the use of American satellites, Coast Guard cutters, the US Navy, and the intelligence services of several South American governments.[37] Migrant-filled ships were forced to stop at sea, such as the *Esperanza* in February 2002 carrying twenty-six Iraqis and, apparently, Feda Ahmed.

"When one was discovered, I would detain them," Barreno said of SIAs in his country. "They were always turned over to the Americans."

The operations rolled up large smuggling organizations involving dozens of Salvadorans, Nicaraguans, and Colombians. Some had names like Fagr Ibrahim Mohammed Almat, Amin Omar Said Ahamad, and Ashrah Ammed Abdallah Bashar. These were Middle Easterners, smugglers, who lived and worked moving SIAs in bulk numbers out of Guatemala, El Salvador, and Ecuador until the smugglers were extradited to the United States for prosecution, or tricked into going there, where US law enforcement could arrest them.

Ironically, controversy over a group of Jordanians would lead to the joint program being shut down, Barreno said, which illustrates one reason American efforts in Guatemala remain an uphill slog. One day in early 2005, US and Ecuadorian intelligence officers alerted Barreno to the expected arrival in Guatemala of two wanted Jordanians.

After the safe houses were uncovered and the Jordanians arrested, the investigation turned up links between senior government officials and the smuggling ring, he said. Constant interference in the case eventually led to Barreno's ouster and cancellation of the American program, he said.

The Americans were contending with their corrupt environment as best they could. Santos Cuc Morales, Guatemala's National Director of Migration in 2007, told me a story that helps illustrate how bad the mire was for the gringos. Earlier that year, Morales told me, American embassy officials in Guatemala City approached him and asked whether his immigration officers could stop Iraqis "because of terrorism and the situation in Iraq."

The gringos provided intelligence, including lists of stolen passport numbers, and they offered training and money to Morales's immigration agents. But Morales said he couldn't help the gringos with their war on terror. Most of his 450 agents stationed along the nation's borders and at airports and seaports were on the take from the smuggling organizations, he told me, and wouldn't respond to orders. With a shrug, Guatemala's top immigration enforcement official said he wished he could help the Americans avert another attack.

"I hope that doesn't happen. It would be terrible, but it could happen because of the corruption here," Morales told me all those years ago. "It's the reality of things."

Still, the Americans have persisted where and when they could. Operations with the vetted local law enforcement groups continued through the years, though these evolved from the ambitious early ones as smugglers downsized from the pre-9/11 industrial scale of the smuggling and adjusted their tactics to evasion. Suspected jihadists have long been among the catch, the gold flakes in the bottom of the pan that American homeland security prospectors work so hard for.

By my count, the United States has prosecuted about twenty-five SIA smugglers inside the United States since 9/11. That's less than a couple a year but the number is misleadingly small. Uncounted are a great many other takedowns and disruptions that may well have been spearheaded by the Americans behind the scenes but were left to allied governments like Panama, Brazil, Colombia, and Mexico to prosecute.

In 2019, Brazil finally passed its first comprehensive anti-smuggling laws and funding. The Americans beefed up their presence in the country to take advantage of the new opening. In August of that year, a joint US-Brazil investigation centered in Sao Paulo rolled up three important SIA smugglers—a Somali, an Algerian, and an Iranian—and began Brazil's first SIA smuggler prosecution.[38] For years, these three had been flying SIAs from their homelands into Brazil on counterfeit Brazilian visas and passports of East African countries and then facilitating their travels northward to the US border.[39] Although details were tightly cropped, the Brazilian government's announcement of these operations let it be known that among the migrants sent to the US "are two Somalis arrested by the US police over suspected terrorism."[40]

In September 2020, the Brazilians bagged their second major SIA smuggler—this one specializing in moving Iranians to the American border. With ICE-HSI, federal police found Reza Sahami, a dual citizen of Canada and Iran guiding a group of seven Iranians in the city of Assis Brasil on the border with Peru.[41] Sahami had been smuggling "criminals" across international borders for more than 10 years, ICE Attaché for Brazil Bolivia Robert Fuentes said.[42]

ROUTES OF LEAST RESISTANCE THROUGH NO-MAN'S-LAND

The deployments generally followed the SIA routes. From a study of US court prosecutions of twenty-five SIA smugglers, I found that SIA smugglers and the DHS investigators who followed them chose some of these countries, in part, out of geographical necessity; for instance, the often unavoidable Panama offers the only land-based exit northward from South America.[43] Guatemala acts as an almost unavoidable funneling chute into Mexico. In turn, Mexico is obviously unavoidable as the only country from which to access Texas, California, New Mexico, and Arizona.

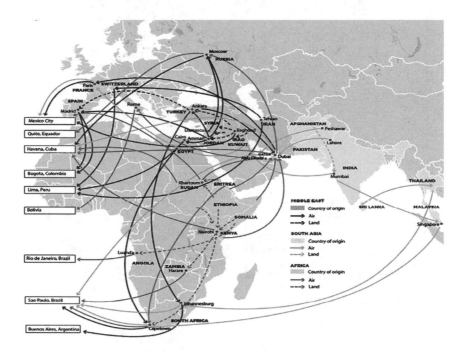

Departures from Middle East, Africa and South Asia
and Initial Landings in the Western Hemisphere

But once the Americans showed up, the smugglers drifted their operations to countries diplomatically estranged from the United States, where American officers couldn't work. Socialist and leftist Cuba, Venezuela, Bolivia, and Nicaragua fit that bill, and to an extent, Russia. One popular route from Syria, for instance, was a flight from Damascus to Russia, then Cuba, and finally Guatemala, skipping along a stepping-stone path through no-America go-zones.

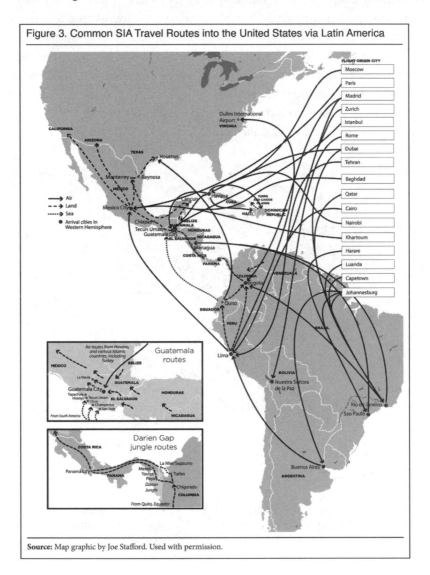

Figure 3. Common SIA Travel Routes into the United States via Latin America

Source: Map graphic by Joe Stafford. Used with permission.

SIA smugglers seemed to appreciate working in countries intrinsically indifferent to American homeland security values and concerns or in those simply too poor to do anything about SIA transit even had they wanted to.

The DHS army of special agents, in league with their homegrown proxies, faced daunting challenges in these physical and political landscapes.

US court prosecution records showed that when they had a choice, SIA smugglers most often routed their customers through the same six transit or staging countries in Latin America: Ecuador, Brazil, Colombia, Panama, Guatemala, and Mexico. There are others, of course. But these six nations feature geopolitical factors that grease the forward mobility of SIAs at minimal risk of arrest to their smugglers.

Except when they were spurred, these governments have often shown passive indifference to trans-migration and US security concerns. Most have insufficient budgets and resources to do much on their own even if they wanted to. All feature vast swaths of ungoverned borderland and territory. All host highly corruptible border and airport customs officials.

Some formal government policies and practices supercharge the SIA smuggling.

A flagrant example is Ecuador, whose president, Rafael Correa, in 2008 eliminated all visa requirements for foreign travelers in the service of an idealized "universal citizenship" where sovereign borders were regarded as archaic. Overnight, the country became a powerful magnet for SIA smugglers looking for a landing zone that didn't require expensive fake or bribed visas and didn't draw unwanted questioning from airport inspections officers.

In 2013, Ecuadorian pro-immigration advocate researcher Luisa Feline Freier published some (unintentionally) disturbing findings from interviewing hundreds of migrants and senior government leaders about the visa-free policy's first five years.[44] For one thing, she confirmed the obvious, which is that global human smuggling networks immediately shifted their thousands of US-bound immigrant clients straight to the Ecuadorian landing zone, including floods of SIAs from South Asia, North Africa, and the Middle East.

It wasn't long before the SIA surge had seriously alarmed the Americans, who had deployed their SIA hunters to the region a few years earlier. From her interviews with miffed Ecuadorian leaders, Freier found that the Americans had threatened to withdraw US foreign aid if Ecuadorian leaders did not resurrect visa restrictions on ten nations, among them Afghanistan, Bangladesh, Eritrea, Ethiopia, Kenya, and Pakistan. Ecuador supposedly complied in 2010. But, citing secret US diplomatic cables published by WikiLeaks, Freier learned that American diplomats, unsatisfied with Ecuadorian enforcement of the list, demanded an operation in 2011 that saw mass arrests in Quito of Muslim immigrants and FBI agents interviewing Pakistanis.

American alarm over Ecuador's visa-free policies persisted well into 2019, when the Trump administration found that the four suspected ISIS operatives from Iraq and Egypt had entered the hemisphere through Ecuador's international airport in Quito. In a barely reported move, the Trump administration pressured Ecuador to add Syria, Iraq, and Libya, among other countries, to its list requiring visas.[45]

The Americans also had to contend with high-transit countries of Colombia, Panama, Costa Rica, and Mexico, whose indifferent governments always seemed to need a little American goading. These countries adapted what I call "catch, rest, and release" safe passage policies wherein governments started to feed, house, and medically treat SIAs, then provide temporary visitor's visas that legalize their remaining travel to the next country. Colombia, Panama, Costa Rica developed these programs to such a fine point that they even arranged for affordable bus transportation to government rest camps along the way and handed out fliers filled with helpful tips about where to find money transfer services.[46]

As I've already described above, I found during a 2018 reporting trip that Panama and Costa Rica were running a well-oiled controlled flow assembly line that was moving migrants coming off the Darien Gap trail through to the Nicaraguan border on commercial buses. The government of Panama deflected months of my requests to discuss this 2016 policy, then seeing I wasn't going away, finally formally declined on national security grounds. But those doing the work in jungle outposts talked plenty.

"There is a thing the world does not see, and it is the work we do," a ranking Panamanian military police commander told me in the end-of-highway Darien Province town of Yaviza whose troops regularly collected the migrants. "No other country, or, I believe, any country in all of Latin America, does what Panama does. And that is to receive [foreign citizens], to aid them, give them medication and to organize them" for transport to

Costa Rica. When I asked if terrorists may be placed on this human conveyor belt, the officer offered, with a knowing chuckle, "Maybe!"

Several Panamanian National Assembly members explained how the policy works in the interests of both Panama and the migrants in removing a lot of the illicit smuggling that had been going on in places like the Hotel Miami.

"Panama is like a bridge or passway to another country," Juan Carlos Arrango of the ruling coalition Panamanian Popular Party explained to me one day in Panama City. "Wherever they come from, by boat, plane, or walking through the Darien jungle, they're very vocal in saying, 'We don't want to stay in Panama. We want to pass through, to the north.'" So, Arrango told me, the government is happy to see to that.

Until pausing the practice under pressure from the Trump administration in 2019, Mexico employed the same catch, rest, and release safe passage policy, providing SIAs respite for a couple of weeks and then legal papers and release to finish the trek to the US southern border. After Trump, Mexico is likely to go back to this model. An ICE agent testifying in one of the smuggling prosecutions described the Mexican practice this way:

> "Most of them, all the East Africans and many from the Middle East, they will surrender at Tapachula (in the state of Chiapas bordering Guatemala). The Mexicans will hold them for, you know, ten to 15 days, and then they will give them an order of deportation, and they are given 30 days to leave the country at that point."[47]

SIA smugglers regarded these policies as akin to government business subsidies. A Bangladeshi migrant who had just made it to the Texas border told me his smuggler required, under pain of a $5,000 fine, that he and his group turn themselves into the Mexicans as soon as they could because the Mexico pit stop would lower the smuggler's risks and costs for bribery, food, and shelter.

As he explained to me: "Mexico has a lot of checkpoints, and [these cause] lots of problems for the smugglers. It's [Mexican detention] a month of free room and rest, then the paper," referring to the short-term transit visas Mexico for years handed out.

A Pakistani migrant preparing to board a bus to Nicaragua
as part of Costa Rica's "Controlled Flow" free passage
policy, December 2018. Photo by Todd Bensman

As a bonus, Mexican immigration detention officers directed the Bangladeshi to a location where he would quickly find a smuggler for the last leg of the trip to the US border.

For all of these lemons, the gringos tried to make lemonade. The American government handed out equipment and trained immigration officials and police in the catch-rest-release nations to collect fingerprints and retinal scans, as well as facial-recognition photographs. As we've seen, these have paid national security dividends in the form of deported terrorist suspects in Mexico and Panama.

American counterterrorism thinking resulted in some unexpected projects. For the wide-open border between Panama and Costa Rica, the Americans funded, trained, and equipped a Costa Rica border patrol, yet another component of America's covert far war to deter jihadist infiltration and SIA smuggling. In 2018, some of those American-made Costa Rican border guards took me on patrol, in a US-funded jeep, through the unfenced, rarely demarcated wildlands between the two countries where anyone who didn't want to surface and register for controlled flow benefits could simply waltz across.[48] I came away impressed by the officers but wondering how, at the troop strength I saw, they could possibly sew up that border even a little with what they had. But it was a solid start.

Beyond Panama and Costa Rica, in Nicaragua on north, lay classic human smuggling territory. North all the way to the US border is the least-known battlefield in America's covert border war. Here, a most unusual kind of human smuggler—wily, educated, sometimes downright cosmopolitan, and often quite colorful as caricatures—faces off with the Americans hunters.

CHAPTER SIX

CAT AND MOUSE: THE KINGPINS

Despite the heroic efforts of our law enforcement colleagues, criminal organizations are constantly adapting their methods for trafficking across our borders. While there is not yet any indication that the criminal networks involved in human and drug trafficking are interested in supporting the efforts of terrorist groups, these networks could unwittingly, or even wittingly, facilitate the movement of terrorist operatives… toward our borders, potentially undetected and almost completely unrestricted. In addition to thousands of Central Americans fleeing poverty and violence, foreign nationals from countries like Somalia, Bangladesh, Lebanon, and Pakistan are using the region's human smuggling networks to enter the United States. While many are merely seeking economic opportunity or fleeing war, a small subset could potentially be seeking to do us harm.

—Gen. John F. Kelly, US Marine Corps
Commander, US Southern Command
testifying before Congress, 2015.[1]

On March 10, 2011, Ecuadorian law enforcement officers stepped off a plane at the Miami International Airport, escorting thirty-seven-year-old Irfan Ul-Haq, a longtime American quarry.

The prisoner was an SIA smuggler who'd based his operations in Quito, Ecuador. Right up until this point in time, Ul-Haq for years had run a profitable, globe-spanning human smuggling network transporting mostly fellow Pakistanis willing to pay his $60,000 fee to cross the US southwestern border. ICE Homeland Security Investigations agents had been chasing the Pakistani across the globe for months as part of a high-wire intercontinental undercover sting.[2] The far-flung investigation run out of the US attaché office in Quito had involved the insertion of undercover informants into the Ul-Haq organization. It had proven diplomatically complicated working in league with Latin American governments like Ecuador. By comparison to all that had gone down during the Ul-Haq investigation, this final handoff to HSI agents was almost anticlimactic. The Ecuadorian officers simply transferred custody to the American agents, who slapped cuffs on and took him to jail in Washington, DC, to face charges. No drama.

The HSI investigation had been lengthy, expensive, and, at times, touch-and-go, but also nothing all that new to HSI; the ICE division had been hunting and arresting SIA smugglers like Ul-Haq for a decade already, as part of an operation virtually unknown to the American public.

But this investigation had been unique.

The prosecutors and agents decided to test a theory about SIA smugglers. Was Ul-Haq willing to smuggle avowed terrorists into the United States?

To test the proposition, three undercover informants posing as smuggling brokers proposed to Ul-Haq that he transport several fictitious members of the notorious terrorist group Tehrik-e-Taliban, known as the Pakistan Taliban, across the US-Mexico border. They explained that Pakistan had "blacklisted" the terrorists. The first one was willing to pay $35,000. Ul-Haq didn't bat an eye.[3] He took the cash.

He responded that he couldn't care less about what the terrorists would do once in the US—hard labor, sweep floors, wash dishes in a hotel…

"Or, blow up. That will be up to them."

Ul-Haq and two co-defendant subordinates arranged for the first reputed terrorist to secure a bogus Ecuadorian passport, ensuring that it bore someone else's fingerprints, lest the terrorist's real ones flag in a database along the way. He then planned the trip from Lahore, Pakistan, to Dubai, UAE, then on to Cuba, the Dominican Republic, and Haiti for the final leg to the US.

In this case, the Americans were able to tease out the national security danger inherent in these long-haul smuggling networks and in the unusual men and women who tend to operate them. In January 2012, Ul-Haq was sentenced to fifty months in prison on a charge that was rare for an alien smuggler: material support for terrorism. In press releases all along the way, almost entirely ignored by American media, senior homeland security officials, one after the other, emphasized the national security stakes at the southern border and hinted at the existence of a much broader American counterterrorism project in Latin America far from the actual border.[4] As usual, there were few takers.

"These defendants sought to smuggle someone they believed to be a member of a terrorist organization from halfway around the world into the United States," said Assistant Attorney General Lanny A. Brewer. "For financial profit, they were willing to jeopardize the safety and security of the American people. Human smuggling operations pose a serious risk to our national security, and we will continue to work closely with our law enforcement partners at home and abroad to combat this dangerous threat."

The prey at the heart of America's counterterrorism "far war" referenced by Mr. Brewer is an exotic smuggler like no other. They are what I would call "SIA smuggling kingpins." Commanding hard-to-duplicate linguistic, financial, leadership, diplomatic, and organizational skill sets, they are masters of cobbling together dynamic supply chains that deliver human beings to the US border *with* political asylum claim stories that ensure they get into the United States and stay in.

In addition to the national security stakes inherent in the American counterterrorism operation, the Ul-Haq investigation illuminates the uniqueness of the kind of quarry it tracks and hunts.

Ul-Haq was born into a family of two brothers and five sisters; his father was a leather salesman who could barely support them all in Pakistan. Ul-Haq worked hard to get an education as a youth. He graduated from high school, managed to earn an undergraduate degree (types are not described in court documents), and then even an advanced graduate degree. He worked at various entrepreneurial ventures in Dubai, Cyprus, Turkey, Venezuela, and finally Ecuador, where he picked up a third language, Spanish (besides Urdu and Arabic), and discovered that these skills almost perfectly suited the true calling he discovered in South America: human smuggling.[5]

For years, Ul-Haq used his language skills and dual passports to occupy the apex of a profitable international human smuggling network that had transported scores of his fellow Pakistanis into Quito, Ecuador, and then northward through Panama and the rest of the way to the US southern border.[6] With the proceeds, he could afford two wives and two sets of children, one in Pakistan and one in Ecuador, in line with accepted Islamic practices.

THE KINGPINS OF ULTRA-DISTANCE SMUGGLING: PROFIT OVER IDEOLOGY

Fortunately for US homeland security, SIA smuggling kingpins are very hard to replace, at least compared to regular thugs that move drugs in Latin America. When SIA kingpins are caught, the organizations they built and solely enable tend to fall apart, at least for a time. Their indispensability and the kind of people they move made them a prime HSI target from the first days after 9/11. Knocking out one of these smugglers was regarded as akin to blowing the bridge in conventional army-on-army warfare.

SIA smugglers like Ul Haq are the pillars undergirding that bridge. They neutralize the key difference between SIA travel to Europe and to the United States: the Atlantic Ocean. Unlike the boats and overland transportation necessary for Europe-bound SIAs, US border-bound migrants sometimes stow away aboard commercial vessels that dock in Mexican or Central American ports. But the vast majority have to *fly* across an ocean to get within hemispheric striking distance of the United States. Making it over the Atlantic Ocean hump, the obstruction de jour, is the first order of business. Travelers of limited personal horizons who may never have ventured far from homelands, as well as jihadists who would want to slip the radars of governments along the way, usually don't know how to do it. They need the SIA smugglers and their copyrightable knowledge.

But SIA smuggling kingpins are smart, often educated, incredibly mobile, and not easy to fool. These attributes make for intriguing cat-and-mouse games between HSI and the smugglers all over the world.

SIA smugglers are at root entrepreneurs, motivated mainly by profit and much less so out of devotion to violent jihad. Their indifference to ideology, or secondary deference to it, makes what they do for a living just as dangerous as if they were committed jihadists themselves.

"What I have done was motivated by money and what I have earned so far exceeds my qualification," the Bangladeshi smuggler Moktar Hossain told an HSI agent (who was himself from Bangladesh) after his November 2018 arrest in Mexico and deportation to George H. Bush Intercontinental Airport in Houston. "I did help people coming to this country; whatever I did, I did it for money."[7]

But enough of them, like Ul-Haq described earlier, don't mind moving jihadists if they can make an extra buck.

Gauchan, the Mexico City-based Nepalese smuggler who charged clients up to $40,000, told an undercover HSI agent in 2013 that she believed a Pakistani client she smuggled into Arizona from Mexico was a terrorist, but she transported him anyway for the $3,500.[8] This information prompted yet another frantic, belated FBI hunt for the migrant inside the United States. Later, American investigators confirmed the Pakistani was real. They found him. He was from the embattled region of Kashmir and had been granted asylum. Agents interviewed him, but the court records that tell this story, as usual, omit whether Gauchan's instinct was correct.

Eritrean smuggler Habtom Merhay, a prolific smuggler of people from the Horn of Africa, is the one who, in 2010, brought over the California border nine watch-listed Somalis, Eritreans, and Sudanese mentioned in Chapter Three, according to government records I reviewed about that case. It's unclear from his court prosecution or those records whether Merhay was aware of his customers' backgrounds. But if he was aware, it's a safe bet he wouldn't have cared.

One prolific smuggler of Middle Easterners did care, though more for his own welfare than American national security. The Iranian American smuggler, Mehrzad Arbane, had moved Iranians, Syrians, Iraqis, and Jordanians into the United States for years before 9/11. After the attacks, though, he told an associate, he feared he "may have smuggled two of the hijackers who flew the planes into the towers in New York on September 11, 2001."[9] He was so worried about the coming American heat that he got out of the business entirely and went into cocaine trafficking instead. It turned out not to be the case that Arbane smuggled in 9/11 hijackers, as is commonly known now, but Arbane's associate was so alarmed by his suspicion at the time that he became a US government informant and, in 2002, helped investigators arrest Arbane for smuggling not only the coke but the SIAs as well.

As a motivation, sympathy for the jihad can't be entirely ruled out, of course.

Enough Somalis on the US terrorist watch list for their al-Shabaab involvements seem to trace to the same smuggling ring in Zambia. The commonalities could not be lost on the American SIA hunters that something was different about this Zambia operation. Abdulahi Sharif, the Somali terrorist who entered California in 2011 and went on to conduct a double-vehicle ramming attack in Edmonton, Alberta, was among those smuggled from Zambia, as was the watch-listed Somali terror suspect caught in Costa Rica's El Golfito camp in 2017, among several others who traveled with him. Any reasonable observer would wonder if that network is controlled by the terrorist group for the purpose of moving its operatives.

As described at length earlier, the Somali smuggler Ahmed Dhakane, who came across the Texas border with a fraudulent asylum story in 2008 after smuggling scores of East Africans from Brazil, not only was an AIAI guerrilla fighter and the group's trusted financial "hwaladeer" but also later admitted that he smuggled men who he knew were ready to die for the jihad inside the United States the moment they were asked. Clearly, Dhakane was a terrorist sympathizer even if he also liked to make a buck.

What seems certain is that a single-minded thirst for profit among SIA smugglers makes them a danger to US national security, whatever their personal affiliations or ideological predilections. Ul Haq seemed more interested in his $35,000 fees to move Pakistani Taliban terrorists than whether any of them might decide to "blow up" in the United States.

In the court prosecution files, federal prosecutors most often wrote of the motivation in boilerplate language. This seemed to be the case of the terrorism-linked Jordanian smuggler Maher Jarad, even though he was tied to Hezbollah and an Egyptian terrorist group. He ran his business, the prosecutors said, "for the purpose of commercial advantage and private financial gain, knowing and in reckless disregard of the fact that said aliens had not received prior official authorization to enter."[10] In the prosecution of the Iranian smuggler Mohammed Hussein Assadi, prosecutors wrote that, "evidence at trial clearly showed that Assadi was driven in his illicit business purely by monetary gain and exercised no discretion at all with respect to the character or potential motives of those whom he helped smuggle into the U.S."[11]

Those characteristics explain why the American government chose a long time ago to chase them down and break up their networks. But doing so is a premier challenge as far as missions go. The smugglers and their clients are slippery prey, the territories through which they glide often ungoverned places where corruption, incompetence, and indifference are the rule.

HUMAN BRIDGES TOO FAR

In this kind of extreme-distance smuggling business, handshake bargains are struck for journeys on other continents for the all-important false identity documents to board transatlantic flights, to pay bribes at Mexican consulate offices in Beirut, to illegally buy real visas in Middle Eastern casbahs and in Kenyan refugee camps, and to pay Brazilian airport inspection officers to look the other way for a moment. SIA smugglers coordinate a complexity of variables over greater distances to navigate a constantly shifting labyrinth, made riskier by the entrance of American hunters.

SIA smugglers get their clients out of international airport customs in the Eastern Hemisphere and through customs in the Western Hemisphere. But that high-price achievement is only the first of many marketable commodities. The real journeying then occurs, seen and unseen, in the unpoliced jungles of Colombia and Panama, in speedboats off the Pacific coast of Guatemala, through the ungoverned borderlands of developing African nations by foot or horseback, and in the bus depots of Bolivia and Peru. It must all be arranged in advance, money directed to the right places at the right times.

To bridge such vast geographies, with their diversity of customs, border inspections, visa requirements, and American agents with their informants, the SIA smugglers have to be more sophisticated, innovative, and elusive than any drug-smuggling network.

Once migrants land in the Western Hemisphere, they need places to stay, transportation north, and guides to navigate not only landscapes but the different kinds of border controls of countries through which they'll transit. These smugglers arrange it all, often with confederate subordinates and in league with indigenous Spanish-speaking groups and individual specialists.

The smugglers tend to cast a more colorful aura than ordinary, law-abiding human beings. Like a Peruvian national known to homeland security and his clients as "Peter." He was a world-class golf pro. Peter supplied high-quality false passports representing countries like Canada, Cuba, Guatemala, India, Spain, and Venezuela for SIAs. He lived and conducted his operations in Quito and Lima. But as a golf pro, he played in international tournaments, networking opportunities the gloved, golf-shirted smuggler was always able to leverage to generate business for his document factory.

My study of these human smugglers and the global networks their cash mortars together comes from what investigators learned about them, and what prosecutors later allowed to be put in the court records of more than twenty-five cases prosecuted in the United States. For starters, SIA smuggling is not simply one-stop shopping. Like any other industry, fees and services cater up or scale down depending on clients' ability to pay. Those wishing to reach the United States may choose services that range from all-inclusive, doorstep-to-doorstep guided journeys to more piecemeal arrangements that cost less.

An FBI agent who worked SIAs in San Diego told me that during the Syrian civil war starting in 2011, a number of wealthy Syrians paid $100,000 to be transported in first-class flights through passport-controlled airports, five-star hotels, luxury vans for long road trips, a two-week luxury rest vacation in Cancun, and then delivery over the California border with well-practiced asylum persecution stories. Such full service, guided, origin-to-destination journeys are arranged in advance. That requires sound strategic planning skill. The kingpin smugglers usually field sales forces in origin countries to recruit and vet customers. Next, they provide travel documents, air tickets, lodging, and accompanied transportation along each stage. Screw-ups can be expensive as news of these travel back to wealthy clients through the word-of-mouth grapevine.

It doesn't take much for smuggler and client to find one another. During a reporting trip to Syria in 2007, which was awash in hundreds of thousands of Iraqi war refugees willing to buy new lives in Western countries, I interviewed dozens of refugees who knew the price lists and services for US border trips well enough to recite them by heart.

"If you are an Iraqi and you stand by the corner of the Grand Mosque [in the Old City of Damascus], they'll come right up to you and say, 'When do you want to go?'" said one refugee who had saved enough money for such a smuggler and was getting ready to go. "All you have to do is stand there."

Author with SIA migrants in Paso Canoas, Costa Rica, December 2018.

During my 2018 reporting trip Panama and Costa Rica, I decided to find out for myself just how easy it might be to find a smuggler. I was on the Costa Rica side of the Panama border in Paso Canoas, a smuggler's haven of a shared, binational town. I tried my luck at the spot where Panamanians dropped off busloads of SIAs several times a week for their transfers to Costa Rican buses.

It was three o'clock in the morning when I crossed over to a spot just a short distance from where the SIAs process in to Paso Canoas, a place dotted with cheap motels and eateries. I was quickly accosted by different smugglers offering services. In terrible Spanish, I explained to one of them that I was trying to find someone to bring my Guatemalan friend (my interpreter in actuality) on through Costa Rica, Nicaragua, and Mexico to the American border. The smuggler said "no problem" and that it would cost

$1,000 to get as far as Nicaragua, where a new smuggler would be arranged to take the handoff for the next stage of the route.

I expressed a feigned disbelief at the $1,000 price tag for this. But the smuggler and a buddy who joined him explained that, because my supposed friend had no proper passport or visas, some of the money would have to be used to pay off police at roadblocks along the way to Nicaragua and again at the border.

It was that easy.

Many prospective migrants pay large fees in home countries so that they don't have to arrange piecemeal segments of journeys like my attempt; the kingpin smugglers often arrange segment handoffs well in advance, reducing the risk of rip-offs and other mishaps that are bad for new business in home countries.

These smugglers bring to bear preexisting collaborative relationships with all sorts of independent networks, often Spanish speaking but sometimes of their own ethnicity and language, which just work sections of the route and to whom the travelers are handed off like batons in a team foot race.

One of the first ICE takedowns, Detroit-based smuggler Neeran "Nancy" Zaia's case, exemplifies the full-service organization type. A dual US-Jordanian citizen, Zaia and her husband moved Middle Easterners into the United States for $50,000 each until their 2004 arrests.[12] The Zaia organization controlled a travel agency in Jordan, which recruited clients with advertisements and through word of mouth. A subcontractor provided fraudulent passports and purchased airline tickets. Other subordinates accompanied paying customers to South Africa, handing them off to other subordinates who cared for and then accompanied the migrants to Ecuador. From there, additional conspirators took over at the airport, accompanying them on the next leg of travel. The operation proceeded this way in an unbroken, guided journey to the US border, where still other conspirators would meet and transport them to American cities.[13]

I interviewed several Bangladeshis in ICE detention who described how the smuggling kingpin had them don blue baseball caps when they arrived in Latin American bus stations so that new Spanish-speaking local smugglers could recognize and collect them for the next trip to another country, where they would don the cap for the next smuggler pickup.

Some SIA smugglers specialize in one segment of the route. The Americans don't discriminate; they'll arrest those too if they are moving SIAs, such as the Somali smuggler Mohamed Abdi Siyad, a.k.a. "Hassan," who was indicted in August 2018.[14] But DHS sources tell me Hassan staved off US justice by slipping into Canada and successfully battling extradition. From his base in Sao Paulo, Brazil, Hassan and co-conspirators provided the connecting bridge by which hundreds of Somalis and other Horn of Africa migrants—extremists almost certainly among them—traveled from the African continent to the California and Texas borders.

His network in Brazil was one of three interconnected cells passing the human batons through their regions. The originating Africa network, for example, charged $2,500 to transport clients by air to Hassan in Sao Paulo, the cost of fake documents and visas baked in to that. If they wanted to keep going using his organization, Hassan would charge $500 each to hook them up with his Colombia-based compadre. They usually did. He'd snap photos of the migrants and text them downrange using WhatsApp so the Colombia smuggler could recognize them. That smuggler would then move them through Peru, Ecuador, and into Colombia via taxi, bus, horseback, boat, and air. Another segment chief would pick them up in Central America to keep them going so long as they kept paying.

Hassan's operation also fed clients into an entirely different route out of Brazil by two Bangladeshis, Moktar Hossain and Milon Miah.[15] Both smugglers kind of kept things in the ethnic family; their pipeline segued to the Texas border. Miah worked out of a restaurant in Tapachula near the Guatemala border. It was called The Bangladesh Restaurant. There, Miah would fetch Bangladeshis fresh in from Guatemala who knew to go meet him there. He'd house and feed them. Then, he would buy them airline tickets to cover the hundreds of miles to the northern Mexican industrial city of Monterrey. There, his partner Hossain would fish them out of the airport and arrange drivers to transport them the two or three hours north to the Rio Grande, with someone on the payroll there to swim them over the Rio Grande. Both were busted in 2019 in a joint HSI-Mexico counter-smuggling investigation.

Some months after their arrests when I was in Tapachula, I found the restaurant where Miah ran his operation. Bangladeshis still frequented it, dishing out heaping helpings of meat and rice concoctions from common buffet-style trays. I couldn't find anyone willing to talk (or who could speak English) about whether organized smuggling still happened there.

Nationality-based streams and strands of people moved between the wider riverbanks. A small Mexico City–based group run by Rakhi Gauchan, a dual citizen of Mexico and Nepal and a career smuggler, kept the flow of Pakistanis and Afghans going for some time through just Belize and Guatemala into Mexico.[16] Until HSI agents arrested the Nepal-born Gauchan in 2013, her network maintained alliances with other networks to the south that guided Pakistanis and other South Asians into Central America. From her Mexico City base, Gauchan would accept an average of ten referred migrants a month from upstream and transport them to the Texas border for about $3,500 each. Business was no doubt good because Nepalese migrants, who move along the trails too, would likely feel overjoyed to deal with her in their native tongue so far from the old country. Her business made sense because as a Mexican citizen, the entrepreneur certainly knew the terrain and officials who needed to be bought off, and they knew and trusted her back.

Reflecting the lowest end of the scale are those who provide the single service of providing a visa or identity document enabling a self-propelled SIA to cross the Atlantic. Sometimes, the smuggler's primary competitive advantage is marketing a single key service, such as trading on relationships with a corrupt consul officer or a document-forger or passport thief. Sometimes, one of those things was all a budget traveler needed to cross the Atlantic and do what I did in Paso Canoas, that is, to hire a smuggler on the street for a few-country passage.

Speaking of self-propelled budget SIA travelers, the Iraqi I met at the Texas border back in 2007, Boles, described how he did it. He paid $750 to a smuggling group's facilitator in Syria to buy a Guatemala visitor's visa in next-door Jordan. But that was as much as Boles could really afford and still eat along the way. It was just enough. The visa and a one-way air ticket got him over the Atlantic Ocean hump. He then piecemealed together a journey the rest of the way to Texas, mostly by bus. He briefly took a job in Guatemala City, then kept going to Texas. Total cost: $4,000 over nine months.

The US citizen and convert to Islam Anthony Joseph Tracy, as mentioned earlier, was convicted of providing identity documents to 272 Somalis before his 2010 bust, while he was living in Kenya. These were fraudulently obtained Kenyan passports, which would enable the migrants to land in South American and Central American countries that accepted Kenyans but not so much Somalis, who usually had no passports. Tracy had a highly valuable service to trade after which his hands were washed of them. To get his clients the Kenyan passports, Tracy used local collaborators to create fake identity cards, bank records, and citizenship documents to defraud the Kenyan passport offices into providing the document, all necessary to exit the region by air and get over the ocean.[17]

Most journeys sit somewhere in the middle of the sliding scale in partial-service variations of one or two journey stages.

An apt example involved a family of Iraqi Christians I interviewed in their Detroit apartment about their Syria-to-Texas journey in 2007.[18] The Iraqi couple had taken refuge from the war in Damascus, Syria, with their two young boys. They took an offer by a Jordanian man. For $10,000, the Jordanian provided authentic Guatemalan and Cuban visas, likely obtained from Guatemala's consulate office in Amman and from Cuba's embassy in Damascus. The smuggler also provided Damascus-Moscow-Cuba-Guatemala City airline tickets, and then a referral to a woman who ran a safe house in Guatemala City. That's as much as the $10,000 bought for a vulnerable family of four. But through the woman who ran the safe house, who took a shine to the boys, they found an unaffiliated local independent smuggler who, for $15,000, personally escorted the family of four the rest of the way to the Rio Grande, which they swam into Texas as he looked on from the opposite bank to make sure they got over okay.

SOPHISTICATED INTERNATIONALIST ENTREPRENEURS

Instead of the comprehensive vetting process required by immigration law, smugglers of course do not vet the backgrounds of the people they smuggle, except to determine how much money they will pay to enter the U.S. illegally.

—Deputy Assistant Attorney General David Rybicki, speaking at a press conference on April 29, 2019, announcing the sentencing of an SIA smuggler.[19]

Most of these men and women are, at heart, international entrepreneurs and not motivated by Islamic extremist ideologies. As smugglers go, they are sophisticated, multilingual internationalists who understand the value of dual citizenships and bi-hemispheric residencies. Their maneuverability makes them slippery adversaries. The full-service SIA smuggling kingpins get ICE agents the most bang for their buck, based on the belief that the full range of capabilities simply go to jail with them and are not easily succeeded, at least not as quickly as ordinary drug traffickers.

Actually, it's unclear how long it takes for successors to replace arrested SIA smuggling kingpins or for restoration of their operations; that's a subject worthy of future study. As mentioned previously, SIA smuggling remains fairly consistent from one year to the next despite busts and disruptions. Still, the thinking that SIA arrests can sever a bridge over the Atlantic and, with constant law enforcement pressure, suppress overall volume holds merit. Perhaps the fact that SIAs continue to arrive in steady numbers testifies more to a need to flood the zone with more investigators and resources. A US immigration officer provided one entirely anecdotal clue when he testified in a Mexican court prosecution of the Tijuana-based Lebanese smuggler Salim Boughader-Mucharrafille in 2003. That organization had moved hundreds of Lebanese into California for years, including several Hezbollah-affiliated migrants. The US officer said that "several months" passed before other smugglers returned to helping Lebanese nationals enter California from Tijuana,[20] though it was unlikely in the high numbers as when Boughader-Mucharrafille was running the show.

Other case records revealed that underlings do lie in wait for kingpins to be deposed, although timelines were not available to indicate delay times. For instance, the 1997 arrest of a "legendary" Ecuador-based alien smuggler named George Tajirian, responsible for smuggling hundreds of Middle Easterners into the United States during the 1990s, was followed by a competition for the helm among numerous successors.[21] The Iranian smuggler Assadi won out and ran his own highly lucrative network until his own arrest in 2002.

My research shows these men and women lead less by violence and intimidation than by centrally controlling cash flow; communications; key competitive advantages, such as corrupt government officials; and major logistical decisions, such as when and where travel will occur.

Many also have developed singular relationships with corrupt officials and document forgers. With these specialized skills and assets, they legally maneuver through origin and transit nations at will, manage clients and underlings, and personally direct recruitment, staging, and all the needs associated with long-haul travel. A case in point was Moayad Heider Mohammad Aldairi, sentenced in 2019 to three years in prison for running the smuggling network that brought Yemenis over the Texas border,[22] including several on the US terror watch list. Aldairi was a Jordanian who obtained Mexican citizenship and lived in Monterrey, Mexico. He kept residences in Mexico and in Jordan. In addition to Arabic, Aldairi spoke Russian, Spanish, and English. He could speak to his clients and to other smugglers as necessary, comforting both and enabling relationships.

Another case in point is the Pakistani smuggler Sharafat Ali Khan, a classic kingpin operator who moved Bangladeshis, Pakistanis, and Afghans along corridors from Brazil to Texas and California until his 2016 arrest.

Among his smuggled clients were several linked to terrorism, DOJ noted in the typical truncated press releases that dropped the terrorism bomb and then abandoned readers to unrequited speculation.

Khan was uniquely situated to provide the travel capability that any extremist from his home region could have exploited for $15,000 or less. The thirty-three-year-old smuggling entrepreneur had legal residency in Brasilia, Brazil, and an Ecuadorian passport. HSI investigators learned he worked full-time at the Sao Paulo, Brazil, international airport. The dual residency, multiple passports, and airport job helped Khan communicate in Urdu with other smugglers in Pakistan and to conduct multinational operations. Khan charged his clients between $3,000 and $15,000 for the Brazil-US border travel. He ran a sub-network of smugglers all through Latin America who guided his customers by bus, foot, and airplane to the US border along variations of a Brazil-Venezuela-Peru-Ecuador-Colombia-Panama-Costa Rica-Nicaragua-El Salvador-Guatemala-Mexico route. The journey could take as long as nine months.

Mohammed Kamel Ibrahim, a Ghanaian citizen, co-managed a major SIA smuggling network from Mexico City, while a partner coordinated in Belize. He typified how SIA smugglers use their global mobility and linguistic flexibility to secure fraudulent documents, access corrupt officials and associate smuggling groups, and establish safe houses. Ibrahim was a naturalized Mexican citizen who spoke fluent Spanish and was able to travel frequently between Mexico and Africa on his passports, recruiting clients and tending his houses and apartments, with nary an alarm sounded. The Ibrahim network moved hundreds of Somali and Eritrean migrants through to the US border on his ability to legally travel and speak multiple languages.

Prosecutors described the versatility of a different SIA smuggler, the Eritrean-born Habtom Merhay in this almost admiring way: "The defendant is believed to be a citizen of Great Britain, to reside in the United Arab Emirates, and to travel frequently to London, England," and therefore "has contacts with fraudulent document vendors, human smugglers, and travel agents in numerous countries."[23]

American and British passports, given their acceptability in the widest range of nations, proved to be of particular value to Merhay and several other kingpin smugglers. For example, the Ecuador-based Syrian smuggler Nizar Kero Lorian held US citizenship but maintained residences in Guatemala and Mexico, enjoying unfettered legal travel throughout Latin America and the United States working directly with customers, subordinates, and his favorite corrupted officials.

Investigators noticed that the American passport of naturalized US citizen Neeran Zaia, who was also a citizen of Jordan and spoke Arabic, Spanish, and English, showed extensive travel to the Middle East and throughout South America.

Most of the smugglers appeared to make significant use of their knowledge of the most valuable languages, Spanish and the fairly universal English to operate effortlessly among both cultures and nations. The prolific Iranian smuggler Mohammed Hussein Assadi, who lived in Ecuador, prosecutors noted, was fluent in other applicable, valuable languages: Arabic, Spanish, and "other languages" as well.[24]

The Americans are after the full-service SIA smugglers but aren't choosy about who they'll take down. Each cog plays an important role without which a network may be debilitated for a time. They will take down single-segment route operators or facilitators of false visas and documents, especially if they can turn one into an informant.

NONVIOLENT BUT DANGEROUS

SIA smuggling kingpins are considered a US national security danger for another reason too: because of language and cultural affinities, their clients tend to come from their own home countries, where violent jihadist groups proliferate.

In the examined court cases, smugglers choose their fellow citizens and co-religionists for recruitment, likely due to shared language and culture but also because they are positioned to understand local demand back home and exploit community ties to recruit business. Such ethnic affinity was in evidence in almost all of the twenty-five cases I studied. SIA smugglers transported compatriot clients from their home tribes, countries, or geographical regions. They only opportunistically strayed from this business model on occasion. The Guatemala-based Egyptian smuggler Ashraf Ahmad Abdallah, regarded in 2004 as one of ICE's most wanted smuggling kingpins, for instance, recruited clients from the area around his home community of Bata in the Egyptian province of Qaubiya; he transported at least one hundred of them through Guatemala and Mexico over several years.[25]

The Indian smuggler Kaushik Jayantibhai Thakkar mostly transported fellow Indians.[26] Sammy Lovelace Boateng and Mohammed Kamel Ibrahim were natives of Ghana operating a smuggling network from Mexico City and Belize City that moved hundreds of Africans to the US border during the mid-2000s until their 2008 arrests.[27] In one case, a naturalized US citizen who emigrated from Jordan to Detroit used her ties with immigrant communities in Michigan to recruit clients in Jordan.

The rule is not without exceptions, though, since smugglers were regarded as primarily motivated by profit. The Associated Press once quoted Assistant US Attorney Laura Ingersoll, who has prosecuted numerous SIA smuggling cases for federal court in Washington, DC as saying that "people from places in the Middle East will hear about who to go through, and they tend to be people from their same country, but once you get into the system we saw associations that really were driven by, 'What's the most effective way for me to move my product?'"[28]

Another key difference between SIA kingpin smugglers and drug traffickers is that they do not generally rule with an iron fist as do typical organized crime bosses. They're not above throwing out a threat. About as rough as it gets was when the Ecuadorian-based smuggler Nizar Lorian told an undercover agent, who asked what would become of a migrant if his family did not deliver $24,000 in overdue fees, that "there's no fucking around with me, on me" and to tell the smuggled migrants that if they try to leave, "I tell them you are going to be our barbecue tonight if anything!" In none of the court cases did information suggest that Lorian followed through with any physical coercion.

There was one case that definitely caught the attention of American authorities. After serving a search warrant on the home of Dearborn, Michigan-based smuggler Nancy Zaia, investigators recovered an auto-biographical manuscript. In it, Zaia outlined in great detail her intention and efforts to murder the lead special agent whose investigation of her a full decade earlier had led to a first conviction for alien smuggling, bribery, and visa fraud, according to one of the government motions later filed in her court case.[29] In her manuscript, Zaia explained how she had gone so far as to hire a private investigator to follow the immigration enforcement agent so that she could find out where he lived. After finding the home, she obtained a firearm and staked it out with an intention to murder him. She stood watch long enough one day to watch his wife come and go. She only abandoned the plot after a friend talked her out of it. Zaia wasn't charged with this old crime, though it was used as a factor in her sentencing.

There is some information to suggest that an established kingpin smuggler based in Brazil threatened the Somali underling smuggler Ahmed Dhakane, who, as we've seen, was an AIAI operative who decided to quit his smuggling business in Brazil and come over the US border himself. Dhakane's boss threatened him after learning that he had been transporting clients and taking their fees without the boss's knowledge, always a no-no.

For the most part, SIA smuggling kingpins relied on finesse, personal relationships, and negotiation to get it done.

But the SIAs keep coming despite HSI agents and their proxies in Latin America busting them. In addition to having deployed too small an army in too vast an area, another plausible explanation is that the smugglers know how to evade in worlds that are more hospitable to them than to their American hunters.

ANTENNAE FOR CHANGE AND EVASION

Evidence presented during prosecutions indicated that SIA smugglers fig-uratively deployed antennae sensitive to any information about changes in threat and opportunity. After 9/11, several of the major SIA smuggling net-works knew the Americans would come for them wherever in the world they lived and worked. They were correct in that, of course. But the smug-glers also very quickly learned that agents along the physical land border had begun systematically working their former customers for intelligence about them.

The smugglers adapted to the new environment. This is a typical devel-opment in all interplay between cops and robbers. But if the cops are always a step or two behind the robbers, this classic elasticity is likely exaggerated in the Latin American smuggling battlefields, given how vast, ungoverned, and unpredictable are the geopolitical circumstances of government and diplo-matic wind shifts.

The telltale indicator that something is not right in the prosecution of the American far war is the steadily increasing number of SIA apprehensions at the border.

The organizations morphed and anticipated after 9/11 and continue to do so, ensuring American vulnerability if nothing changes on the cop side. For instance, one smuggler pointedly had his clients dress and look like Europeans to avoid US law enforcement profiling they presumed would follow the attacks; women were told to dye their black hair blonde, the men to shave their beards, and for both genders to discard any personal artifacts that might make them "appear Arab."[30] Cops hoping to detect this sort of thing need to know about it and then look for the telltale indicators that it is happening.

Most smugglers put a wet finger to the wind and pivoted as needed to keep going.

When one of his East African clients expressed concern that a new American border fence would foil his crossing, the Mexico-based Ghana smuggler Mohammed Kamel Ibrahim showed he had already shifted gears. Ibrahim replied to the worried migrant by email in 2007, after the US Congress approved funding for border wall construction, long before the idea became so divisive: "There is a lot of rumor here, but there is still a way to enter. Don't worry about that. The wall will start building next year. It is still OK from now to February next year."[31]

In May 2005, a change in Ecuadorian government caused corrupt airport officials to charge substantially more to let Syrian smuggler Lorian's clients exit the country by air. So Lorian ordered an associate to establish a new smuggling route from Lima, Peru, and to quickly transfer a large group of clients to it. Lima was chosen not only to avoid excessive payoffs in post-9/11 Ecuador, but also because it was the only Peruvian city with direct flights to US cities, comporting with Lorian's business model at that time of flying clients directly into those cities. That's not as easy now because Americans have figured out ways to check passenger lists for signs of fraud.

SIA smugglers learned American agents were interrogating their clients at the border and would become potential informants and witnesses against them. So most of the smugglers coached, exhorted, or financially threatened clients to bite their tongues once they were apprehended at US destinations or in transit. Smugglers started using aliases to cloak nationalities they believed would draw attention to them after 9/11. The Egyptian smuggler Ashraf Abdallah told clients to wire money to him in the name of "Juan Manuel."[32] The Eritrean smuggler Samuel Abrahaley Fessahazion tried to obscure his African origin by alternatively using the names "Sammy," "Alex," and "Alex Williams." Mehrzad Arbane went by the name "El Turco," "Achi Saba," or just "Tony."

Some of the smugglers admonished or threatened their clients into silence once the Americans were interviewing them. The smuggler Rakhi Gauchan, who used the alias "Niki," told her clients "not to provide detail to U.S. immigration officials about being smuggled to the United States or otherwise cooperate in human smuggling investigations." Gauchan also has said she believes she could be prosecuted and imprisoned for human smuggling if arrested by the United States."[33] Other smugglers demanded that, for the final US crossing, clients eliminate phone numbers from cell phones, throw away notes, and destroy any fraudulent travel documents to eliminate clues. The Ghanaian smuggler Boateng emailed a subordinate on September 4, 2006, saying in part, "They should not carry any phone number from USA or Belize and Mexico. They are only vacation here.... No mention of my name."[34]

Some also sought to forcibly leverage the silence of clients caught en route. The Jordanian-Palestinian smuggler Maher Jarad, who used many aliases, instructed one migrant, who later testified against him at trial, that if he or other members were apprehended in Guatemala or Mexico, "they should not provide his name to the authorities as being involved in smuggling them, warning that if they did they would lose their money, and Jarad would not attempt to smuggle them to the United States."[35] The smuggler Assadi told clients that they should destroy all their fraudulent passports and documents and "surrender to U.S. immigration without disclosing either their true place of origin or Assadi's role, a government press release explained."[36]

The smugglers started using operational security methods to better hide their communications and money transfers too. Most used Western Union offices throughout Latin America and the United States to receive and send money, but also sometimes commercial mail services like DHL and Federal Express. Some ordered wire transfers in small amounts, believing they would not attract the attention of regulators and investigators. The Syrian smuggler Lorian, worried about law enforcement detection, told his underlings in late 2001 not to deposit more than $9,000 at a time "because after $9,000 there is always an investigation and so…deposit eight, or seven, five, or eight."[37]

Kingpin smugglers used false names or subordinates to send and receive money, again to mask nationalities they believed would raise national security flags. The smuggler Lorian once sent a $2,000 Western Union wire to a Kwik Chek Mart in Houston, Texas, under the name "David Philippe Paul Gouman," in hopes that such a name might not attract law enforcement attention.[38] Sometimes, smugglers used real names, if the sums to be transferred were small. The Eritrean smuggler Fessahazion had one of his subordinates instruct "Alien T.W. to have $400 wired to Guatemala in the name of Samuel Abrahaley."

THAT WHICH WORKED

The border interviews and investigations of SIAs form the connective tissue between the near war and the far war.

The smugglers ducking and running in Latin America eventually came to realize their own clients posed great danger. That's because those travelers, once journeys were completed, became the most prevalent source of intelligence information about their former smugglers. Despite exhortations by their smugglers that they not inform on them, the migrants consistently did just that during the detention center interviews.

For example, during the 2016–2017 HSI investigation of Pakistani kingpin smuggler Sharafat Khan, some of the more than one hundred of his Afghan, Pakistan, and Bangladesh customers dimed him out, including some of his subordinates.[39] One customer, for instance, spilled the beans at the border port of entry in Pharr, Texas. He described how Khan flew him from Pakistan to Sao Paulo and rested up in Khan's house in Brasilia and how Khan would tell him via WhatsApp where to go, whom to contact, and when to give more money to Khan confederates along the way. Khan had urged this particular witness to delete all the WhatsApp conversations and never mention his name if caught at the US border.[40] But loyalty seems to end with the trail and at the beginning of new American lives. I interviewed more than my share of migrants who presumed I might be someone who, in exchange for their helpful cooperation, could help them stay in the country forever.

The investigation and 2014 prosecution of Habtom Merhay relied on fourteen cooperating witnesses, all of whom Merhay smuggled but who clearly felt no loyalty afterward. Their bits of independent testimony helped investigators piece together the whole Merhay operation. In an Assadi case government-sentencing memorandum, prosecutors credited Assadi's former clients for candidly describing the smuggler's role in their transportation. Wrote the government attorneys: "But for these cooperating witnesses, who represent but a fraction of the aliens smuggled by Assadi, the government would have been unable to bring Assadi to justice."[41]

In addition to testimony at court, some of the smuggled have been used as active participants in investigations against their smugglers. In 2009, for instance, "ALIEN P" agreed to let law enforcement agents in Houston consensually monitor and record a conversation with a major co-conspirator in the Annita Devi Gerard smuggling network, enabling investigators in Florida to nab their quarry in two days.[42]

SIA interviews did not take place only on US soil, as I have shown. Mexico City–stationed US law enforcement and intelligence agents, accompanied by Mexican counterparts, usually conducted these interviews. The migrants seemed just as eager sometimes to dime out their smugglers there too.

THE INFORMANTS

The court case files suggest that many investigations began as a result of tips from law enforcement informants, sometimes in foreign countries, but also that informants were key to investigative and prosecutorial success. For example, a confidential informant working with ICE's attaché office in Mexico City provided some of the earliest information that Gauchan's principal occupation was smuggling people into the United States. It was a confidential informant who, concerned that the smuggler Arbane was pretty sure he'd smuggled in two of the 9/11 hijackers, went to law enforcement authorities and helped the ensuing investigation. Also, when the US-based Iranian smuggler Zeavadale Malhamdary, who once inside the United States himself smuggled as many as sixty Iranians in behind him, went to Mexico to shop for a smuggler, he was introduced to a confidential informant for the United States named "Gabriel, who broke open the investigation," prosecutors wrote in court documents.[43]

Sometimes, the best tips and leads came from rival SIA smugglers who had been arrested and were willing to inform on their rivals. A number of them cooperated with investigators in exchange for time off sentences or other benefits. Smugglers pretty much are defined by the fact that they have no loyalty. For all their worldliness and business acumen, SIA smugglers were quite inclined to turn on one another once they saw bars, as in the case of against the Ghanaian smuggler Boateng.

In a memorandum arguing for a lesser sentence, Boateng's defense attorney argued, "He has provided the government with as much information as he possessed and held nothing back, including his own use of false travel documents. Likely, his willingness to testify played a role in the decision of his co-defendant (clearly a more culpable participant) to plead guilty."[44] During the 2002 District of Columbia prosecution of the Ecuador-based Iranian smuggler Assadi, prosecutors had the Ecuador-based Jordanian smuggler Jarad testify against his former associate.[45]

As discussed previously, the Ecuador-based Pakistani smuggler Irfan Ul-Haq was arrested and convicted on terrorism charges after talking about how he didn't care if one of his clients blew himself up in America. What did him in was that ICE deployed three local Ecuadorian undercover informants to help him smuggle that blacklisted terrorist from Pakistan to the

United States. This was one of about a dozen cases since 9/11 in which US law enforcement inserted sworn undercover agents or paid confidential informants into SIA smuggling operations.

The snitches and undercover agents collected evidence that may never have otherwise been had, given the natural camouflage and mobility smugglers enjoy in distant jurisdictions. Once undercover agents were accepted into a network, however, they were able to discover highly granular operational details. An undercover ICE agent who busted one of these smugglers once described to me how he sneaked into the smuggler's apartment bedroom while his target went to the bathroom. The agent opened up the smuggler's briefcase and feverishly snapped photos of every piece of paper he could, fingers jittery. Then, as the toilet was flushing, the agent spotted a trove of stolen passports in the case and snapped photos in a rushed heady frenzy. The agent got out before the smuggler emerged, and those passports turned out to be the prosecutorial noose.

Informants and undercovers recorded phone calls, stored email and other communications, videotaped direct observations, identified otherwise hidden coconspirators, and developed new leads. Undercover agent operations have also enabled search warrants for smuggler cell phones, email, computers, homes, and businesses.

One case in point involved a long-term, deep undercover insertion of ICE undercover agents into the organization of Ecuador-based Nizar Kero Lorian, which was responsible for moving hundreds of Middle Easterners to the US border. Over time, the agents collected audio and videotaped documentation that revealed the organization's inner workings, to include manner and means of smuggling, hierarchy, identification of other individuals who worked for Lorian, money transfer habits, and fees.[46] Lorian had no chance.

Through a recorded telephone conversation with an undercover operative, US investigators learned that the Arizona-based Iranian smuggler Malhamdary was selling Mexican visas for $12,000 each to fly Iranians into Mexico for transport over the Arizona border.[47]

American agents were able to manipulate smugglers to travel to US territory so they could be arrested and prosecuted there. This was also the case with an undercover agent inserted into the Nepalese smuggler Gauchan's organization, running a Mexico City–based arm of a larger network. Posing as a prospective business partner, the El Paso, Texas–based agent in 2012 lured Gauchan to enter the United States for a business meeting; she was arrested instead, avoiding a time-consuming extradition process.

In two separate important terrorism infiltration cases already described in these pages, paid FBI undercover informants of Somali descent were inserted into Texas detention facilities, where they collected intelligence about Somali SIAs that led to the terrorism-related immigration fraud prosecution of Ahmad Dhakane, Omar Fidse, and his wife, Deka Abdalla Sheikh. It was a lucky strike because it turned out they were hard-bitten terrorists.

CHAPTER SEVEN

LATIN AMERICA'S FOREIGN EMBASSIES: WITH FRIENDS LIKE THESE AND ENEMIES LIKE THOSE

As part of my earliest research into SIA smuggling and terror travel in 2007, I found myself in Amman, Jordan, capital of the tiny Arab kingdom nestled in the tough neighborhood between Israel, Iraq, and Syria. I'd come to town looking for something I wasn't sure even existed. The city's central business district seemed a logical place to ask around. The very first pedestrian smiled at my question and pointed one hundred yards up the street. And sure enough, there it was, a totem that did not belong at all in an Arab kingdom: a twenty-foot-tall metal pole at the top of which proudly waved the national flag of Guatemala. I said "*shukran*" (thank you), one of the only Arabic non-curse words I knew, and headed for the flag.

That year was the height of the American war in Iraq and of a massive refugee crisis that sent about 600,000 Iraqis into Jordan and Syria. I'd come to the Middle East as part of my first journalistic investigation into how some of them had been able to travel so far to cross the Rio Grande border into my home state of Texas. The United States had put tight quotas on Iraqi refugee visas. So did other Western countries. The Iraqi refugees couldn't go forward to new lives, nor could they return to their old ones just yet. Stuck. That circumstance, predictably, had led to a booming human smuggling trade to the countries that didn't want them. Demand for travel documents and know-how had escalated.

Several Iraqis who'd been forced into these neighboring countries and then made the trip to Texas had told me they were able to get there, in part, by paying $750 or more to smuggling intermediaries in Syria to secure for them Guatemalan tourist visas somewhere in Amman. With these, they could fly to the Central American country, pass inspection at its airport, and then make their way to the American border. DHS friends had slipped me a hot-off-the-presses Law Enforcement Sensitive 2008–2013 "Homeland Security Threat Assessment," which warned that "ease of access to human smuggling and fraudulent document networks 'likely would' underpin an increase in the coming years of Iraqi refugees pooling in Syria and Jordan over the US land borders due to Europe's tight caps on the numbers they'd take." It noted that in 2007, CBP had apprehended 392 Iraqis illegally crossing the US border, and many more were getting caught with fraudulent passports en route.

The Iraqi asylum seekers I interviewed had no idea where their inter-mediaries secured the visas, only that they were real, legal ones and were stuck to pages inside their government-issued passports. So I'd driven the 150 miles from Damascus, Syria, where other Iraqi refugees knew of the Guatemalan visas, to find who was selling them and from where. Now, a Guatemalan flag flapped above me, its two sky-blue stripes symbolizing the Pacific Ocean and the Caribbean Sea that sandwiched the country, with a white stripe down the center, which I knew represented one of the world's busiest human smuggling corridors. Accompanied by an Arabic interpreter, I opened the glass door of the nearest building.

It was a furniture store. A woman was working with a customer over some papers at a heavy oak desk right in front. She motioned for us to give her a moment, and when the customer left, I approached.

"Um, is this the Guatemala consulate?"

"Yes, it is," the woman in her midthirties answered, curious and suspi-cious at once. "I am the honorary consul of Guatemala. How can I help you?"

Her name was Patricia Nadim Khoury. The honorary consul title was inherited from her Guatemala-born father after he died, and this was some-thing she did part-time, she explained. She made her living selling the fur-niture, but Jordanian, Syrian, and Iraqi students and businesspeople needed her "honorary consul" duties to travel to and from Guatemala City, home to a significant Arab diaspora.

I disclosed that I was a journalist visiting Jordan to interview war refugees but didn't immediately let on that some of them told me they paid for Guatemala visas in Amman. First, I wanted to know the official process for issuing visas. Still leery, Khoury nevertheless explained that all visa applicants had to show up for an in-person interview with her and bring along personal financial records, like bank statements, to demonstrate they had something to return to in the region. Application processing cost about $60.

"I don't give visas to people who don't come personally here," Khoury insisted.

Guatemalan Honorary Consul Nadine Khoury's Amman, Jordan office in 2007.
Photo by Jerry Lara of *The San Antonio Express-News,* reprinted with permission.

Things turned ugly when I asked her why at least five Iraqi refugees in America told me they gave in excess of $750 to strangers who got Guatemalan visas in Amman and then headed for the US border.

"If someone came and asked, I would kick him out," she said. "I can maybe get the police."

As I pressed, Khoury suddenly demanded that we leave her store immediately. Kicked out, my interpreter and I left with that as an answer.

A CHINK IN AMERICA'S BODY ARMOR: THE HOSTILE FOREIGN CONSULATES AND EMBASSIES OF LATIN AMERICA

My research, both on the ground in places like Jordan and Syria and in the court prosecution records, shows that Latin American diplomatic missions in countries such as Jordan, as well as in Lebanon, Dubai, Saudi Arabia, Thailand, India, Russia, Kenya, Turkey, Singapore, and many more, reveal a profound hole in the border security net that will need to be sutured if American homeland security leaders want to retard European-style border crossings by migrant-jihadists.

The distant foreign consulates, embassies, and diplomatic representatives of Latin America in migration jump-off nations provide the passports and visas that are essential for SIAs and terrorists to board aircraft and make Western Hemisphere landings within striking distance of the US border. This vulnerability—Latin America's foreign consulates and embassies providing the documents necessary for SIA intercontinental travel—is a one of the most unimagined surprises of my research and field reporting over the years.

Not all South American and Central American nations maintain foreign consulates in all high-risk source countries. Among those that surfaced from the data, however, were the foreign consulates of Mexico, Guatemala, Honduras, Belize, Ecuador, Bolivia, Brazil, Venezuela, Cuba, and the Dominican Republic. Court records from the SIA smuggler prosecutions and my many interviews with SIA migrants showed that they often bought real visas and authentic passports outright from corrupt consular or embassy officials in distant Eastern Hemisphere nations and handed them over to ineligible travelers.

Sometimes, smugglers or the travelers themselves obtained the documents legally and cheaply due to a Latin America country's inherent indifference to American security concerns or inept vetting processes, when these existed at all.

Perhaps even more ominously, though, other smugglers and SIA travelers knew they could always depend on countries that were diplomatically hostile toward the United States and, therefore, purposefully uncooperative in counterterrorism and helpful to its enemies.

CUBA

I came face-to-face with this attitude in 2007 at Cuba's embassy in Damascus, Syria. But I also know, from interviews I've conducted with SIAs in Panama, Costa Rica, Mexico, and Texas, that hostile nations and regimes remain pivotal in SIA smuggling today.

Author (in doorway) in Syria reporting about SIA smuggling, 2007.

In Damascus, during the same 2007 reporting trip when I found Guatemala's "honorary consul" in Amman, I also visited Cuba's embassy to check out the stories of Iraqi refugees who told me that, once their high-priced Guatemalan visas were in hand, they had flown through Moscow (no transit visa required) and then through Cuba to get to the Central American country. They needed Cuban transit visas for that and said they had filled out an application, paid $70, and walked out with the visas with no questions asked. I cabbed over to the Cuban embassy's three-story whitewashed building in central Damascus just three blocks from the American embassy and soon found myself in front of Cuba's consul at the time, Armando Perez Suarez.

He told me his country happily granted visas to any Middle Easterner in Syria and in the wider region who asked for one and had the $70 fee, "because America doesn't give anyone the opportunity to take refuge, especially after 9/11.

"But we work another way. We put conditions on the American people who are making war with everyone. The Arab people are the peaceful ones. We give visas to anybody who wants to visit our country."

Suarez said he was well aware that Cuba, with its economic problems and poverty, was not anyone's idea of a final destination.

"After that, if he wants to travel to any other country, the U.S. or Central America, that is not our problem," Suarez said. "It's not our burden."

He scoffed at American concerns about terrorist infiltration over the Texas border where I lived and worked.

"I'm sorry your president is from Texas," he said, referring to President George W. Bush, who was in office at the time and had served as the state's governor. "Now you're receiving your own medicine. The problem started in Texas, and it's finishing in Texas."

The consul in Damascus was hardly the only one so free with visas. A year after 9/11, federal investigators busted three smugglers—a Pakistani named Iqbal Munawar and Canadian citizen and Sri Lankan native Sri Kajumukam Chelliah for transporting hundreds of Middle Eastern migrants through Cuba and into South America. But the third smuggler working with them, Indian national Nathu Babu Dhamelia, had an interesting resume.[1]

Dhamelia was an honorary consul for Cuba, and he had used this position to issue more than 1,500 Cuban visas "without regard to the person's eligibility for such visas," according to a court document from the case. During the 2012 smuggling investigation, Indian customs officials once intercepted a package addressed to Dhamelia in India and found fifty-five blank Cuban tourist visas inside.

The availability of Cuban visas has not subsided with time. In fact, the spigot seems stuck on wide open. One of the smugglers, the Sri Lankan, Chelliah, went back to smuggling after serving an American prison term on that case, opening a sea route that brought at least 1,750 Sri Lankans into Cuba, then by sloop through various Caribbean islands and then to the shores of Florida until his second smuggling arrest in August 2020.[2] Flying them to Cuba would have required visas.

In 2016, the *Washington Post* reported that Afghans who were finding their passages into Europe blocked by terror-shocked governments started showing up at Kabul travel agencies bearing Cuban visas suspected of having been issued in Iran or acquired on the black market. The visas were clearly to be used to travel on to Mexico, then the United States or Canada.[3]

Travel agents in Kabul reported a spike in interest in Cuba, and UN officials in the northern Afghan city of Kunduz told the newspaper they recently encountered an entire family with Cuban visas. The shifting travel plans of Afghans signaled the probable next phase in a "migration crisis that is rattling world leaders."

"They are not staying there. The only option is to move forward, probably on to Mexico and then America…," one travel agent was quoted.

Even if Cuban counselor officials are willing to give a legal visa to anyone who pays the nominal processing fee, a black market for them also is evident. The American fraudulent document provider, Anthony Joseph Tracy, was able to provide hundreds of Cuban visas to Somalis while he was living in Kenya by bribing two employees of the Cuban embassy in Nairobi, Kenya, identified in court records as "Consuela" and "Helen."[4] Reportedly, Cuba fired both after Tracy was arrested in 2010 but only because they had provided information to American law enforcement in a show of traitorous disrespect to the Cuban revolution.

Cuba remains a source of SIA transit visas to this day.

VENEZUELA

Also knowing that Venezuela was a popular landing country for US border–bound Middle Easterners, I stopped in at the embassy in Damascus to see what was going on. After his 1999 election, leftist populist Venezuela President Hugo Chavez shifted the oil-producing country to an antagonistic relationship with the United States and nurtured relationships with American nemeses such as Iran and Syria, which the US had designated as state sponsors of terrorism. Venezuela never participated in international counterterrorism coalitions after 9/11 and does not as of this writing in 2020.

On the day I visited its Damascus embassy, its walls bedecked with large portraits of President Chavez, Syrians packed the lobby and formed a line of applicants for one hundred yards outside on the sidewalk. The consul declined interview requests, but several of the Syrians in line described the nine different types of tourist and business visas offered inside as easy and affordable to receive.

Venezuela has remained a spigot of cheap, easy visas for migrants from countries of American terrorism concern. For instance, I more recently interviewed a Pakistani named Mohammed from the Punjab district. Some extremism and political violence beset Punjab, though it is one of the more settled and prosperous of the Pakistani states. Mohammed explained that he'd been working as a laborer in Saudi Arabia when he decided to cross the American border.

For $2,500, a smuggler took him to the Venezuelan embassy in Iran, where he picked up a visa, then caught a direct flight from Damascus to Venezuela's capital city of Caracas with three other Pakistanis bound for the US border. Another Pakistani named Tahir told me a relative "arranged with a guy" to also secure a Venezuelan visa in Iran. For that matter, Venezuela and Cuba for many years offered Iranians visa-free travel. According to one 2011 government threat assessment, the illegal migrants use their own valid Iranian document for that portion of the trip and obtained a different fraudulent passport, usually a stolen European one, for the remainder of the travel to the US border.[5]

In December 2018, I met four US-bound Iranians in Costa Rica, but they had all flown into Ecuador, which required no visa either, as revealed and discussed earlier in this book.[6]

BOLIVIA

The willingness of hostile embassies and consulates to grant travel visas to just about anyone, with little regard for US sensitivities or perhaps with sadistic intent, underscores the expansive role that these diplomatic outposts have played in the years since 9/11. For instance, Bolivian visas have often figured in SIA smuggling schemes as both a landing and stepping-stone country to the US border. Leftist governments in the South American country aligned for many years with Venezuela against United States interests, although a more recent change in government has attenuated its overtly hostile attitudes toward the US. Before he quit smuggling SIAs in expectation of drawing US counterterrorism attention in 2002, the Iranian smuggler Assadi was able to secure hundreds of Bolivian visas from the Bolivian embassy in Beijing as part of a smuggling operation that also transported Middle Easterners.

A Bangladeshi migrant told me of a smuggling pipeline that fed on Bolivian visas either bought through bribery or which were granted with no vetting. The Bangladeshi paid this smuggler $12,500 for a package of services that included a visa that the smuggler's agents obtained in Bolivia to put in a stolen passport. The smuggler then sent the migrant's photos to Bolivia, where the subordinate substituted them in the other passport, and sent the passport back to the Bangladesh capital of Dhaka with a real Bolivian visa inside. The migrant then used it to board an aircraft in Dhaka and fly to Bolivia.

WITH FRIENDS LIKE THESE...

In some ways this open sieve should be predictable for US enemies, even expected. Perhaps less can be done about the hostile nations. But the embassies and consulate offices of American friends and allies also enable the smuggling schemes. As the old saying goes, with friends like these, who needs enemies?

In 2016, the Honduran newspaper *La Prensa* published an investigative exposé that found the country's consulate in Barcelona, Spain, had sold at least one hundred passports to Palestinian Arabs and Syrians as part of an international SIA-smuggling network.[7] The scheme allowed for these Arab nationals to buy Honduran birth certificates and then the passports that made them eligible to enter the United States later on tourist visas, or simply enabled them to get to Honduras for the overland trip north.

The smuggling organization involved kept corrupt Honduran government workers on their payroll, in rural areas of the country, to sell them Honduran citizenship documents, sometimes claiming the identity of dead people or using the real identities of Hondurans who had not yet gotten their own official ID documents. The whole caper apparently was found out when Syrians carrying their new Honduran identities showed up at US embassies to request tourist visas, but not before scores flew into Honduras and crossed the US border.

Just the previous fall, six military-aged men were caught at the airport in Tegucigalpa, Honduras, carrying stolen Greek passports, which they used to travel first through Brazil, Argentina, and Costa Rica.[8] It's unclear which of those countries gave them visas for their stolen Greek passports or whether any of the men had terrorist ties, but all planned to make their way to the US border.[9]

HIGH-VALUE MEXICO PAPER

The most consequential of the offenders is Mexico and its surprisingly expansive archipelago of consulates and embassies across the globe. Compared to the visas of twenty-six South American, Central American and Caribbean island territories, states and colonies, Mexican visas and passports are the most prized and valuable on the SIA smuggling market.

It's easy to understand why; a migrant's ability to land in the country closest to the American border makes for the fastest, easiest ride, albeit not the cheapest. For smugglers, close-in landings shorten treacherous distances and reduce their own costs and risks of law enforcement detection. Mexico landings not only accomplish those efficiencies but also would be the most desired of all the landing zones for its well-known catch, rest, and release treatment of those SIAs it catches. But as with any other commodity, demand and value inevitably lead to irresistible corruption, and that's what has happened throughout Mexico's diplomatic archipelago.

My first exposure to just how valuable Mexican visas and passports are came during the same illuminating 2007 reporting trip to Syria and Jordan. After my encounter with Guatemala's honorary consul in Amman, I managed to track down and interview Mexico's "honorary consul" in Jordan's capital, only about a mile away from the Guatemala flagpole.

His name was Raouf N. El-Far, a Jordanian businessman who had been appointed Mexico's consul to Jordan in 2004. El-Far was a reporter's dream: friendly, amusing, and candid. I asked him if, with hundreds of thousands of trapped Iraqi refugees in the country, anyone ever offered him bribes for Mexican visas.

"I've been offered lots of money—thousands of dollars," he told me.

The bribe offers came from Iraqis, Syrians, and Jordanians, many of whom openly disclosed their plans to get themselves smuggled over the US border once inside Mexico. One man had just earlier that week offered $10,000 for a tourist visa to give to another Iraqi. If all went well, the man told El-Far, he would bring him ten Iraqis per month at the same price. That, of course, would amount to $100,000 per month.

"Are you tempted?" I asked El-Far, stunned that he had revealed this information to me on the record.

He chuckled and answered, "Yes, I am." But suddenly serious, El-Far said he won't take the bribes "because it's against my principles."

"What about the guy you replaced a few years earlier?" I asked.

"That guy…?" El-Far said, pausing with a tight smile in search of the right words. "That guy wasn't so principled."

The Americans found out what was happening and forced the Mexican government to oust him and conduct an intelligence background investigation on the man's replacement, which was…El-Far. The Mexican intelligence service investigation was so thorough "they wanted to know how many times I kissed my wife before I go to bed."

The move to replace the predecessor with El-Far was undoubtedly connected to a broader Mexican scandal in next-door Lebanon at that time. The case is emblematic. In the high-tension days not long after 9/11, the Americans had busted the Lebanese smuggler Boughader-Musharrafille for smuggling hundreds of Lebanese into California, including known Hezbollah operatives. The investigation found that Boughader-Musharrafille had been able to keep his pipeline full of California-bound clients by routinely bribing employees of Mexico's large Beirut-based embassy for visas.

In November 2003, the year before El-Far replaced his unnamed predecessor in Amman, the Mexican government took steps to fire and prosecute some of its Beirut embassy employees, including its head of mission, for selling visas and blank passports to Boughader-Musharrafille's California-bound clients.[10] The investigation proved one employee sold the passports for up to $4,500 each.[11] The same investigation turned up evidence that Mexican visas and passports also were being sold out of other unspecified Mexican consulate offices, including the one in Cuba and obviously the one in Amman.

Despite the fact that Mexico discovered how widespread the scheme is across its global consulate network, illegal sales of Mexican visas and passports have continued long after this 2003 investigation. The 2005 smuggling prosecution of the Iranian smuggler Zeayadale Malhamdary, whose operation was predicated on acquiring Mexican visas by hook or by crook, offers one of many cases in point. Malhamdary was an Iranian émigré himself, having been caught in the California desert after a border crossing from Mexico in 1998. Having achieved US asylum in 1999 on grounds that his conversion to Christianity endangered him in the harsh Iranian theocracy, he must have thought the idea was scalable.

Malhamdary, while living in Arizona, turned to smuggling other Iranians through Mexico to repeat his asylum success. He would fly to meet clients in Tehran or European cities, collect their passports, and deliver them to a third party, who would somehow obtain and insert Mexican visas. These were inserted into the passports. Applicants were not physically present at any Mexican embassy or consulate office as is required. Malhamdary customers were willing to pay $12,000 each for just the Mexican visas.[12] Obviously, the premium he charged his Iranians customers for the Mexican visas was worth every penny because the documents shortened what would otherwise have been arduous journeys through, say, Panama's Darien Gap.

That lasted until 2005 when an undercover Border Patrol agent infiltrated his network and busted him on alien smuggling charges. At one point, Malhamdary boasted to the undercover agent that he had smuggled sixty Iranians over the Mexico-Arizona border on the Mexican visas.[13]

Mexican consulate offices in the Middle East remain leaky document sieves. Those who can get their hands on Mexican passports and visas will even go to some lengths to, as former FBI Director Robert Mueller once testified to Congress, pose as Mexicans themselves.

One internationally convoluted March 2008 case shows how that works. It happened in the transit section of the Kuwait airport when an alert customs agent pulled aside three male travelers just in from New Delhi, India, and heading to board another flight to France with a final destination of Mexico City. The trio were carrying valid, bar-coded Mexican passports, brand-new.[14] Each passport bore a Spanish name and photo of its carrier. But the customs officer took a good look at their bearers and asked the men to speak some Spanish. Two of the three could not, sparking an intercontinental investigation.

At the time, I was a reporter working in San Antonio when I spotted a short foreign press blurb about this case. I went to work and soon was on the phone interviewing India's federal police case agent in Mumbai.

The three travelers, I would go on to report for my newspaper, were actually Afghans on their way to the US border.

One of them was a Mexico-based smuggler of the other two. They had purchased altered but genuine Mexican passports for $10,000 each at Mexico's consulate office in, of all places, Mumbai, India. V. G. Babu, superintendent of immigration police at Mumbai's Cochin International Airport told me at the time that the presumed smuggler did speak some Spanish, as well as other languages, and also was in contact with corrupt Mexican embassy personnel in New Delhi. Here, Mexican travel documents had somehow gotten tangled up in an octopus of countries and agencies in Afghanistan, Kuwait, Mumbai, New Delhi, and France. An investigation made for very strange bedfellows of police in Kuwait, India, Mexico, the FBI, and God knows who else.

Ricardo Alday, the spokesman for Mexico's embassy in Washington, DC, at the time, tried to assure me that Mexico "has applied strong measures and invested considerable resources to continuously improve the security of its travel documents" and also that "Mexico is a committed partner with the U.S. in ensuring our borders are not used to threaten or undermine our common security."

There can be little doubt that's true to some extent as the Beirut and Amman episodes show.

But over my years of investigating SIA smuggling, I could seemingly turn over no rock without finding Mexican travel documents in the unlikeliest of places. Years after the Beirut embassy fiasco, in 2009, ICE let me and an Arabic interpreter into their detention facility in Pearsall, Texas, to interview three Iraqi Kurds who'd just been caught on the border. They told me they'd gotten to within striking distance of the Texas border on Mexican visas. A Turkish smuggler named "Murat" charged them $20,000 apiece to secure those, along with airfare. The way it worked, they explained, was that they gave Murat their Iraq passports and then the next day met him at the Mexican embassy in Ankara, Turkey. They did as they were told. At the embassy, the smuggler handed them back their Iraqi passports. Inside were fresh Mexican visas.[15] And here we all were, a few weeks later, together inside a Texas detention facility.

Likewise, Mexican documents turned up in the Boateng SIA smuggling operation, run by two Ghana nationals who transported hundreds of Somalis and Eritreans to the US border until their 2010 arrests.[16] Bear with me here; it gets a little complicated:

One of the Ghanaians, Mohammed Kamel Ibrahim, was based in Mexico City. His partner, Sampson Lovelace Boateng, lived in Belize. Recruiters working for them in Kenya and other African countries would steer US-bound African migrant customers to Ibrahim in Mexico City. Mexico's foreign consulate offices figured like this: First, the migrants would wire thousands of dollars in smuggling fees to Ibrahim in Mexico. Next, they would send their passports to Boateng in Belize, just next door on Mexico's southern border. In Belize, Boateng had a corrupt Mexican consulate employee on the payroll. That employee would stamp the passports with valid Mexican visas.

The passports were sent back to the paying clients in Africa, along with plane tickets to Mexico City. Voilà. Once the migrants arrived in Mexico City, Ibrahim was there to take over. Charter bus employees on his payroll transported the immigrants in sleeper or luggage compartments to the border. Mexican coyote smugglers would ford them over the river.

Sometimes, corruption and high smuggling fees weren't even necessary. I interviewed an Uzbekistani migrant once who told me he decided to cross the US border after "a friend said there was a way to get political asylum in the US." The Muslim-majority Uzbekistan is a known country of national security concern because of violent jihadist groups that operate there. The way to America, apparently, was the Mexican embassy in Moscow. The Uzbekistani said he simply picked up a Mexican tourist visa for $36 and flew in to Mexico City to meet a regional smuggler, who flew him to Reynosa, Mexico, and paddled him over the Rio Grande.

A Pakistani I interviewed once told me his smuggler flew him to Bangkok, Thailand. Sure enough, there was a Mexican consulate in town, a pretty big two-story building with a giant Mexican national flag flying overhead in the central business district. He filled out the forms, paid the small fee in Bangkok, flew to Mexico City on the visa, and was on the American side, all in a couple of days.

Still another Pakistani I once interviewed in ICE detention told me he paid a smuggler $9,000 for his US border crossing. He and the smuggler had to meet first in the Gulf State city of Dubai, in the United Arab Emirates. Why? Because Mexico had an embassy there. The asylum seeker told me he flashed some employment records from a previous job and "lied" that he needed to go to Mexico on company business. He paid a $32 processing fee for the visa and flew in.

The Brazil-based Somali smuggler Ahmad Dhakane gave up some inter-esting details of his document operation when an undercover FBI informant planted in his detention center quarters posed as a potential smuggling spon-sor for a supposed brother still in Somalia. As already described, Dhakane had deep ties to a Somali terrorist organization and had already trans-ported several men whom he believed were committed jihadists. Dhakane explained to the informant while a recording device rolled that, through his connections with a church in Nairobi, Kenya, he obtained six-month Brazil missionary visas and then, with those, secured ninety-day Mexican visas for clients, who typically paid about $9,000 each for the complete US trip.[17]

As a bonus, Dhakane let the informant know that missionary visas also enabled his clients to obtain free traveler's health insurance.

NOT JUST MEXICO

Other country consulates often enable SIA travel and smuggling. Ecuador, Trinidad and Tobago, the Dominican Republic, and Belize have all come up in court prosecution records, in my interviews with SIAs, or both. The Guyanese smuggler Annita Devi Gerald, who had citizenship and a house in Belize like any good SIA smuggling kingpin, worked with a co-conspirator named Dhanraj Samuel of Trinidad and Tobago. The partnership profited by moving Indians and other South Asians from Singapore to Houston, Texas. The Belize consulate office in Singapore made it all work. The smug-glers had a corrupt source there who would provide fraudulent Belize busi-ness visas. They didn't need Mexican visas, but just to make life easier for the paying customers, the two smugglers secured Mexican visas in Belize so they could fly into northern Mexico for easy access to the US border. The whole package deal cost $20,000, a steal considering everyone involved got to avoid the Darien Gap.[18]

Brazil, too, has long figured in providing Atlantic-crossing travel doc-uments, legally and illegally. The BBC and other media reported that in 2014, for instance, Brazilian embassies in Beirut, Amman, and Istanbul processed 2,077 Syrian asylum requests, quadruple the number since 2011. That's not a problem if the Syrians plan to stay in Brazil. But Brazil's history as a landing and staging area for trips to the US border is hard to set aside. Furthermore, twice that number of Syrians entered Brazil through "alternative" means, meaning they used the usual fraudulent documents and bribery to reach the infamous staging country, almost assuredly as a way station to the US border.[19]

Clearly, the question of how to attack this fail point in the SIA smuggling chain is not going to keep Latin American allies and enemies up at night, since ISIS and other Islamic terrorist groups see the American homeland as the golden target and not these countries of passage. Interest in earnestly cleaning up their diplomatic stations is scant.

American homeland security strategists should consider ways to heighten the self-interest so that these countries might actually want to police their foreign consulates and embassies on behalf of their northern ally, the United States.

The apparent ease with which SIA smugglers secure travel documents from the foreign diplomatic redoubts of southern neighbors reflects more than just missed opportunity. It is one of many data points suggesting that America's covert border war is not well, is not thought through, and is probably mismanaged. The Achilles' heel of the infiltration-enabling US asylum system, as described in Chapter Four, reflects another symptom of illness.

But other evidence abounds of a covert war that is clearly flailing in the absence of public attention.

CHAPTER EIGHT

HOLES IN THE DOUBLE NET

If the good guys can come, you know, then so can the bad guys. We are at risk. You'd like to think at least you're catching one out of 10. But that's not good in baseball, and it's certainly not good in counterterrorism.

—Steven McCraw, former assistant director of the FBI's Office of Intelligence and executive director of the Texas Department of Public Safety, interview with the author.

In Paso Canoas, a small town split in two by the Panama and Costa Rica border, I found Pakistani migrant Jawad Ali and another Pakistani basking in the shade of an outdoor migrant processing center. This was during my December 2018 reporting trip to the region. The two Pakistanis were among one hundred other migrants from a dozen countries—who volunteered to me that they were Iranians, Iraqis, Bangladeshis, and other Pakistanis—that Panama had just bused in from its side of the Panamanian border for a handoff to Costa Rica. These daily handoffs happened under the bilateral "controlled flow" agreement already described. Knowing the answer, I asked where the Pakistanis were going, as a kind of conversation ice-breaker.

Speaking enough English to give an answer, twenty-one-year-old Ali replied: "I am going to New York."

Two Pakistani migrants in Costa Rica, Jawad Ali at left.
Photo by Todd Bensman, December 2018

"Where are you two from?" I asked. He explained that he and his traveling companion hailed from Pakistan's Swat District.

I instantly recognized the region as a former redoubt of the Pakistani Taliban, a US-designated terrorist organization.[1] The hardline Islamist militant group took over the district in 2007 and, rather infamously, used it for years to kill American troops battling away in next-door Afghanistan.

"Why did you two leave?" I asked, expecting to hear an asylum persecution story of some kind.

Ali said he left because of "some severe problems." He demurred when I asked for specifics, which was unusual. If Ali knew the US asylum process, he'd have a persecution story ginned up and practiced by now.

"Sorry, I can't tell you right here. Sorry."

"How did you get this far?" I asked, shifting tack. They had hired a smuggler named "Musa" in Pakistan and paid $10,000 each. Musa brought them back Brazilian visas, flights there, and guides up to the Colombia jump-off, where the smuggler Musa knew the Panamanian and Costa Rican governments would take over.

"What's the plan now?" I asked.

"Of course we are seeking political asylum over there."

I asked how he knew to do that.

"Because a lot of people have been in asylum over there, and they are now safe and secure. They didn't have any problems." Ali explained. "This is why I leave my country, because I have a lot of friends go over there [the United States]."

I knew the Americans would be interested in any Pakistani, let alone those from the militarized Swat District. Back in Texas among intelligence workers, all Pakistanis got hard-interview treatment. I asked questions I would have asked him when I worked for DPS. Had he and his friend provided fingerprints, retinal scans, and facial-recognition photos to the Panamanians after exiting the Darien jungle? The answer was yes. I asked if any Americans had interviewed them so far in the Panamanian camps, which sometimes happens. That answer: "No, you are the first."

I asked whether he thought the American immigration officials had any reason to feel suspicious of him after he crossed the US-Mexico border.

"Of course, I am from Pakistan.... Maybe they'll think I'm interested in some type of attack," Ali acknowledged, then quickly added, "but we are a peaceful people. We don't have any problem. I know that I...everything is clear. I am going there without any problem."

I didn't mention to Ali and his companion that I knew they hadn't come this far without less-visible kind of contact with the American cordon. I knew the Panamanians would have mainlined the biometrics they'd collected to US intelligence analysts for checks against criminal and terrorism databases. I knew the Pakistanis and the Americans had fairly good cooperation protocols on sharing information about known terrorists. The Americans up at the southern border might even have gotten word that these two were on their way and to be on the lookout for when they arrived. I knew it was even possible US intelligence had already run the database checks on these two and got no "hits," hence the fact that they were still traveling free rather than detained and deported. Remember the Yemenis the Arizona State University students found stuck in a remote Panamanian village under long investigation by the Americans.

The fact that the biometrics of these Pakistanis from Swat District—and thousands of SIAs like them over the years—had been collected and imported into American systems scores as a national security achievement for the Americans. What the Pakistanis did not know was that they were moving through a layered defense, that the Mexicans could interview them and ask that they fill out a questionnaire for the Americans. Or that once they reached the American border, well-trained federal officers were going interview them before they could go anywhere near New York.

But I also knew something else as I interviewed Ali and his friend (and later four Iranians traveling with them): one or both could sail right through as terrorists anyway. Gaping tears mar the double-netting of detection along the Latin American routes and at the physical border too. The main factor to consider is that probably only a fraction of the world's jihadists ever make it into a Western nation's terrorism database. Large numbers are not going to be in the proverbial "system," not by their real names, aliases, fingerprints, or retinas. They're ghosts, and they like it that way. Pakistan's intelligence services almost surely do not know every jihadist in their territories, and there are a great many there. Pakistan is a country with an actual government and, despite split-loyalty issues, remains a somewhat capable, intact intelligence service more often willing to share than not. Other countries in the neighborhood don't even field real governments or intelligence agencies the Americans can phone up for a database check.

Consider if the Taliban had chosen to send these Pakistanis on a mission because they were "clean" of terrorism databases, or that they were unaffiliated solo jihadist entrepreneurs coming on their own. Ali and his friend stood decent odds of slipping slip right through into the American interior on the hapless asylum system described in Chapter Four. One good consistent yarn, a clear background, and a fake name are all it would take.

With preparation and just a little luck, America's double-netted cordon has paid a far greater public safety dividend than did pre-2015 Europe in the capture and deportation of many jihadists and questionable travelers. However, intelligence systems are very far from perfect, and the ways through the cordon are many, as I'll show next. It seems only a matter of time before the wrong one finally ambles right through the thinning, gap-filled front lines of America's covert border war.

'IT JUST DIED' AND OTHER TROUBLES FOR THE NEAR WAR

For basic health and fitness, government programs need at least audits, critical evaluations, and adjustments. Critical examination informs how to discern flaws, fix them, and appropriately resource and coordinate programs to the ever-evolving problems they exist to solve. But if any US government agency ever holistically evaluated all the components of the American counter-infiltration enterprise described in these pages, I could find no evidence of it. Congressional subcommittees, offices of inspectors general, and the Government Accountability Office have hit bits and pieces of it but do not seem to have weighed in on either the near or far wars in any holistic way.

By contrast, oversight, evaluation, and auditing attention is practically lavished on the various conventional enforcement campaigns that manage Spanish-speaking migration flows and drug trafficking. All indications are that SIA traffic and infiltration, a threat issue far too tailored and unique to benefit from those, has become a neglected stepchild at risk of veering off the straight and narrow. High consequences of the sort Europe has suffered are in the offing if the trend continues in that direction.

Former CBP Commissioner David Aguilar, a key author of the near-war effort, said he was not aware that counterterrorism programs were ever audited through to the time he left government service in 2013. ICE Homeland Security Investigations Chief James Dinkins told me he too was unaware of any government audit or evaluation of his agency's SIA-hunting far war in Latin America, through to the time he left government service in 2014.

Dinkins told me he had answered questions about the program before Congress a number of times but that "I've never seen a comprehensive congressional investigative report, no."

Another indication that America's counter-infiltration projects have languished without audit or evaluation can be found in DHS Secretary Jeh Johnson's 2016 memo calling for a renewed and unified project. In it, he seemed to recognize the inherent discordance of its many components. Johnson asked his agency chiefs, before they did anything else, to assess presumed "shortfalls, limiting factors, and potential areas for improvement" so that effort could move forward as a single collaborative in a dedicated, effective manner. Alas, Secretary Johnson's ideas for an everyone-on-the-same-page-right-now effort ended when the election of President Trump swept most of the memo recipients out of office, including Johnson. The whole new enterprise "just died," one of those involved directly in the start of it told me.

In my own effort to evaluate the totality of the covert border war's various elements, I found discombobulation everywhere. Even basic common definitions and terms necessary to operate in unison across agencies have eluded all of them across time. Different agencies under different administrations haven't even been able to agree on the term "special interest aliens." Different agencies have called them "aliens from special interest countries," "third country nationals," and "aliens from specially designated countries." Nor is there even a commonly agreed-upon list of countries by which to tag illegal immigrants as one of those things for enhanced screening (SIAs, ASICs, TCNs…or whatever). In congressional testimony, DHS officials have interchangeably used the terms "special interest country," "countries of national security concern," and "country of interest."

Naming convention disparity is less a fatal problem than an indication of deeper issues.

More problematically, the number and names of countries on those lists have fluctuated almost wildly at political whim, which in turn whipsawed the frontline troop decisions about which migrants from which countries they are to investigate and interview.[2] The earliest-known "specially designated country list" trotted out in 2004 was fifty-two, then winnowed to thirty-five in CBP Chief Aguilar's 2004 memo ordering that SIAs from those countries be flagged and investigated.[3] The number of listed countries was twenty-five during the Trump years.

In the years since the 2004 Aguilar memo, the country lists have fluctuated wildly depending on diplomatic and political winds. In August 2011, for instance, a DHS Office of Inspector General report disclosed that Obama administration officials decided the 2003 list was "outdated" and had to be "eliminated" because it was "not based on any judgment that the states listed supported, sponsored or encouraged terrorism." The Obama administration felt it was time to eliminate the list because "many of the states listed are important and committed partners of the United States in countering terrorism."[4]

This narrative runs counter to what Aguilar told me, which is that agencies of the nation's intelligence community had recommended which nations should be on the list based on rigorous analysis eight years earlier of terrorist organization activities within them.

The absence of any universal understanding of basics like this indicates neglect.

In his interview with me in May 2020, Aguilar warned against such unguided meandering from his original program, whose prescriptions he said remained just as needed and relevant today as they were back in 2004.

"Has it ebbed and flowed? Yes. But we can't allow it to do that," Aguilar told me of the way his original border program was set up. "It needs to be revisited on a regular basis. One of the things that always concerns me is that we get complacent as a nation. That's how we got to 9/11. Complacency starts to take hold over time if we allow it. It's up to leadership that we stay focused, stay prioritized and recognize the continuing need."

In 2017, researchers for the *Small Wars Journal,* among the few who are in the know about SIAs, criticized the apparent lack of a more dedicated whole-of-government approach to countering the SIA-terror infiltration threat.[5] They observed an absence of a unified, dedicated, and resourced approach (maybe like what Secretary Johnson ordered). The authors concluded that this represents a "strategic and operational level failure…a consequence of not having the requisite strategic leadership and policy guidance."

FAILING TO INTERVIEW SIAS

To quickly recap the near war basics, after 9/11, legislation required the nation's border security agencies to figure out ways to stop terrorists from infiltrating over the land borders. At the American borders, Congress funded walls, a doubling of Border Patrol agents, and more technology and air and marine assets. DHS agents with Border Patrol and ICE started singling out special interest aliens apprehended annually for enhanced security screening, such as terrorism and criminal database checks, notifying the FBI and National Counterterrorism Center when they were in custody for the all-important face-to-face threat assessment interviews. CBP deployed Tactical Terrorism Response Teams to zero in on SIAs deemed especially problematic. When these efforts revealed strong enough intelligence information to suspect terrorist involvements, the migrants were quietly deported or publicly prosecuted for various non-terrorism crimes, such as immigration fraud.

The goal was always that the DHS agencies and the FBI fully screen and interview 100 percent of those apprehended SIAs, which ranged from 1,500 to more than 3,000 a year at just the southern land border (by my very conservative count of thirty-seven countries) and share what was learned with one another. But inconsistent application has bedeviled these crucial migrant national security screening processes. Over time, the number of SIA debriefing interviews began to decline. By how much is unknown because no known audit has ever been conducted about this.

But I know this because sometime around 2011, FBI agents responsible for the duty in Texas told me headquarters had called them off universal interviews with all SIAs. Whereas agents used to interview every single one, they pulled back to prioritize select ones from the war zones where American troops operated—say, if they were from Afghanistan, Iraq, or Pakistan—while turning over responsibility for the rest to ICE Enforcement and Removal Operations (ERO) intelligence officers stationed inside the detention centers.[6] I have good reason to believe ICE ERO intelligence officers in the detention facilities were unable to reach anywhere close to their 100 percent interview goals before detainees bonded out into the American interior, taking whatever they knew about terrorists and SIA smugglers with them into the ether.

I came to learn this firsthand during my service with Texas DPS when I canvassed officers working in three border detention facilities. I asked how many SIAs were interviewed before the migrants bonded out on asylum claims. The answer seemed to be about a third. That number struck me as so low that I felt obliged to help in my Texas DPS capacity. With my leadership's approval, I launched a program to train and send my state analysts into the detention facilities to help them knock out more interviews and capture at least some of the intelligence that would otherwise flow out the back door.

Before any trip down to a border detention facility, I'd request a list of the SIAs who had not yet been interviewed. Pages would come back, filled with single-spaced names and nationalities of the multitudes who had never been interviewed and never would be.

Whatever my small team could accomplish in any given month amounted to a drop in the bucket. We could pick maybe three or four names, then head down to the facility for one or two days of interviews. But even these seemed a worthy net gain over nothing. It remained this way through to the end of my service in mid-2018.

BLIND SPOTS EVERYWHERE

Even when the FBI, ICE, or my own analysts did interview SIAs in detention, our abilities to discern terrorism connections or to detect discrepancies and lies were far from foolproof.[7] That's because far from all travelers with terrorism history, connections, or proclivities are even known to authorities and so would not be entered into any intelligence database. Plenty floated around undiscovered in Europe until it was too late.

Recall that many SIAs show up with no identification from anarchic countries like Somalia or Libya, which have no governments that keep official records of even births and deaths, let alone terrorism intelligence databases. Other countries haven't worked with American intelligence or law enforcement for decades for various reasons, like Muslim-majority Sudan (once home to Osama bin Laden and his al-Qaeda group) even when they had functioning governments. (Sudan was listed as a US-designated State Sponsor of Terrorism for years.) Still other countries, like Iran, Syria, Cuba, and Venezuela, have proven so hostile toward the United States that they would never deign to take a call from the Americans asking for some help from harm. These countries *like* the idea of American harm.

As discussed earlier in this book, American agents conduct as many security threat interviews as possible, not only in US detention facilities after they have already crossed the border but in Mexico, Costa Rica and Panama too. Yet FBI and DHS have only been able to episodically interview SIAs inside the all-important Mexican facilities after 9/11.[8] Limited staffing in Mexico never allowed for more than a few interviews at a time anyway. Often, interpreters were in short supply for obscure dialects, leaving most of the SIAs to continue on to the American border without debriefing interviews to the US detention centers, where they also stood a good chance of passing through into the interior without a trained agent grilling them.[9]

As detailed in Chapter Four, the US asylum system won't find terrorists as things stand either. The security vetting in that asylum system is so broken that the system can only aid and abet terrorist embedding. To end up largely free to plot inside the United States, all a determined jihadist from a country like Pakistan would have to do is hew pretty consistently to a fabricated persecution story that possibly won't be vetted anywhere along the way, including at the last-line of defense immigration courts. Recall the case of Fidse and Sheikh, where an immigration judge granted her asylum within three months of entry on a fake story and after she simply pretended not to know her terrorist husband.

This isn't only my assessment. A 2006 DHS Office of Inspector General audit report about ICE detention and removal practices noted this inherent problem of vetting total strangers moving in and by revolving door.[10]

"The effectiveness of these background checks is uncertain due to the difficulty that CBP and ICE have in verifying the identity, country-of-origin, terrorist or criminal affiliation of aliens in general," the report said. Therefore, the release of SIAs "poses particular risks."

Or as one FBI agent told me once when complaining of these same circumstances: "You interview them, run every database possible, fingerprints, watch lists, check their stories.... Could we be fooled? Of course."[11]

It gets worse. Keeping in mind that ICE detention centers are the last possible line of defense before SIAs are released into the nation's interior on their own recognizance, a 2011 DHS Office of Inspector General audit discovered that ICE wasn't consistently following DHS policy that it run database checks on all detained SIAs from "specially designated countries" before their release to determine if they were wanted by anyone.[12] That wasn't done in more than half the 116 cases the auditors randomly checked.

A more worrisome finding was that no one checked 100 percent of the time even to find out whether SIAs were on terrorism watch lists. The number of oversights was small, only 3 percent of the cases randomly checked. But as I and the auditors knew, small numbers portend unacceptably grave consequences. The auditors noted that failures to check the terror watch list foretold such consequences.

"Although we found only two cases in which ICE officers did not properly screen aliens, releasing a single known or suspected terrorist could have serious ramifications," the 2011 OIG report observed.

Fast-forward a half dozen years to a January 2018 follow-up DHS audit report that found more egregious inconsistencies in the terrorism vetting process at the detention centers. With some understatement, the audit report is titled *ICE Faces Challenges to Screen Aliens Who May Be Known or Suspected Terrorists*. It tracks with what I experienced working with ICE while at Texas DPS.

OIG auditors found a different system in place to accomplish the same objective to identify SIAs on the watch list so that other interested agencies could be notified in time to act on that intelligence. The idea by then was to comport with a November 2014 policy issued by then-DHS Secretary Johnson, which specified that "aliens engaged in or suspected of terrorism, or who otherwise pose a danger to national security, are the highest civil immigration enforcement priority to which DHS should direct its enforcement resources."

Unbelievably by 2017, the OIG picked forty cases and found problems with the handling of every one of them. In eighteen of the cases, ICE did not run background checks (biometric and biographic) at each required point during the SIA's detention, most importantly before they were released from custody. Many of the other cases where the checks were run were conducted off-schedule and late, some just before release into the country, as though more of an afterthought rather than the "highest civil enforcement priority."

In six other cases where they did confirm the migrant was on the watch list, ICE couldn't show it reported that to the FBI and other interested agencies so they could act on it. One impediment was that "the majority of ERO offices" did not have access to DHS classified networks by which to communicate derogatory information about suspected terrorist SIAs to other agencies that needed it. In ten of the forty cases, ICE officers didn't log any of the required information into case management systems or file reports to ICE headquarters in a timely manner.

While ICE attributed these problems to "human error" and a lack of familiarity with policy, the auditors blamed "limited program oversight and weak management controls" that prevent ICE ERO from "effectively screening all aliens in ICE custody for terrorism connections."

Any homeland security worker or leader who lets an SIA terrorist slip through because of seemingly arcane and bureaucratic oversights like these will no doubt find themselves later with right hands up swearing oaths before Congress to tell the whole truth as to how their failures enabled a terror attack.

Persistent imperfection did not plague only the near war.

YAWNING HOLES IN THE FAR WAR

In January 2020, I found myself at the center of Mexico's southernmost city, Tapachula, inside one of the many seedy restaurants that provide thousands of migrants moving through it with cheap eats. I was studying the walls, which intelligence agency contacts had told me about stateside.

A thumb-tacked Eritrean dollar bore dated signatures. I studied photos of smiling people tacked up too, obviously taken here at some point. Those hung under scribbled home nations right on the wall itself, like "Somalia," "Ethiopia," and "Bangladesh." One large scrawled traveler's note read, "Thank you Mama Africa," reflect an appreciation for her cheap and often free food, floor space for sleeping, and reputed smuggling connections. Right about then, a narrow-framed woman tapped my shoulder, introduced herself as the apparently famed Mama Africa and asked if she could help.

I knew American intelligence had already identified or busted other "Mama Africa" women smugglers in Nicaragua and Colombia, a moniker that African migrants seem to apply to any local woman who consistently provides assistance.[13] I was in this Mama Africa's restaurant, "The Bangladesh," just a few months after a US-Mexico counter-smuggling operation bagged a Bangladeshi human smuggler who worked for her in the restaurant.[14]

"Ahh, so nice to meet you," I said. "I just have a few questions."

She invited me to sit on a wobbly plastic chair at a wobbly plastic table and waited as the matronly Mexican entrepreneur bustled to and fro in an eatery that, despite the recent bust, obviously still drew customers fresh off a global underground railroad, who still seek her out when they hit town.

"There are more Africans coming now than I have ever seen before," she told me a little while later as the place filled with Bangladeshis, Haitians, and Nepalese. One migrant woman sitting at a table wore a bright blue hijab head covering and spoke on a cell phone in an unrecognizable dialect.

Mama Africa denied she was involved in smuggling; just feeding, caring, and sometimes "giving some advice" on travel. She told me Iranians, Syrians, and Somalis were in town at the moment, all pushing on to the American border.

If judging only from business at The Bangladesh and outside on Tapachula's streets, the health of SIA traffic and the demand for smuggling services were undeniable in 2020. Whatever the Americans were doing, including arresting Mama Africa's own employee for smuggling Bangladeshis, certainly was not deterring anyone, like problematic Pakistani Asef Khan, whom I found outside a little way down the street.

The bearded and road-unkempt Pakistani national was loitering in a downtown park down the street. At the time, in a nod to President Trump's demand that Mexico end the latest Central American mass migration crisis, Mexico happened to be in a rare moment of using its national guard troops to block Central American migrant caravans from continuing north from Tapachula. Mexico has always been a welcoming transit country for US-bound migrants and will become one again after Trump. But for now, all migrants entering Mexico were required to register and apply for Mexican asylum or be deported.

But SIAs like Khan knew Mexico couldn't deport them because that required diplomatic agreement from home countries that was hard to secure, and also expensive intercontinental flights for which Mexico wasn't willing to pay. They also knew that, if they could just get by the Mexican troops, they'd be let in at the American border on the usual asylum claims because all US push-back policies were geared to Central Americans. The SIAs had been forgotten and exempted.

Assuming, of course, that was his real name, "Khan" told me he was an engineering school graduate from Peshawar and had evaded the Mexican requirements, looking for a way around it all. He was off the grid, looking for a way to an American border that was still open to people from Pakistan.

"I'm waiting for something good to happen," he said.

I knew that once he was caught and detained, while the Americans may or may not interview him, they'd need to. Khan clammed up when I pressed him about why he left Pakistan and wanted to go to America.

"I had some problems" with Pakistani authorities was all he would say about it.

Remember that, at the same time that American homeland security agencies started screening arriving SIAs for terrorist infiltrators among them at the physical border, they'd also set up other operations abroad. DHS deployed hundreds of ICE Homeland Security Investigations (HSI) officers to hunt down SIA smugglers transporting those SIAs in from the Middle East, South Asia, and North Africa. HSI developed a proxy army of vetted and trusted local law enforcement groups in countries all along the smuggling routes to do the work. The FBI and other US intelligence community agencies, such as the CIA, and the US military's Coast Guard, Southern Command, Northern Command and Joint Task Force West provided intelligence and assets such as satellites, naval vessels, and personnel, the latter to interview suspected noncitizen jihadists apprehended in the custody of Panama, Costa Rica, and Mexico. Jihadists strained from the flow were deported.

Whichever theory is true, all indications suggest the American enforcement strategy, though successful at detecting some terrorists, may not be properly resourced or take into account certain geopolitical circumstances: SIAs have reached the US southwestern border in relatively steady, increasing, annual numbers since the start of the American post-9/11 operations as described in Chapter Two.

One reason is that, short of constant evaluation and improvement, the American effort will naturally lag behind the adaptations of their quarry.

Numerous scholars and experts on the global crime economy write persuasively that US efforts abroad have utterly failed to keep step with the new realities of international criminality. The argument is that the international black-market economy has boomed alongside the legitimate economy due to an explosion of trade agreements and technological advancements in communication, transportation, and finance. But law enforcement never really did. In their book about this, *Deviant Globalization, The Black Market Economy in the 21st Century*, editors Niles Gilman, Jesse Goldhammer, and Steve Weber write that smuggling organizations in particular have quickly grown to unprecedented dimensions in recent decades, energized and made more elusory by vast increases in cross-border flows of people and freight.[15]

The expansion, pace, and technology ushered in a historic boom in global black markets, a true golden age far exceeding the capacities of conventional law enforcement, which is not driven by the same powerful incentives, they write. Naím Moisés, in the book *Illicit: How Smugglers, Traffickers and Copycats Are Hijacking the Global Economy*, sums up the problem by noting the United States has become virtually hapless in countering clandestine industries because they operate in "geopolitical black holes where they live and thrive…pushing our world in new directions that so far have eluded our capacity to comprehend, let alone arrest."[16] Naím argues that uninformed flailing at transnational smuggling only causes prices, profits, and incentives to rise, further feeding demand for more enforcement in an endless, self-defeating cycle.

Terrorism scholar John Rollins writes that the American lack of "appreciation of global complexities" and confused organizational responsibilities have led to "inefficiencies, actual and near tragedy, and continuing challenges in detecting, responding or recovering from a security-related issue."

He believes the American transnational law enforcement efforts against terrorism, which include how to fund and most efficiently target quarry, have to be well informed by understanding shifting ground realities.[17] Rollins calls for a more significant US commitment to a transnational approach that "entails understanding and addressing the interrelationship of global risks to a nation's short- and long-term strategic interests."[18] He also believes a more informed American transnational effort will help leaders know how to apply funds and other resources in a more efficient and targeted manner.

Assuming that even some of these dystopian assessments are correct, America's covert border war is in desperate need of care if the country wants to maintain its remarkable track record of shielding.

MISSING GOALPOSTS

What are the war's objectives, anyway? Perhaps the truest measure of downstream effectiveness of the American foreign effort might well be SIA apprehensions at the border. But this number, no matter who is calculating it or how, has risen steadily for the last decade without respite. The rise of those numbers indicates poor performance. Another outcome measure might be how often SIA smugglers are caught and brought to American justice. Yet there's no objective benchmark for how many SIAs is too many—underscoring an absence of much recent deep thinking about it.

On the ground in Latin America and working with American intelligence agencies as described earlier in this book, HSI should be commended for the smuggling investigations its agents *have* completed; they are complex, intercontinental affairs buffeted by the politics and diplomatic tiffs of foreign countries where they unfold.

But by my count, HSI investigations have produced only some twenty-five US prosecutions of major kingpin smugglers since 2001 (not counting subordinate coconspirators), or one or two per year since 9/11. To be fair, HSI is not typically credited for additional cases and busts it caused because these were given over to partner nations like Mexico and Brazil to prosecute, so the number of kingpin smugglers busted and prosecuted is most certainly higher.

But because the US government has conducted no known accounting of whether HSI staffing in Latin America—human capital resources—

is appropriate to actual rates of SIA smuggling and apprehension rates, a gaping unknown, it's perennially unclear whether the number of personnel actively working on the problem set is appropriate. In short, no one knows if we're winning the war.

That kind of information is important to know because some evidence suggests the 200 or 300 HSI agents stationed along SIA routes are diverted to and distracted by a variety of investigations in Latin America that have nothing to do with SIA smuggling. The ICE-HSI investigations are complex affairs, spanning various countries in collaboration with foreign law enforcement and intelligence services. But operating in the secrecy necessary for operational security (to keep the bad guys in the dark about how they are to be caught), ICE-HSI foreign operations have been vulnerable to diversion.

A 2010 GAO report titled *Alien Smuggling: DHS Could Better Address Alien Smuggling Along the Southwest Border by Leveraging Investigative Resources and Measuring Program Performance* questioned whether ICE (its pre-HSI Office of Investigations, OI) had spent too little time on counterterrorism alien smuggling investigations.[19] Auditors interviewed the chiefs of all the ICE-OI offices along the southwest border, officials in six Border Patrol sectors, and officials in all five US Attorney's districts. They also analyzed court records and ICE case management data.

The GAO found that, at the time, ICE investigators were conducting "immigration-related activities that are not consistent with the primary mission of conducting criminal investigations." The percentage of time investigators spent on alien smuggling investigations versus other investigative areas, such as drugs, was 16–17 percent over the previous four years.

After any successful attack on the homeland, that 16–17 percent figure should become the butt of congressional hearings as to what went wrong and why. It is true that SIA smuggling is but one of many HSI-worthy crime categories the agency is required to tend, such as human trafficking, child exploitation, and drug trafficking. However, it will be useful for policymakers and the American public to know, on the day after smuggled SIAs succeed in conducting an attack, that HSI has room to reprioritize and reposition its forces in Latin America. Some might argue this should be done preemptively, counting me.

Post-attack commissions and congressional interest would escalate quickly into the red zone over a variety of other government accountability reports that looked at narrow portions of the overall enterprise. These indicate inconsistent or uncoordinated attention to the problem set and always the scant oversight that could have further remedied the risks.

NOT KNOWING THE KNOWABLE

Because the US government apparently has never comprehensively audited all the counter-SIA enterprises as a whole, no one seems to know whether US intelligence agencies, foreign government partners, and ICE-HSI have blown the SIA-smuggling bridges and therefore reduced the haystacks within which needles could then could more easily be found.

Richard Best, writing for the Congressional Research Service in 2010, noted that the potential for terrorists coming across the border had led policymakers to "reach beyond law enforcement agencies to seek out information acquired by intelligence sources." In doing so, however, "much of the contribution of intelligence agencies to the border security effort is classified, and few details are publicly available."[20]

"There is no public assessment of the intelligence contribution," Best lamented.

But in an "Issues for Congress" section, Best also observed that none was on the horizon since a profusion of different congressional committees and subcommittees provided oversight to all the different agencies involved in preventing terrorist infiltration.

"Congress does not oversee a self-contained entity known as 'border security,' rather, components and aspects of the effort are considered by a number of different committees…Congress authorizes and oversees intelligence activities separately from other governmental activities."

That should prove troublesome to the involved agencies after any attack if this shortfall was left unaddressed, which it probably has been.

What is almost certain is that, short of dedicated study and comprehension of the interplay between total threat picture and the American effort, SIAs and jihadists among them likely will keep coming. The vulnerability that these flaws and imperfections conspire to create keeps the drawbridge down and clear for Trojan horses.

What can be done the day after an attack, or preferably before?

CHAPTER NINE

REMEDIES

America had the reputation of being non-ideological, super pragmatic, problem solvers par excellence. This image of the United States was an earned image, of people seeing America do almost a wondrous series of things.... We became known as the can-do country. If you contrast that with the image of the U.S. today, it's kind of depressing.

—Former Executive Director of the 9/11 Commission Philip Zelikow, April 2020, regarding the lack of advance preparation for the COVID-19 virus pandemic.

The American counterterrorism project to protect against terrorist border infiltration, to include all of its components holistically, undoubtedly saved many lives since 9/11. But its fitness has declined amid denialism about its existence at a time when the threat it counters is intensifying. More than ever, the project begs evaluation, recalibration, and repair.

Chief among the changed circumstances arguing for attention is the extraordinary success of jihadist border infiltration in Europe from 2015 through to the end of 2020 and going forward. Terrorist organizations and freelance jihadists did not merely notice the successes of border-infiltration in European body count, raging gun battles with antiterrorism police forces, and disrupted plots; jihadists pointedly beheld and regaled the damage in their online chatrooms, forums, and propaganda. But the most important factor to know is that they *noticed the success*. The international jihadist community is aware that people-camouflaged border infiltration will eventually work.

In crime and terrorism, a classic and infallibly reliable law enforcement and intelligence assumption is that street crooks, white collar fraudsters, and terrorists will replicate past successes, especially in spaces where it will not likely be widely expected, and where past thwarting and plot defeats have been denied and never publicized. The United States southern frontier certainly qualifies as such an idyllic space. Foreign observers with violent jihad on their minds had to have noticed, especially during the 2019 Trump-media tussle over whether Middle Eastern migrant border crossers even exist, that America won't look *there* and that opportunity will beckon under Democratic leadership or obstruction. Knowing your adversary's gaze is largely directed elsewhere and that the secretly posted guards are dozing or are ill-prepared are the best preconditions possible for eventual successful surprise attack.

We also know from evidence described in this book that jihadist groups and individuals have held fast to their aspirations to cross the American border and attack. As described in these pages, ISIS and al-Qaeda operatives regularly agitate for US border infiltration; in 2016, ISIS's external operations division actually hatched an infiltration plot involving its Trinidadian fighters. Why would the border, as an avenue of covert approach denied as such by liberal US political leaderships, appeal more strongly now than in earlier years? For several reasons, chief among them that it is now much harder to enter the United States in the old conventional ways used, for instance, by the 9/11 hijackers, and these difficulties have made border crossings much more viable as alternatives.

For a long time after 9/11, conventional wisdom among homeland security analysts held that terrorists desiring to enter the United States would and could fly in like the 9/11 hijackers, on various kinds of non-immigrant and legal immigration visas and that this was naturally preferable to arduous overland journeys fraught with snakes and stinging insects.

That notion should be regarded as unmerited now, passé, in light of changed times and evolved circumstances.

In the post-9/11 decades, many of the immigration enforcement and legal loopholes through which the 9/11 hijackers slipped into the country have been significantly tightened, even if imperfectly. For one small example, passenger manifests on all flights are shared with homeland security and run through databases and terrorism watch lists. Passport security has significantly improved too. Systems for other means of entry, such as refugee resettlement, became even harder to game after the election of Donald Trump. The administration, for instance, put caps on legal migration from countries of interest, so-called "Muslim travel bans," and sharply reduced legal refugee resettlements from Muslim-majority countries.

Very significantly, though, most Trump White House immigration initiatives between 2017 and 2021—caps on visas and refugee admissions, improved overseas vetting, and the travel restrictions on ten countries—only increased pressures to enter through the border. None of these initiatives came with provisions that would address SIAs crossing the US-Mexico border.

Just like in the pressure cooker, steam finds the path of least resistance, the chink in the armor, the hole in the inner tube. Recall that when Syrians suddenly faced restrictions of American tourist visas during their civil war back home, hundreds merely shifted tack and came over the land border instead, where they accessed the asylum system and eventually secured paths to citizenship. When the United States restricted humanitarian visas to Iraqis during the mid-2000s American war, hundreds just came in over the Texas and California borders too like the first Iraqi I interviewed in Brownsville back in 2007, Aamir Boles.

There is more steam than ever under pressure in the cooker too. Historic numbers of migrants have been coursing through the global bloodstream for years looking for new lives in economically developed countries—by most accounts, the most since World War II. In 2020, the United Nations International Organization for Migration noted that the world's top twenty countries with the largest number of internally displaced persons were either in the Middle East or sub-Saharan Africa and predicted the pattern of mass migration to economically developed countries was "likely to remain the same for many years into the future."[1] Like the relentless rise in the number of SIAs to date, more of them than ever should funnel into the path of ever-lessening resistance, especially under Democratic Party governance, toward the southern land border. The ever-upward trend of SIA apprehensions at America's land borders should only continue under these friendly conditions, heightening the associated risk of terrorism by sheer numbers in just the same way it did in Europe.

Whether that path becomes more or less resistant depends on which party happens to control the White House, the levers of immigration enforcement, and the counterterrorism project described in these pages. Judging by the political campaigns of every Democratic candidate who ran for president in 2019 and 2020, most impediments to mass migrations over the southern land border, and any of those quite tenuous obstructions put in place by President Trump during his 2016–2021 term, would be dismantled in a new Democratic administration.

By way of example, President Trump in 2019 demanded that Mexico deploy its national guard to halt camouflaging mass migration from Central America and break up new migrant caravans, or else he would impose punishing trade tariffs. Mexico fearfully complied after nearly a million Central Americans had already poured over the southern border. The Mexican troop deployment largely worked, along with other deterring Trump push-back policies at the US border, and the caravans ended. Mysteriously, none of the Trump push-back policies at the border, such as the Migrant Protection Protocols (sometimes known as "Remain in Mexico"), applied to SIAs, who were exempted and continued to cross and claim asylum if they could steal past the Mexican roadblocks.[2] Well-placed senior DHS officials told me that the reason SIAs were exempt was because Mexico had to agree to take back each nationality type and had stalled on SIA nationalities. Still, the removal from the battlefield of massive numbers of Central Americans somewhat cleared away the camouflage and relieved pressure on personnel at the border to at least contend with the SIAs who were allowed to still come over.

Under any Democratic administration, that trade tariff threat would disappear along with the Mexican national guard cordon, effectively clearing the pathway once again to mass camouflaging migration and returning Mexico to the caravan-friendly transit state it had always been. The threat-national guard arrangement was always tenuous anyway, even under Republicans, because the agreement was entirely predicated upon the political whims of whoever holds the Mexican presidency.

Taken all together, conditions and forward-leaning trends only seem poised to stress the already troubled American counterterrorism enterprise. Past success cannot guarantee future performance without evaluation-based repair, upgrades, appropriate resource allocations, and threat comprehension.

REMEDIES

UCLA management professor Richard Rumelt writes in "The Perils of Bad Strategy" that good strategy focuses energy and resources on the judicious selection of one or very few important objectives, rather than on "a scrambled mess of things to accomplish, a dog's dinner of goals."[3] A good strategist, he argues, selects only a few objectives that can be attained with existing resources and competencies. With that principle in mind, I propose strategies in this chapter to confront only some of the more egregious fail points in the American counterterrorism border enterprise.

Preferably, reforms to government programs are implemented preemptively, before surprise terror attacks occur. Preemption is in line with classic homeland security and military doctrine. But face it; the United States most often reacts to smoking aftermaths. Whether preemptory or reactionary on something like The Day After, the balance of chapter stands at the ready.

THE NEAR WAR

Resurrect aspects of Jeh Johnson's 2016 counter-SIA initiative, particularly the call for an enterprise-wide study and assessment of impact and effectiveness. Follow through on its plan to coordinate all involved DHS component agencies, as well as the FBI and military intelligence components of US Southern Command.

In 2016, the DHS Secretary ordered an enterprise-wide threat analysis of SIA travel and terrorist infiltration as well as a comprehensive assessment of how all counter-SIA enterprises currently address the threat. That did not happen. Reinstitute the order and require that it be done biannually with focus on all its moving parts, individually and collectively. Additionally, follow through on the Johnson plan to create standardized and consistent intelligence-sharing protocols, processes to create standardized country list compilations, and term definitions that apply across all involved agencies. Merge currently disaggregated agency efforts to counter SIA cross-border smuggling and vetting of SIAs at the border and abroad based on the assessment and study.

Establish a single congressional oversight entity to ensure the border counterterrorism enterprise remains updated and impactful, with clearly stated goals and annual outcomes reports.

As shown, different congressional oversight committees and subcommittees provide oversight for different law enforcement and intelligence agencies that might have a role of the counter-SIA project. Organizing the enterprise as an entity under the oversight of a single committee would ensure that the work of intelligence and law enforcement agencies in border security missions is prudently coordinated, organized, and resourced so that agencies aren't working at cross-purposes or duplicating efforts.

Institute extended detention time and potential misdemeanor prosecution for illegal entry of SIAs and SIA asylum claimants, as well as encourage an increase in bonds for SIAs; ensure that bed space availability is commensurate with average SIA apprehension rates so that bed space is consistently available to maintain extended detention necessary for investigative efforts to succeed.

Research indicates that the prospect of lengthier detentions and prosecution for illegal entry between ports of entry, pending adjudication of asylum claims or other legal processes, are regarded as high-consequence deterrents on initial decisions to migrate.[4] Additionally, this policy would increase time in custody necessary to conduct comprehensive security assessments and vetting on all SIAs. White House directives for longer detention time and illegal entry prosecutions for non-SIAs have foundered, in part, on bed space availability. But these strategies can be successfully employed on the smaller numbers of SIAs.

Require that ICE ERO, the FBI, and designated others conduct threat assessment interviews of all SIAs detained inside the United States to assess risk and collect intelligence on routes, smugglers, and terrorism before they bond out or deport. Consider state and local fusion center officers and analysts as trusted partners to assist. Emphatically integrate this effort with CBP's National Vetting Center with its tie-in to the intelligence community.

In past years, ICE intelligence officers and FBI agents were guided by a goal of 100 percent, in-person security vetting assessments of detained SIAs and to collect intelligence about their smugglers. However, the evidence shows that many detainees bond out without enhanced vetting, leaving potentially valuable intelligence uncaptured and releasing dangerous individuals into the US interior. Use state and local law enforcement agencies associated with fusion centers in US states that border Mexico to interview apprehended SIAs, as a force-multiplier, and have the reports provided to federal investigators. Through the national fusion center network, local police have been designated as partners in counterterrorism. Fusion center police officers and analysts often are vetted and trained to share information and have federal security clearances.

Resolve all outstanding Government Accountability Office audit recommendations from 2008 through 2020 as these relate to the ability of all US Citizenship and Immigration Service officers to detect and competently act on asylum fraud, particularly with respect to SIAs. Reform the Fraud Detection and National Security Directorate to grant its agents arrest and investigative referral authorities independent of any other agency.

USCIS bureaucracies have sharply restricted FDNS investigators and line-level asylum officers who conduct interviews with migrants to detect, flag, refer, and investigate asylum fraud indicators. FDNS, for instance, is disallowed from referring asylum fraud cases to US Attorney's offices for prosecution and must instead request that HSI investigate and refer, which rarely happens. Asylum officer interviewers routinely interact with SIA migrants, an unexploited opportunity of proximity. SIA asylum fraud is likely to be frequent as SIAs and their smugglers are deeply invested, financially, in a positive outcome of release into the United States. As well, many jihadist extremists have been found to have abused the asylum process by providing false, coached statements to asylum officers, justifying a harder focus within this cadre to develop fraud detection capabilities aimed at SIAs. Consistent government reporting over time indicates that USCIS officers are largely ineffective, uninterested, and unable to detect and report fraud during their required interactions with these migrants.

Reorient USCIS asylum officers to collect intelligence information from SIAs during other normal courses of duty and create new, standard distribution channels to provide it to appropriate agencies for action. Substantially increase FDNS investigative staffs and asylum officer corps as frontline sensors and require training in national security vetting during credible fear interview processes and during other interactions.

This initiative acknowledges that USCIS officers have unique access to a category of asylum seekers that consistently proves rich in national security intelligence information and about terrorism in foreign nations, their smugglers, and shifting routes and modus operandi of SIA smuggling and travel. The numbers of USCIS officers should be substantially increased. That officer corps should be retrained and given access to systems by which they can capture and log intelligence information that otherwise goes uncaptured. The intelligence information that USCIS asylum officers are uniquely situated to collect can be collated with information collected elsewhere by other means, providing opportunities for corroboration or indications of prevarication. Intelligence information should then be shared with foreign-based ICE investigators and other agencies as necessary. This would require access to database systems necessary to stow and share collected information with other agencies.

Restructure USCIS internal rules to ensure asylum officers are empowered to independently exercise their discretion to decline credible fear claims for SIAs.

As discussed, internal bureaucracies that are subject to external political pressures have sharply limited the independence and ability of USCIS asylum officers to decline credible fear claims. Rather, asylum officers are often required to automatically approve claims en masse, despite strong indications of deception and fraud.

Require US Attorney offices to prioritize and prosecute asylum fraud case referrals. Direct responsible agencies and newly empowered FDNS officers to prioritize asylum fraud detection, investigation, and prosecutorial referrals.

Research shows that SIA smugglers rely on US unwillingness or inability to detect, investigate, or prosecute asylum fraud. The smugglers exploit that to ensure their paying migrant clientele achieve the vaunted asylum legal status after they arrive, which helps ensure SIA smuggling business continuity; therefore, smugglers often coach migrant clients in how to craft fraudulent persecution claims to increase the prospects for approval to pursue asylum. However, a 2015 GAO report found that US Attorney offices usually decline to prosecute asylum fraud investigative referrals, creating disincentives for investigators to do so. Directing an emphasis on asylum fraud prosecution, along with a corresponding requirement that revamped and increased FDNS and asylum officer cadres detect and investigate, would reverse the trend.

THE FAR WAR

Yes, it is true that a lot of aid is given to corrupt governments, but that is by design, not by accident or out of ignorance. Rather, aid is given to thieving governments exactly because they will sell out their people for their own political security. Donors will give them that security in exchange for policies that make donors more secure too by improving the welfare of their own constituents.

—The Dictator's Handbook: Why Bad Behavior Is Almost Always Good Politics [5]

Any strategy to achieve US security objectives in foreign countries is contingent on a singularly important factor: friendly governments must cooperate with American requests for help. DOJ press releases announcing SIA smuggler arrests and major case developments often credit Latin American police forces and governments in playing significant or supporting roles, suggesting a degree of successful bilateral collaborations. In a Brookings Institution analysis investigating how the United States should apply Israel's extensive counterterrorism experience, Dicter and Byman write that, after 9/11, America realized that effective local partners were vital to successful counterterrorism efforts because "not only does the United States lack both the capacity and the desire to be omnipresent, but local partners bring capabilities, knowledge and a degree of political acceptability to their counterterrorism efforts that a foreign country cannot possess."[6]

But achieving such cooperation is never a given. Governments in Latin America should be expected to resist expanding the programs recommended in this chapter; they will also resist shifting their own limited local resources to priorities that primarily serve American interests. To help secure the expanded commitments necessary, the United States should establish or substantially increase security assistance, humanitarian development aid, and training program packages to the six key transit countries: Ecuador, Brazil, Colombia, Panama, Guatemala, and Mexico. New program-specific US infusions of money, equipment, technical assistance, and training would be tied to local government progress necessary to achieve some of these recommendations. Smartly applying security assistance and development aid should provide incentive for local governments to cooperate in bilateral law enforcement initiatives. But a muscular diplomatic initiative should accompany this aid to further leverage cooperation at other, potentially more sensitive SIA smuggling leverage points. Muscular diplomacy in conjunction with aid should be used to leverage the internal *political* will to cooperate with strategic needs that largely defy unilateral US action.

Negotiate an end to catch, rest, and release "controlled flow" policies in Mexico, Panama, Costa Rica, and Colombia. Develop a scheme to fund passenger flight repatriations of SIAs from those countries, that includes funding for detention facilities and legal processing infrastructure in both countries, as well as air transport to origin countries.

Mexico, Panama, and several other common SIA transit countries often practice a form of free passage I call catch-rest-and-release that substantially enables journey continuations. The countries provide food and medical attention for ten to twenty-one days and then release with temporary permits granted in the expectation that migrants will quickly exit their countries, always northward. These policies provide SIA smugglers with critical cost-saving support and incentive for migrant decisions to undertake the journeys. The policies are so beneficial to SIA smuggling that they are incorporated into the smuggling business model. One smuggler of Bangladeshis, for instance, required that his clients turn themselves in to Mexican immigration for the housing and legal documents, or else face a $5,000 penalty, one of the migrants told me.

Because the migrants must funnel through them, Colombia, Panama, Costa Rica, and Mexico present logical chokepoints at which SIA migrants could be detained and deported to home countries, rather than their journeys eased and facilitated. Lack of funding for the necessary bed-space infrastructure and costs associated with intercontinental flights, as well as an absence of necessary diplomatic ties to receiving origin countries probably argue against any aggressive alternative policy in these countries. The United States should supply foreign aid and security assistance for the necessary infrastructure and deportation operations. The United States should also use its diplomatic ties to establish repatriation agreements between these transit chokepoint countries and origin countries or safe third countries. Repatriation would significantly deter smuggling at bottleneck route points and drive up costs to evade them. While other countries along the route also conduct catch-and-release, or allow the traffic to pass through unmolested, Colombia, Mexico, and Panama are especially geographically advantageous and are US allies with longstanding collaborative histories in intelligence and law enforcement operations.

In recent years, repatriation flights have been used to send suspected jihadists to home countries from Panama. In 2019, Mexico sent planeloads of Indian migrants back to India for the first time.[7] But while these experiments are promising, repatriation by air remained a rare exception rather than a rule as of this writing and should be institutionalized and expanded as a permanent deterrent.

Direct and prioritize a surge of SIA smuggling investigations in Latin America by ICE Homeland Security Investigations (HSI); ensure more HSI units target SIA smuggling as a larger percentage of total crime categories in South America, in Central America, and in Mexico.

HSI conducts most SIA smuggling investigations in Latin America but, based on its prosecution numbers relative to SIA apprehension rates, appears to be under-resourced. As well, some government reporting indicates that HSI may be diverted too often to drug trafficking investigations or other priorities. SIA smuggling investigations are time-consuming, expensive, and complex because they must occur in conjunction with the law enforcement and intelligence services of sovereign host countries, and SIA smugglers are especially elusive. However, research shows that SIA smugglers are uniquely multilingual and bi- or even tri-national, with access to sources of fraudulent identity documents and visas. Because of those characteristics, their removal through arrest and prosecution can disrupt smuggling networks for longer periods than, say, the removal of typical contraband smugglers.

Increase the number of American law enforcement screeners able to interview SIAs in the detention facilities of Mexico, Honduras, Panama, Brazil, and other Latin American countries known for the staging and transit of SIAs.

FBI, HSI agents, and some intelligence personnel have been allowed access to detention facilities to conduct interviews with SIAs in Mexico, Panama, Costa Rica, Honduras, and elsewhere. The value of this access has proven crucial to assessing how dangerous individual SIAs might be before their releases to continue on to the southern border. However, staffing for these efforts is under-resourced, and so the effort has been inconsistent.[8] While some advances have been reported in, for instance, Panama to collect biometric information on SIAs, US officers and FBI agents should be required to more emphatically make contact with larger numbers of SIAs.

Establish an Immigration Liaison Officer (ILO) program—a corps of intelligence collectors to be stationed inside both US embassies and local country law enforcement offices in origin and transit countries in Latin America but also in the key air transit hubs of South Africa, and the Gulf states of Bahrain, Qatar, and the United Arab Emirates.

This corps would bolster and complement the tactical work being done by counter-smuggling investigators and ensure validity of intelligence provided by local police. Its focus would be to collect information from local sources on modus operandi and routes used by SIA smugglers, analyze it for actionable intelligence, and ensure it is shared with US investigators and the intelligence community. One key target area, for instance, might be Cape Town and Johannesburg, South Africa, which emerged from the data as important air hubs for North Africans and South Asians transiting to Latin America. ILOs also should be stationed in Gulf State air hubs such as Dubai, which also figured often in SIA smuggling, as well as elsewhere in Africa, Asia, and perhaps in Cuba once diplomatic relations with the United States have stabilized enough for such collaboration.

Again, this concept is not without precedent. It could be modeled after a 2004 program the Schengen countries began expanding in 2014, as the Arab Spring and the Syrian civil war sent greater numbers of migrants toward

European borders. The European ILO program's numbers of immigration officers were increased, and their officers were required to develop their own human intelligence sources; this was intended to enable them to build networks of confidential informants feeding them raw, real-time information about local human smuggling operators, local criminal groups aiding the smuggling, and means of transportation.[9] They also collect field intelligence through other methods, such as interviewing transiting or apprehended migrants in those host countries. [10] As I've shown, apprehended migrants are often a primary source of intelligence on smuggling or material witnesses in smuggler prosecutions.

Consider transactional payments to foreign governments and armed groups for cooperation in origin and transit countries.

Some nations normally refuse to become very interested in interdicting US-bound migrants at their airports or land borders. Others refuse to accept repatriations of their citizens from the United States, Mexico, Panama, and other countries. The US government designates countries that refuse to accept deportees as "recalcitrant countries" or "at-risk" of noncompliance. Among the most uncooperative are Bangladesh, Pakistan, Eritrea, Ethiopia, the Caucuses countries, Iraq, Lebanon, Algeria, Egypt, and Mauritania.[11] Other countries, such as Libya, have no working government capable of diplomatically agreeing to accept migrants. But a European solution to end its mass-migration crisis at source countries such as these was to pay governments, and even armed, non-state militias in Libya, to shelter, patrol, and physically halt migration journeys at their beginnings and to accept deportees. In a move embraced by the EU, Italian Prime Minister Matteo Salvini in 2017 provided various inducements to have Libyan militias patrol the border with Niger and Chad for migrants moving north and to halt boat traffic over the Mediterranean.[12]

Migration from Libya by sea to Italy reportedly fell from 181,376 in 2016 to 4,393 by August 2019.[13] In 2016, the EU struck a $3.75 billion annual accord with Afghanistan to accept repatriations of tens of thousands of deportable Afghans it would not have ordinarily accepted.[14] Europeans struck similar repatriation deals with Sudan, Niger, and even extremist militias in Libya for them to physically prevent outgoing migration in exchange for financial aid or other indirect inducements, such as equipment and millions of dollars in charity.[15] One of the most prominent of these transactional arrangements was a €6 billion Germany-spearheaded EU repatriation accord with Turkey to accept returned migrants in refugee camps on Turkish territory, on the gambit that mass deportations would deter new journeys.[16] The number of migrants trying fell from 1.2 million in 2017 to just over 580,000 in 2018 and continued falling in 2019 and through 2020.[17]

In 2019, President Trump threatened Mexico with punitive tariffs to secure its cooperation in stemming the high volumes of Central Americans migrating to the American border. In fear of punishing economic consequences, Mexico deployed its military to its borders and carried out transportation interdiction operations, detentions, and deportations. But the administration has had less success in persuading other important transit countries to assist in detaining and blocking migrant movements. Here, the European experience may guide future American policy choices.

Create a contingency plan to implement "offshore" asylum processing centers in near and far countries of transit and origin.

To eliminate the same incentive of living in Europe illegally after asylum rejection, European Union countries began establishing offshore processing centers where migrants can be deported to apply for asylum and wait but with food and shelter support. The model is based on an Australian policy in which migrant-filled ships are diverted to the Micronesian island state of Nauru for the duration of asylum processing so that they cannot live illegally inside Australia once claims are rejected.

The first Europe-sponsored centers were built in 2019 in the former colonies of Niger and Rwanda with plans to build an archipelago of other centers across Africa.[18] The offshore centers in Niger and Rwanda serve regional populations contemplating migratory journeys but also as destinations where thousands of migrants can be repatriated by air from Europe to await adjudication with basic life support.[19] The idea is to have a safe zone outside of Europe so that asylum seekers who lose their asylum claim decisions cannot go into perpetual hiding inside the EU, as did scores of Islamic terrorists and so that governments can avoid the expensive costs of tracking them down and deporting them.

Along the same lines, Hungary established such "transit zone" asylum processing centers on its Serbia border where migrants must await the outcomes of their applications, given basic life provisions in the meantime but then find themselves already outside Hungary when their claims are rejected.[20]

Though controversial in the public square, Europe's commitment to the policy of offshore asylum zones offers guidance to US border security policy in the event of terror attackers moving in the migration stream. In 2019, several Trump administration policies intended the same outcomes in returning migrants to other countries to wait out their asylum claims, but drew persistent legal challenge and criticism that threatens its continuation under future administrations.[21] The administration also pursued contested "safe third country" policies, such as denying migrants the ability to seek asylum at all unless they have already done so in another country they first transited, resulting in repatriations of, for instance, Hondurans to Guatemala.[22] But these policies are less sustainable or expandable, in part, because they provide for no basic sustenance while migrants wait "off-shore" in these third countries. The European model of asylum processing centers would eliminate the need for unreliable host nation permissions and provide an alternative location for repatriation flights from the United States but also from "catch-rest-release" countries like Panama, Costa Rica, and Mexico.

Fund the creation or expansion of corruption-vetted mobile customs and border patrol units substantially dedicated to seeking out SIAs in currently ungoverned spaces.

This interdiction and deterrence strategy contemplates implementation in all six identified countries to address internal leverage-point circumstances. The prioritized countries, however, should be Colombia, Panama, and Guatemala—the main land bridges linking South America to Mexico. These new customs and border patrol units, carefully shielded from corruption, quickly shift deployment in remote regions like the Darien Gap between Colombia and Panama, as guided by intelligence, when smugglers' routes shift to avoid intervention. Vetted units would be shielded from such influences and operate independently of the main corps.

Again, the concept of US-backed vetted military and police units is not without precedent in Latin America. The concept has much precedent in Colombia and in Mexico, where they are deployed in joint counter-drug trafficking operations. Since 2000, American security assistance investments of many kinds have amounted to well over $12 billion, almost all of it going to help Colombia (Plan Colombia et al.) and Mexico (The Merida Initiative et al.) to suppress drug trafficking, rather than national security-related human smuggling.[23] In return, those governments have allowed significant numbers of US counter-drug personnel to work in their territories and have helped to create law enforcement units ostensibly vetted for corruption to target drugs and anti-government cartels and militias.

SIAs apprehended by such units would be subject to detention and deportation to home countries. In Guatemala, human smuggling organizations have corruptly co-opted northern and southern border control, creating what has been described as a human smuggling superhighway—an obvious leverage point for law enforcement intervention. Under-resourced federal police in Colombia largely ignore migratory routes through its borders with Central America. Guatemala has struggled with systemic corruption in its border guard and customs cadres due to the size and influence of smuggling industries in the country. The vetted unit program should also expand to any of the other five identified transit countries as resources and bilateral relations allow.

Redirect or deploy CIA officers and other intelligence community personnel to collect information about potentially corrupt foreign consulate personnel who provide visas and passports to SIA smugglers, SIAs, and terrorist suspects.

Assuming American intelligence officers are not already stationed in diplomatically estranged, hostile, or particularly corrupt countries where Latin American embassies and consulates can be found, these officers will provide information to the US State Department and leaderships that are positioned to use diplomatic channels to advocate for action against individuals corruptly providing visas and passports for SIA travel. These efforts should focus particularly on the consulate offices in Mexico, Guatemala, Honduras, Cuba, Bolivia, and Venezuela, and in the Middle East, India, Russia, and Singapore.

Use all tools of state power to ensure that the governments of Mexico, Guatemala, Belize, and Ecuador (and Cuba, once full diplomatic relations are restored) more robustly monitor, vet, audit, investigate, and prosecute corrupt practices within foreign service staffs stationed in consulate offices and embassies in countries of interest.

This strategy would confront my reporting about corrupt or inadequate visa and passport issuance from consulates, which enable SIA travel. The strategy would rely on integrity reinforced by covert intelligence collection operations described earlier. This effort should be included as part of a broader strategy; there is some indication that American pressure has worked in the past to ensure integrity inside the diplomatic missions of other nations, such as Mexico's Beirut and Jordan consulates. As mentioned, it was reportedly under American pressure that a Mexican honorary consul based in Jordan was fired in 2004 for illegally selling visas and that his replacement underwent extensive background checks. Also, Cuba reportedly fired two of its embassy employees in Kenya after American authorities brought to their attention that they were selling visas to the American smuggling facilitator Joseph Anthony Tracy, who then resold them to US-bound Somalis. Other empirical evidence points to a Central and South American desire to have American aid, and to not lose it once gained, making leaders susceptible to US diplomatic entreaties. A case in point was Ecuador after 2011. Researcher Luisa Freier reported that aggressive US diplomacy and threats to withdraw millions in aid had forced senior government leaders to backtrack on a controversial policy that would allow visa-free entry into the country to all newcomers.[24] The visa-free policy immediately sparked a rush of human smuggling activity from countries of interest, causing alarm in American national security circles, Freier wrote. Ecuadorian officials created special visas for SIA nationalities under an American threat to withdraw millions of dollars in aid.

Implement an Information Operations (IO) campaign in source countries to inform populations about the outcomes of high-consequence US immigration deterrence policies.

Mere information has proven to be highly influential in the decision-making processes among those contemplating illegal border entry. In early 2017, information about changes in US border enforcement coming with the election of Donald Trump—such as promises to prosecute for illegal entry and to indefinitely detain apprehended migrants pending adjudication of asylum claims—caused a dramatic decline in illegal entries to a seventeen-year low in apprehensions.[25] Individuals contemplating border entry decided not to do so when faced with long detention times, rather than ordinary release after short periods. Likewise, when information traveled that most of the promised policies were not actually implemented, illegal immigration surged. A dedicated IO strategy, in native languages, would draw attention to deportations, repatriations from mid-route transit countries, asylum fraud and illegal entry prosecutions, higher bonds, and longer detention periods. Information about these outcomes, disseminated on a consistent basis in origin countries, would likely produce similar impacts in the Middle East, North Africa, and South Asia.

AFTERWORD

SANCTUARY OR SECURITY?

Nicholas Winton, the British subject credited with smuggling 669 Jewish children from the coming German Nazi Holocaust, did so by forging their travel documents and transporting them out of occupied Czechoslovakia over nine months in 1939.[1] By the standards of this book and our own era, Winton would certainly qualify as a human smuggler. He had resorted to theft, bribery, blackmail, and the forging of their exit visas to mask the origin of the children because foreign governments, including the United States, had refused to provide timely asylum or legal entry to the Jewish children, who otherwise would almost certainly have been enslaved and probably killed.[2]

Although the Nazis would surely have wanted to detect and deal with Winton as the human smuggler he was, in 2002, Queen Elizabeth instead knighted him for his wartime human smuggling deeds, and he has since been lionized—deservedly—as a humanitarian hero in films and books.

I raise this anecdote as a reminder that American homeland security leaders and their elected overseers, in carrying out the difficult duties described and advocated in this book, should strive to always act with core American values in mind. These are explicitly embodied in asylum law and international agreements that offer sanctuary and safe harbor for the truly hounded and endangered, people like Winton and his Jewish children. It is not the "American Way" to wantonly inflict collateral damage on all the sheep unwittingly masking wolves among them.

But nations are just as morally obligated to protect their citizens from the incoming harm of the sort known to be carried along in uninvited and unwanted illegal immigration flows. We saw this citizen expectation powerfully manifested in Europe's course-altering electoral outcomes after the Paris and Brussels attacks.

Critics of more robust securitization of uninvited immigration from proven higher-risk regions of the world would be wrong to deny the human rights of citizen hosts who also are just as much entitled to live in peace and safety. Those who would subsume citizen rights to the presumed "rights" of unknowable immigrants arriving without invitation as complete strangers stand as much on the wrong side of the scale as those on the other who would indiscriminately deny sanctuary to all.

Thankfully, as it turns out, a balance is possible. The nation can do both well. Destination countries like the United States need not choose between sanctuary or security, one starkly over the other; the United States can do both with the turn of one magic key.

That magic key is the United States' ability to "know" the strangers arriving uninvited at the back door, enough anyway to drive informed decisions as to what should be done with them: deportation and prosecution for those with criminal histories or terrorism intelligence records, or asylum and eventual citizenship for those who authentically warrant those privileges and can't find them anywhere else.

The secret sauce necessary to reach that balance is robust and proficient security vetting, investigation, and intelligence collection. As the Europeans painfully learned, security from terrorist mobility over borders requires policies and good intelligence that can make the invisible more visible, detect true motives, and discern the malevolent from the benevolent.

To do this right when the time comes, or preferably beforehand, the policymakers and general public need to recognize and then comprehend the fact that neither the threat nor the infrastructure built to address the threat is imaginary. Also, that terrorists are not only those who would kill but also those who would provide material support, or war criminals who would hide. For all its life, the American campaign to mitigate the prospect that jihadists would do to America what they finally did to Europe operated under a cloak of secrecy so impenetrable that just the idea of its purpose became something like a butt of jokes. There was a time some months before 9/11 when US intelligence picked up reporting that al-Qaeda terrorists were going to fly planes into American skyscrapers at some unspecified future date and place. No one in leadership took it too seriously, and it is easy to even imagine that some in leadership laughed or smirked at this report. That sort of sentiment can be especially fatal in the arenas of homeland security and public safety; when it comes to schemes a little outside the box, creative bad guys usually end up getting the last laugh.

I am not oblivious to concerns that this book might expose too much to the wrong people, that it could provide an evasion roadmap for those best taken by surprise. As a former law enforcement intelligence official, I know firsthand and greatly respect the need for protecting strategies and tactics from the bad guys these are designed to ensnare. But when I saw the national media punditry class excoriate and mock Donald Trump's late-2018, early-2019 claims that this migration form presented a threat in the American theater, I knew the nation had driven too far off track at the very wrong time. I and many others who labor in classified rooms knew that an American border war machine had been built for a concrete purpose. It just became a victim of its own success in preventing jihadist attack, the continued absence of which allowed a perception to linger that it wasn't needed, in the same way that flooding cops onto an urban drug-trafficking corner does. The drug trafficking disappears for a while. But take the cops away and it reappears.

If denialism-related neglect had produced the growing imperfections and flaws I've described in these pages about this aging covert border campaign, I knew that continued secrecy eventually would favor the bad guys. It is at times like these that light is necessary. The light of broad public knowledge can only bring appreciation for what the campaign has done, which in turn, can foster restoration and refurbishment of its protective function. When the terrorists know the weapon is burnished and aimed, perhaps they'll think twice.

ACKNOWLEDGMENTS

They say writing a book is a labor of love, but this first experience showed it to be a labor of other variables besides.

Collecting the material over a long time span, often in foreign countries ranging from Syria to Guatemala, required the support of editors and bosses. These people cleared time for me to write and space in their pages for running reportage that was often out there all alone on the edge. For all that and the encouragement to just get it written, Mark Krikorian, Executive Director of the Center for Immigration Studies, has my sincerest gratitude. Thanks goes to editor Bernadette Serton for her thirty-thousand-foot-high oversight, vision, and the hard deadlines.

My work in Central America would not have been possible without the expert translations, interpretations, reportorial instinct, and sound field judgement of the Guatemalan journalist Carlos Duarte. For all of that and for keeping us out of trouble several times, Carlos also deserves special thanks for having endured many weeks in close-quarters jungle and urban travel with me through four countries. Along these lines, heartfelt thanks also goes to the Pulitzer Prize-winning author and fellow border rat Jerry Kammer for not only the safety lifeline back home during my travels, but also for the encouragement and expert advice.

The book wouldn't be what it is without the government homeland security worker bees who trusted me to handle sensitive, protected information about the topic. They know who they are. Thank you.

Quite separately, I thank the brave and tenacious men and women of Immigration and Customs Enforcement's Homeland Security Investigations stationed in foreign posts doing this counterterrorism work, as well as those of Customs and Border Protection and the FBI. They are the ones who have suffered the paper cuts when American media insisted insists their work and achievements never happened. Whether or not readers come to appreciate them after seeing their unheralded exploits revealed in these pages, they have at least my heartfelt gratitude for keeping *my* family safer.

Which brings me to them. Nothing at all would be possible without the devoted support of my wife and our two children. They have most of my gratitude, with love, for putting up with long physical absences and the other kind that happens during book writing.

ENDNOTES

Introduction

1. Donald J. Trump (@realDonaldTrump), Twitter, October 22, 2018, 5:37 a.m., https://twitter.com/realDonaldTrump/status/105435107 8328885248; Oval Office press conference statements, October 23 2018, Youtube at 2715 and 29:33, https://www.youtube.com/watch?v=roNkQP8pfq8&feature=youtu.be.

2. Abby Ohlheiser and Lindsay Bever, "How an Old Far-Right Meme about Muslim 'Prayer Rugs' at the Border Became a Trump Tweet," *Washington Post*, January 18, 2019, https://www.washingtonpost.com/technology/2019/01/18/how-an-old-far-right-meme-about-muslim-prayer-rugs-border-became-trump-tweet/.

3. Linda Qiu, "Trump's Baseless Claim about Muslim Prayer Rugs Found at the Border," *New York Times*, January 18, 2019, https://www.nytimes.com/2019/01/18/us/politics/fact-check-trump-prayer-rugs-border.html.

4. Johnathan Silver, "Beto O'Rourke: 'Zero' Terrorists or Plots against Americans Connected to U.S.-Mexico Border," PolitiFact, May 3, 2018, https://www.politifact.com/texas/statements/2018/may/03/beto-orourke/beto-orourke-zero-terrorists-harm-Americans-Mexico/; Brady McCombs and Tim Steller, "Border Seen as Unlikely Terrorist Crossing Point," *Arizona Daily Star*, June 7, 2011, https://tucson.com/news/local/border/border-seen-as-unlikely-terrorist-crossing-point/article_ed932aa2-9d2a-54f1-b930-85f5d4cce9a8.html.

5. Josh Feldman, "Jeff Flake Responds to Trump's 'Unknown Middle Easterners' Tweet: 'A Canard and a Fear Tactic,'" Mediaite, October 22, 2018, https://www.mediaite.com/online/jeff-flake-responds-to-trumps-unknown-middle-easterners-tweet-a-canard-and-a-fear-tactic/.

6   Aaron Rupar, "Trump's Unfounded Tweet Stoking Fears about Muslim 'Prayer Rugs' Explained," Vox News, January 18, 2019, https://www.vox.com/2019/1/18/18188476/trump-muslim-prayer-rugs-tweet-border.

Chapter One

1   Anthony Faiola and Souad Mekhennet, "Tracing the Path of Four Terrorists Sent to Europe by the Islamic State," *Washington Post,* April 22, 2016, https://www.washingtonpost.com/world/national-security/how-europes-migrant-crisis-became-an-opportunity-for-isis/2016/04/21/ec8a7231-062d-4185-bb27-cc7295d35415_story.html.

2   Steven Erlanger, "Brussels Attacks Fuel Debate over Migrants in a Fractured Europe," *New York Times,* March 22, 2016, https://www.nytimes.com/2016/03/23/world/europe/belgium-attacks-migrants.html.

3   "Paris Attacks: Authorities Piece Together Identities of Attackers; Syrian Passport Found Next to Dead Bomber," Australian Broadcasting Corporation, November 15, 2015, https://www.abc.net.au/news/2015-11-15/details-emerge-about-paris-attackers-syrian-passport-found/6941864?nw=0.

4   Jean-Charles Brisard and Kevin Jackson, "The Islamic State's External Operations and the French-Belgian Nexus," *Combating Terrorism Center Sentinel* 9, issue 11 (December 2016): 8, https://ctc.usma.edu/wp-content/uploads/2016/11/CTC-Sentinel_Vol9Iss1113.pdf; Rukmini Callimachi, "How ISIS Built the Machinery of Terror Under Europe's Gaze," *New York Times,* March 29, 2016, https://www.nytimes.com/2016/03/29/world/europe/isis-attacks-paris-brussels.html.

5   Faiola and Mekhennet, "Tracing the Path," 2; John Stevens, "How the Paris Bomber Sneaked into Europe: Terrorist Posing as a Refugee Was Arrested and Fingerprinted in Greece—Then Given Travel Papers and Sent on His Way to Carry Out Suicide Bombing in France," *Daily Mail* (UK), November 16, 2015, https://www.dailymail.co.uk/news/article-3320272/Paris-bomber-sneaked-Europe-posing-refugee-Greece-arrival-given-travel-papers-officials-admit-damning-expose-EU-s-open-borders-policy.html.

6   Stevens, "How Paris Bomber Sneaked into Europe,"; Erlanger, "Brussels Attack," 2; Isabel Hunter, "Master Bombmaker Who Posed as Migrant and Attacked Paris Last Year Is Now Chief Suspect in Belgian Atrocity as

Police Swoop on Home District," *Daily Mail*, March 22, 2016, https://www.dailymail.co.uk/news/article-3504920/Master-bombmaker-posed-migrant-attacked-Paris-year-chief-suspect-Belgian-atrocity-police-swoop-home-district.html.

7   Callimachi, "How ISIS Built the Machinery," 15.

8   Paul Cruickshank, "Raid on ISIS Suspect in the French Riviera," CNN, August 28, 2014, https://www.cnn.com/2014/08/28/world/europe/france-suspected-isis-link/index.html.

9   Ibid; "Belgium Puts Verviers Terror Cell Suspects on Trial," BBC News, May 9, 2016, https://www.bbc.com/news/world-europe-36245504.

10   Aaron Blake, "Analysis | The GOP's Pernicious Link between Terrorism and the Border Wall," *Washington Post*, January 4, 2019, https://www.washingtonpost.com/politics/2019/01/04/gops-pernicious-link-between-terrorism-border-wall/.

11   Sam Mullins, *Jihadist Infiltration of Migrant Flows to Europe: Perpetrators, Modus Operandi and Policy Implications*, (London: Palgrave Macmillan, 2019), https://www.amazon.com/Jihadist-Infiltration-Migrant-Flows-Europe/dp/3030133370.

12   Todd Bensman, "What Terrorist Migration Over European Borders Can Teach about American Border Security," Center for Immigration Security, November 6, 2019, cis.org/Report/Terrorist-Migration-Over-European-Borders.

13   Ibid.; Jean-Charles Brisard and Kevin Jackson, "Islamic State's External Operations," *Combating Terrorism Center Sentinel*, 12; Ibid.; Bensman, "What Terrorist Migration Over European Borders."

14   Robin Simcox, "The Asylum—Terror Nexus: How Europe Should Respond," Heritage Foundation, June 18, 2018, www.heritage.org/terrorism/report/the-asylum-terror-nexus-how-europe-should-respond; "Risk Analysis for 2018" https://www.europol.europa.eu/activities-services/main-reports/european-union-terrorism-situation-and-trend-report-2018-tesat-2018.

15   "'Riesige Dimensionen': Mutmaßliche IS-Terrorzelle in NRW Ausgehoben," *Frankfurter Allgemeine Zeitung*, April 15, 2020, www.faz.net/aktuell/politik/inland/mutmassliche-is-terrorzelle-in-nrw-ausgehoben-16725855.html; Deutsche Welle, "Germany Arrests IS Suspects Plotting Attacks on US Bases," April 15, 2020, https://

www.dw.com/en/germany-arrests-is-suspects-plotting-attacks-on-us-bases/a-53129563.

16   Gerard Couzens, "Killer Busted Brit ISIS Rapper Who Loved Selfies with Decapitated Heads Snuck into Spain by Boat Posing as a Desperate Migrant," *The Sun* (UK), April 22, 2020, https://www.thesun.co.uk/news/11456844/brit-isis-rapper-severed-heads-spain-posing-migrant/; "Islamic State: Rapper Lyricist Jinn Arrested by Police in Spain," BBC News, April 21, 2020, https://www.bbc.com/news/uk-england-london-52374784; "Adel Abdul Bary Pleads Guilty in US Embassy Bombings," BBC News, September 20, 2014, https://www.bbc.com/news/world-us-canada-29282510; Gerard Couzens and Nick Fagge, "British 'Jihadi Rapper' Was 'Snuck into Spain by Boat after Posing as an Undocumented Migrant,'" *Daily Mail Online*, April 21, 2020, https://www.dailymail.co.uk/news/article-8242983/British-jihadi-rapper-snuck-Spain-boat-posing-undocumented-migrant.html.

17   "Police to Investigate Terrorism Link after 2 Die in Knife Attack in Southeast France," RFI, April 5, 2020, http://www.rfi.fr/en/france/20200405-police-to-investigate-terrorism-link-after-2-die-in-knife-attack-in-southeast-france.

18   "Three Sudanese Arrested over French 'Terror' Stabbing," France 24 News, May 4, 2020, https://www.france24.com/en/20200405-three-sudanese-arrested-over-french-terror-stabbing; Peter Allen, "Three Sudanese Refugees Held after Terror Attack in French Town on Coronavirus Lockdown That Left Two Dead and Seven Severely Wounded," *Daily Mail*, April 5, 2020, https://www.dailymail.co.uk/news/article-8189351/Three-Sudanese-refugees-held-terror-attack-French-town-coronavirus-lockdown.html.

19   Frank Jansen, Julius Betschka, and Alexander Frohlich, "Drivers in psychiatry after Berlin autobahn attack," Der Spiegel, August 19, 2020, https://www.tagesspiegel.de/berlin/polizei-justiz/mehrere-verletzte-auf-berliner-a100-fahrer-nach-berliner-autobahn-anschlag-in-psychiatrie/26106672.html

20   Frank Jansen, "Sarmad A. – between fanaticism and mental disorder," Der Spiegel, https://www.tagesspiegel.de/berlin/wer-ist-der-taeter-von-der-berliner-stadtautobahn-sarmad-a-zwischen-fanatismus-und-psychischer-stoerung/26108906.html

21   "*Christian Science Monitor* Breakfast with James Clapper," C-SPAN, April 25, 2016, https://www.c-span.org/video/?408624-1/christian-science-monitor-breakfast-james-clapper, minute 31:16 and minute 39.

22   Adam Lebor, "Angela Merkel: Europe's Conscience in the Face of a Refugee Crisis," *Newsweek*, August 5, 2015, https://www.newsweek.com/2015/09/18/angela-merkel-europe-refugee-crisis-conscience-369053.html.

23   Heather Horn, "The Scale of the Refugee Crisis in Germany Is Staggering," *The Atlantic*, September 14, 2015, https://www.theatlantic.com/international/archive/2015/09/germany-merkel-refugee-asylum/405058/; Karl Vick, "TIME Person of the Year 2015: Angela Merkel." *Time*, 2015, time.com/time-person-of-the-year-2015-angela-merkel/.

24   Ibid.

25   Reuters in Berlin, "Angela Merkel Stands by Refugee Policy Despite Security Fears," *Guardian*, November 25, 2015, https://www.theguardian.com/world/2015/nov/25/angela-merkel-stands-by-refugee-policy-syria-despite-security-fears.

26   Marcus Walker and Anton Troianovski, "Behind Angela Merkel's Open Door for Migrants," *Wall Street Journal*, December 9, 2015, https://www.wsj.com/articles/behind-angela-merkels-open-door-for-migrants-1449712113.

27   Anton Troianovski, "Paris Attacks May Unsettle EU's Debate on Migration," *Wall Street Journal*, November 14, 2015, https://www.wsj.com/articles/paris-attacks-may-unsettle-eus-debate-on-migration-1447510975?mod=article_inline.

28   Reuters, "Angela Merkel," 8.

29   Axel Von Spilcker, "Er Bastelte Schon Das Bekennerfoto! 16-Jähriger Syrer Bekam Bombenanleitung Im Chat," FOCUS Online, December 4, 2016, https://www.focus.de/politik/deutschland/16-jaehriger-islamist-stelle-bomben-her-und-lass-sie-bei-euch-explodieren_id_6293689.html; www.zeit.de/zustimmung?url=https%3A%2F%2Fwww.zeit.de%2Fgesellschaft%2Fzeitgeschehen%2F2017-04%2Flandgericht-koeln-fluechtling-terror-anschlags-planung-jugendstrafe.

30   "Anis Amri," Counter Extremism Project extremism database, https://www.counterextremism.com/extremists/anis-amri.

31   Melissa Eddy, "One Dead in Knife Attack at German Supermarket," *New York Times*, July 28, 2017, https://www.nytimes.com/2017/07/28/world/europe/one-dead-in-knife-attack-at-hamburg-supermarket.html.

32   Anton Troianovski, "Hamburg Stabbing Suspect Is Known Islamist, German Authorities Say," *Wall Street Journal*, July 30, 2017, https://www.wsj.com/articles/hamburg-stabbing-suspect-is-known-islamist-german-authorities-say-1501332136?mod=e2tw.

33   Melissa Eddy, "Germany Arrests 2 Syrians on Terrorism Charges," *New York Times*, March 2, 2017, https://www.nytimes.com/2017/03/02/world/europe/germany-arrests-terrorism-nusra-front.html.

34   Melissa Eddy, "Afghan Teenager Spoke of Friend's Death Before Ax Attack in Germany," *New York Times*, July 19, 2016, https://www.nytimes.com/2016/07/20/world/europe/germany-train-ax-attack.html.

35   Kirsten Grieshaber, David Rising, and David McHugh, "Refugee Teen in German Train Attack Seemed to Be Adjusting," Associated Press, July 20, 2016, apnews.com/437f6d6e83d64c028a4717b2df5c44d3.

36   Jennifer Newton and Allan Hall, "ISIS Train Axe Attacker Is a 'Pakistani' Who LIED about Being Afghan to Get Higher Immigration Status in Germany—as He Is Pictured at a Music Festival Wearing a Pink Wig," *Daily Mail Online*, July 20, 2016, https://www.dailymail.co.uk/news/article-3698818/Did-ISIS-axe-attacker-LIE-Afghanistan-Claims-train-jihadi-hid-Pakistani-background-higher-immigration-status-Germany.html.

37   Dragana Jovanovic and Bill Hutchinson, "Suspect in Stabbing of 2 Americans in Amsterdam Claims He Was Seeking Vengeance for the Prophet Muhammad: Prosecutors," ABC News, September 3, 2018, abcnews.go.com/US/man-suspected-terrorist-motive-stabbing-american-tourists-amsterdam/story?id=57572294.

38   Associated Press, "Islamic State Suspects Face Terrorism Charges in Germany," *Oklahoman*, March 8, 2017, oklahoman.com/article/feed/1181080/islamic-state-suspects-face-terrorism-charges-in-germany.

39   Anthony Faiola, "Germany Arrests 3 Suspected Syrian Terrorists, Foils Possible Islamic State Plot," *Washington Post*, June 2, 2016, https://www.washingtonpost.com/world/europe/germany-arrests-3-suspected-syrian-terrorists-foils-alleged-islamic-state-plot/2016/06/02/31e29767-6df7-496b-aa47-5b8911459f13_story.html.

40 Allan Hall, "Police Arrest Suspect Who Planned Terrorist Atrocity after Seeking Sanctuary in Germany," Express.co.uk, August 11, 2016, https://www.express.co.uk/news/world/698831/refugee-suspect-terrorist-plot-seeking-sanctuary-Germany.

41 Ruth Bender, "Germany Accuses Asylum Seeker of Aiding Paris Attacks Leader," *Wall Street Journal*, July 7, 2016, https://www.wsj.com/articles/germany-accuses-asylum-seeker-of-aiding-paris-attacks-leader-1467904592.

42 Rukmini Callimachi, Alissa J. Rubin, and Laure Fourquet, "A View of ISIS's Evolution in New Details of Paris Attacks," *New York Times*, March 20, 2016, https://www.nytimes.com/2016/03/20/world/europe/a-view-of-isiss-evolution-in-new-details-of-paris-attacks.html.

43 Marco Pasciuti, "Attack in Barcelona, the Name of Ahmad Alkhald Appears: 'He Made the Bombs Used for the Massacres of Paris and Brussels'" (translated from Italian), *Il Fatto Quotidiano*, August 22, 2017, https://www.ilfattoquotidiano.it/2017/08/22/attentato-barcellona-spunta-il-nome-di-ahmad-alkhald-confeziono-le-bombe-usate-per-le-stragi-di-parigi-e-bruxelles/3807136/.

44 "Attacks in Paris and Brussels: The Main Explosive Device on an American List of 'Terrorists,'" Europe 1 News (translated from French), August 17, 2017, https://www.europe1.fr/international/attentats-de-paris-et-bruxelles-le-principal-artificier-sur-une-liste-americaine-de-terroristes-3413507.

45 "State Department Terrorist Designations of Ahmad Alkhald and Abu Yahya Al-Iraqi," US Department of State, April 29, 2020, https://www.state.gov/state-department-terrorist-designations-of-ahmad-alkhald-and-abu-yahya-al-iraqi/.

46 "German Police Arrest Three Iraqi Refugees on Suspicion of Islamist Bomb Plot," *Telegraph*, January 30, 2019, https://www.telegraph.co.uk/news/2019/01/30/german-police-arrest-three-iraqi-refugees-suspicion-islamist/.

47 Christophe Bourdoiseau, "Berlin: a driver causes several accidents, a 'probably Islamist attack,'" Le Parisien newspaper, August 19, 2020, https://www.leparisien.fr/faits-divers/berlin-un-chauffard-provoque-plusieurs-accidents-un-acte-islamiste-19-08-2020-8369955.php

48 Ibid.

49   Lisa Ferdinando, "Breedlove: European Security Situation 'Serious,' 'Complicated,'" US Department of Defense, March 1, 2016, https://www.defense.gov/Explore/News/Article/Article/683569/ breedlove-european-security-situation-serious-complicated/.

50   Julia Gelatt, "Schengen and the Free Movement of People across Europe," Migratory Policy Institute, October 1, 2005, http://www.migrationpolicy.org/article/schengen-and-free-movement-people-across-europe; "Roles and Responsibilities," Frontex, http://frontex.europa.eu/operations/roles-and-responsibilities.

51   "European Border and Coast Guard Agency Risk Analysis for 2018," Frontex, page 8, https://reliefweb.int/sites/reliefweb.int/files/resources/ Risk_Analysis_for_2018.pdf.

52   "The Future of Schengen," European Council on Foreign Relations, https://www.ecfr.eu/specials/scorecard/schengen_flash_scorecard; "How Costly Would Inner-European Border Controls Be?" Deutsche Welle, December 7, 2018, https://www.dw.com/en/how-costly-would-inner-european-border-controls-be/a-44647255; "Temporary Reintroduction of Border Control," Migration and Home Affairs— European Commission, December 6, 2016, ec.europa.eu/home-affairs/ what-we-do/policies/borders-and-visas/schengen/reintroduction-border-control_en; Erlinger, "Brussels Attacks Fuel," 2.

53   Elizabeth Pineau, "Hollande Opens French Doors to Refugees Despite Opposition," Reuters, September 7, 2015, https://www.reuters.com/ article/us-europe-migrants-france/hollande-opens-french-doors-to-refugees-despite-opposition-idUSKCN0R70WC20150907.

54   Andrew Higgins, "Belgium Confronts the Jihadist Danger Within," *New York Times*, January 24, 2015, https://www.nytimes.com/2015/01/25/ world/europe/belgium-confronts-the-jihadist-danger-within.html.

55   "France Thalys Train Attack Gunman Was 'Unable to Kill,'" BBC News, May 9, 2018, https://www.bbc.com/news/world-europe-44053410; Ruth Bender, "Germany Accuses Asylum Seeker of Aiding Paris Attacks Leader," *Wall Street Journal*, July 7, 2016, https://www.wsj. com/articles/germany-accuses-asylum-seeker-of-aiding-paris-attacks-leader-1467904592.

56   Jean-Charles Brisard and Kevin Jackson, "The Islamic State's External Operations and the French-Belgian Nexus," *Combating Terrorism Center Sentinel* 9, issue 11 (December 2016).

57   Steven Erlanger, "Profile Emerges of Suspect in Attack on Train to Paris," *New York Times*, August 22, 2015, https://www.nytimes.com/2015/08/23/world/europe/thalys-train-attack-france-moroccan-suspect.html; "France Train Shooting Suspect Profile: Ayoub El-Khazzani," BBC News, August 25, 2015, https://www.bbc.com/news/world-europe-34032218.

58   Leigh Thomas and Gerard Bon, "Tapped Phone Led Paris Attack Leader to His Death," Reuters, November 21, 2015, uk.reuters.com/article/uk-france-shooting/tapped-phone-led-paris-attack-leader-to-his-death-idUKKCN0T40DY20151121.

59   "France Arrests Man in 'Advanced Stages' of Terror Plot," CBS News, March 25, 2016, https://www.cbsnews.com/news/france-arrests-man-in-advanced-stages-of-terror-plot/.

60   Aurelien Breeden, "Attack at Marseille Train Station Leaves 2 Women Dead," *New York Times*, October 1, 2017, https://www.nytimes.com/2017/10/01/world/europe/knife-attack-marseille.html.

61   "Marco Orioles, "Anis Hanachi, Who Is the Brother of the Terrorist ISIS of the Marseilles Attack," *Formiche*, October 10, 2017 (translated from Italian), https://formiche.net/2017/10/anis-isis-marsiglia/; "Brother of Marseilles Attacker Was Foreign Fighter in Syria," Thelocal.it, October 9, 2017, https://www.thelocal.it/20171009/brother-of-marseilles-attacker-was-foreign-fighter-in-syria.

62   "Anti-terrorist Call in Brest. The seven suspects indicted and imprisoned," *Ouest-France*, January 20, 2020, https://www.ouest-france.fr/societe/police/coup-de-filet-antiterroriste-brest-les-suspects-transferes-au-siege-de-la-dgsi-6703514; "Brother of Marseille Attacker Fought in Syria: Police," Agence France-Presse, https://www.arabnews.com/node/1175006/world.

63   "Anti-terrorism strike in BrestLe Syrien Arrêté à Brest Soupçonné D'avoir Appartenu à L'État Islamique," *Le Télégramme*, January 23, 2020, https://www.letelegramme.fr/bretagne/le-syrien-arrete-a-brest-soupconne-d-avoir-appartenu-a-l-etat-islamique-23-01-2020-12485879.php; "Anti-terrorist Call in Brest."

64   Sports+, DH Les, "Coup De Filet Antiterroriste En France: Sept Hommes Interpellés," Retour à La Page D'accueil, January 22, 2020, https://www.rtbf.be/info/monde/detail_coup-de-filet-antiterroriste-en-france-sept-hommes-interpelles?id=10412725.

65 "National Strategy for Counterterrorism of the United States of America," White House, October 2018, p. 8, https://www.whitehouse.gov/wp-content/uploads/2018/10/NSCT.pdf.

66 Anna Ercanbrack and Jussi Rosendahl, "Finland's Millionaire Prime Minister Offers His Home to Refugees," Reuters, September 5, 2015, in.reuters.com/article/europe-migrants-finland-pm/finlands-millionaire-prime-minister-offers-his-home-to-refugees-idINKCN0R50RT20150905.

67 Reuters, "Finland's Prime Minister Offers His Home to Refugees," Huffington Post, September 5, 2015, https://www.huffpost.com/entry/finland-prime-minister-offers-home-refugees_n_55eaee42e4b093be51bbaa81.

68 Finish Immigration Service, https://statistics.migri.fi/index.html#decisions?start=553&end=564.

69 "Finnish Court Names Knife Attack Suspect as Abderrahman Mechkah," *Guardian*, August 21 2017, https://www.theguardian.com/world/2017/aug/21/finnish-court-names-knife-attack-suspect-abderrahman-mechkah.

70 Sewell Chan and Mikko Takkunen, "Finland Attack Suspect, a Moroccan Youth, Was Flagged for Extremist Views," *New York Times*, August 21, 2017, https://www.nytimes.com/2017/08/21/world/europe/finland-turku-abderrahman-mechkah.html.

71 "Finnish Court Names Knife Attack Suspect"; "Moroccan Asylum Seeker 'Targeted Women' in Finland Terror Stabbing," *Straits Times*, August 19, 2017, https://www.straitstimes.com/world/europe/moroccan-asylum-seeker-targeted-women-in-finland-terror-stabbing.

72 "Four Suspects Remanded in Custody over Turku Knife Attack, One Man Freed," YLE (Finland), August 23, 2017, https://yle.fi/uutiset/osasto/news/four_suspects_remanded_in_custody_over_turku_knife_attack_one_man_freed/9790767.

73 "Finland: Extremism & Counter-Extremism, Counter Extremism Project," publication date unknown, https://www.counterextremism.com/countries/finland.

74 Tony Barber, "Stefan Löfven Rebukes Eastern Europe over Refugee Crisis," *Financial Times*, November 3, 2015, https://www.ft.com/content/108f9de6-8209-11e5-a01c-8650859a4767.

75 "Radicalized Uzbek Akilov to Address Court over Stockholm Terror Attack," The Local (Sweden), February 20, 2018, https://www.thelocal.se/20180220/radicalised-uzbek-akilov-to-address-court-over-stockholm-terror-attack.

76 "Stockholm Truck Attack: Who Is Rakhmat Akilov?" BBC News, June 7, 2018, https://www.bbc.com/news/world-europe-39552691.

77 Tore Hamming, "The 2016 Copenhagen 'Matchstick' Terror Plot and the Evolving Transnational Character of Terrorism in the West," Combating Terrorism Center at West Point, February 28, 2020, ctc.usma.edu/2016-copenhagen-matchstick-terror-plot-evolving-transnational-character-terrorism-west/.

78 Ibid.

79 "ISIS Claims Unremarked Arson Attack in Malmö," The Local, 2016, https://www.thelocal.se/20161021/isis-claims-swedish-arson-attack-that.

80 "Malmö Man Found Guilty in Denmark 'Matchstick' Terror Case," The Local, 2019, https://www.thelocal.com/20190411/malm-man-found-guilty-in-denmarks-matchstick-terror-case.

81 "Denmark: Syrian Man Gets Jail for Terror Planning," Associated Press, May 20, 2019, https://apnews.com/01c22598b8ac47eab3932bcdb6f54a6b.

82 *European Union Europol Terrorism Situation and Trend Report 2017*, page 14, https://www.europol.europa.eu/activities-services/main-reports/eu-terrorism-situation-and-trend-report-te-sat-2017.

83 *European Union Europol Terrorism Situation and Trend Report 2018*, page 28, https://www.europol.europa.eu/activities-services/main-reports/european-union-terrorism-situation-and-trend-report-2018-tesat-2018.

84 "Sweden: Extremism & Counter-Extremism." Counter Extremism Project, https://www.counterextremism.com/countries/sweden.

85 Luke Harding, "Refugees Welcome? How UK and Germany Compare on Migration," *Guardian*, September 2, 2015, https://www.theguardian.com/world/2015/sep/02/refugees-welcome-uk-germany-compare-migration.

86 Alex Massie, "How Terror Threatens the EU," *Slate*, March 25, 2016, https://slate.com/news-and-politics/2016/03/brussels-brexit-and-the-future-of-the-european-union.html; Ned Simons, "Brexit Will Keep UK Safer from ISIS Terror, Says Justice Minister Dominic Raab in EU Referendum Speech," Huffington Post, March 29, 2016, https://consent.

yahoo.com/v2/collectConsent?sessionId=2_cc-session_9a46efec-403d-4c57-ae9b-2181d0880377; Barcelona Centre for International Affairs, "Brexit: Causes and Consequences," October 20, 2016, https://www.cidob.org/en/publications/publication_series/notes_internacionals/n1_159/brexit_causes_and_consequences; Robert. Hutton, "The Roots of Brexit," Bloomberg News, March 20, 2019, https://www.bloomberg.com/quicktake/will-uk-leave-eu.

87 *Frontex Risk Analysis for 2020*, Risk Analysis Unit, reference number 1218/2020, p. 54, March 2020, https://frontex.europa.eu/assets/Publications/Risk_Analysis/Risk_Analysis/Annual_Risk_Analysis_2020.pdf.

88 William Booth and James McAuley, "Britain deploys military drones to stop migrants in rafts from crossing English Channel," *Washington Post*, September 3, 2020, https://www.washingtonpost.com/world/europe/britain-deploys-military-drones-to-stop-migrants-in-rafts-from-crossing-english-channel/2020/09/03/0709643c-edf7-11ea-bd08-1b10132b458f_story.html; "Migrants could die crossing Channel, ex-chief inspector warns," BBC, May 30, 2016, https://www.bbc.com/news/uk-36410828.

89 Ian Cobain, "'A Duty to Hate Britain': The Anger of Tube Bomber Ahmed Hassan," *Guardian*, March 16, 2018, https://www.theguardian.com/uk-news/2018/mar/16/a-duty-to-hate-britain-the-anger-of-tube-bomber-ahmed-hassan.

90 Ibid.

91 Seth Jacobson, "Foster Carers of Parsons Green Tube Bomber Sue Council for Negligence," *Guardian*, March 8, 2019, https://www.theguardian.com/uk-news/2019/mar/08/foster-carers-of-parsons-green-tube-bomber-ahmed-hassan-sue-council-for-negligence.

92 Patrick Grafton-Green, "Tube Bombing Suspect Said 'It's My Duty to Hate Britain,' Court Hears," *Evening Standard*, March 12, 2018, https://www.standard.co.uk/news/crime/parsons-green-bombing-suspect-told-mentor-its-my-duty-to-hate-britain-court-hears-a3787986.html.

93 Emma Snaith, "Man Who Plotted Terrorist Attack Using Explosive Driverless Car Jailed for 15 Years," *The Independent*, July 24, 2019, https://www.independent.co.uk/news/uk/crime/farhad-salah-trial-sheffield-bomb-terror-attack-jail-driverless-car-a9019006.html.

94   "Driverless car bomb plot man Farhad Salah found guilty," BBC News, July 12, 2019, https://www.bbc.com/news/uk-england-south-yorkshire-48924715.

95   "Farhad Salah Jailed over Driverless Car Bomb Plot," BBC News, July 24, 2019, https://www.bbc.com/news/uk-england-south-yorkshire-49095955.

96   Todd Bensman, "ISIS Commander Arrested in Hungary Held Refugee Passport Enabling Unrestricted Air Travel," Pjmedia.com, May 19, 2020, pjmedia.com/homeland-security/todd-bensman/2019/03/25/isis-commander-arrested-in-hungary-held-refugee-passport-enabling-unrestricted-air-travel-n101439.

97   Chris Pleasance, "ISIS 'Butcher' Is Charged with Crimes against Humanity in Hungary," *Daily Mail Online* and Reuters, September 3, 2019, https://www.dailymail.co.uk/news/article-7422187/ISIS-butcher-charged-crimes-against-humanity-Hungary.html.

98   "Syrian Hassan F Accused of Mass Murders Denies Charges," Hungary Today, November 13, 2019, https://hungarytoday.hu/syrian-hassan-f-terrorist-murder-charges/; Sandor Pedo, "Hungary Detains Syrian Islamic State Member Accused of Killings," Reuters, March 22, 2019, https://www.reuters.com/article/us-hungary-isis/hungary-detains-syrian-islamic-state-member-accused-of-killings-idUSKCN1R31PQ.

99   "COMMENTARY—Turkey Intel-Linked ISIL Man Posed as a Refugee, Went through Greece, Registered in Germany," Stockholm Center for Freedom, May 11, 2017, stockholmcf.org/turkey-intel-linked-isil-man-posed-as-a-refugee-went-through-greece-registered-in-germany/; "Aggravated Life Sentence for 9 Suspects in Ankara Massacre Case," ANF News, August 3, 2018, anfenglishmobile.com/news/aggravated-life-sentence-for-9-suspects-in-ankara-massacre-case-28717.

100 Thomas Pany, "Kriegsverbrechen: Bundesanwaltschaft Geht Gegen Al-Nusra-Mitglieder in Deutschland Vor," Heise Online, June 12, 1970, https://www.heise.de/tp/features/Kriegsverbrechen-Bundesanwaltschaft-geht-gegen-al-Nusra-Mitglieder-in-Deutschland-vor-3741658.html; "Al Nusra Member Committed Suicide in Prison," ANF News, August 31 2017, anfenglishmobile.com/news/al-nusra-member-committed-suicide-in-prison-21856.

101 "Finland Detains Iraqi Twins over IS Massacre in Tikrit," BBC News, December 10, 2015, https://www.bbc.com/news/world-

europe-35067187; "Finland: Extremism & Counter-Extremism," Counter Extremism Project, August 21, 2017, https://www.counterextremism.com/countries/finland.

102 Alison Smale, "Iraqis' Arrest in Finland Highlights Difficulties in Prosecuting Distant Crimes," *New York Times*, December 24, 2015, https://www.nytimes.com/2015/12/25/world/europe/finland-iraq-refugees-isis.html.

103 Alexi Teivainen, "Finnish Court Acquits Iraqi Twins of Massacre Charges," *Helsinki Times*, May 26, 2017, https://www.helsinkitimes.fi/finland/finland-news/domestic/14782-iraqi-twins-acquitted-of-massacre-charges-by-finnish-court.html.

104 John Mueller and Mark Stewart, "Terrorism and Bathtubs: Comparing and Assessing the Risks," presented at annual convention of American Pohttps://www.heise.de/tp/features/Kriegsverbrechen-Bundesanwaltschaft-geht-gegen-al-Nusra-Mitglieder-in-Deutschland-vor-3741658.htmllitical Science Convention, August 13, 2018; Alex Nowrasteh, "Terrorists by Immigration Status and Nationality: A Risk Analysis, 1975–2017," Cato Institute, May 7, 2019, https://www.cato.org/publications/policy-analysis/terrorists-immigration-status-nationality-risk-analysis-1975-2017; Alex Nowrasteh, "Center for Immigration Studies Shows a Very Small Threat from Terrorists Crossing the Mexican Border," Cato Institute, November 28, 2018, https://www.cato.org/blog/center-immigration-studies-shows-very-small-threat-terrorists-crossing-mexican-border.

105 "Counter-Terrorism Module 14 Key Issues: Effects of Terrorism, 2018," United Nations Office of Drugs and Crimes, https://www.unodc.org/e4j/en/terrorism/module-14/key-issues/effects-of-terrorism.html; Marco Hafner et al., "The Cost of Terrorism in Europe," RAND Corporation, 2018, https://www.rand.org/randeurope/research/projects/the-cost-of-terrorism-in-europe.html.

106 Ibid; "The Fight against Terrorism, Cost of Non-Europe Report," European Parliamentary Research Service, May 2018, p. 41, https://www.europarl.europa.eu/RegData/etudes/STUD/2018/621817/EPRS_STU(2018)621817_EN.pdf.

107 Richard Wike, Bruce Stokes, and Katie Simmons, "Europeans Fear Wave of Refugees Will Mean More Terrorism, Fewer Jobs," Pew Research Center's Global Attitudes Project, Pew Research Center, May

31, 2020, https://www.pewresearch.org/global/2016/07/11/europeans-fear-wave-of-refugees-will-mean-more-terrorism-fewer-jobs/.

[108] Ibid.

[109] "Autumn 2016 Standard Eurobarometer: Immigration and Terrorism Continue to Be Seen as the Most Important Issues Facing the EU," European Commission, December 22, 2016, ec.europa.eu/commission/presscorner/detail/en/IP_16_4493.

[110] Phillip Connor and Jens Manuel Krogstad, "Many Worldwide Oppose More Migration—Both into and out of Their Countries," Pew Research Center, December 10, 2018, https://www.pewresearch.org/fact-tank/2018/12/10/many-worldwide-oppose-more-migration-both-into-and-out-of-their-countries/.

[111] "A Majority of Europe's Voters Do Not Consider Migration to Be the Most Important Issue, According to Major New Poll," European Council on Foreign Relations, April 1, 2019, https://www.ecfr.eu/article/european_voters_do_not_consider_migration_most_important_election.

[112] "Some Schengen Countries Are Extending Internal Border Controls to Year's End," Schengenvisainfo News, April 13, 2020, https://www.schengenvisainfo.com/news/some-schengen-countries-are-extending-internal-border-controls-to-years-end/; "Germany extends border checks to halt refugees," The Local, October 13, 2015, https://www.thelocal.de/20151013/ministry-extends-border-controls-to-curb-refugee-flow; Johan Ahlander and Mansoor Yosufzai, "Sweden Intensifies Crackdown on Illegal Immigrants," Reuters, July 13, 2017, https://www.reuters.com/article/us-sweden-immigration-crackdown-idUSKBN19Y0G8.

[113] Paulina Neuding, "So Long to Swedish Political Stability," Politico, April 18, 2019, https://paulinaneuding.com/2018/09/10/politico-long-swedish-political-stability/; Jon Henley, "Sweden Gets New Government Four Months after Election," *Guardian*, January 18, 2019, https://www.theguardian.com/world/2019/jan/18/sweden-gets-new-government-more-than-four-months-after-election.

[114] "The Latest: Populist party amazed by Finland election result," the Associated Press, April 14, 2019, https://apnews.com/5d0c2d290dc14ce7a6519a184c1b12d3; "Social Democrats Claim Narrow Win over Populists in Finland Election," France 24, April 15, 2019, https://www.france24.com/en/20190414-social-democrats-

claim-narrow-win-over-populists-finns-party-finland-election; "Finland Elections: The World's Happiest Nation Is Slipping to the Far-Right," TRT World, April 22 2019, https://www.trtworld.com/ magazine/finland-elections-the-world-s-happiest-nation-is-slipping-to-the-far-right-26074.

115 Emily Schultheis, "What Right-Wing Populists Look Like in Norway," *The Atlantic*, September 12, 2017, https://www.theatlantic.com/ international/archive/2017/09/norway-progress-party-populism-immigration/539535/.

116 Martin Selsoe Sorensen, "Denmark Election Is Fueled by Anger on Climate and Immigration," *New York Times*, June 4, 2019, www. nytimes.com/2019/06/04/world/europe/denmark-election-climate-immigration.html; "Denmark's Left-Wing Bloc Triumphs in Election as Far Right Suffers Losses," The Local, 2019, https://www.thelocal. dk/20190606/denmarks-social-democrats.

117 James Reynolds, "Italy Election: What Does the Result Mean?" BBC News, March 5, 2018, https://www.bbc.com/news/world-europe-43291390; Ritula Shah, "Italian Election Dominated by Immigration Debate," BBC News, February 26, 2018, https://www. bbc.com/news/world-europe-43167699.

118 "The Future of Schengen," European Council on Foreign Relations, date unknown, https://www.ecfr.eu/specials/scorecard/schengen_ flash_scorecard; "How Costly Would Inner-European Border Controls Be?" Deutsche Welle, July 12, 2018, https://www.dw.com/en/ how-costly-would-inner-european-border-controls-be/a-44647255.

119 Todd Bensman, "Progress Report from Hungary's Fenced Borderlands," Center for Immigration Studies, April 3, 2019, CIS.org, 2019, cis.org/ Bensman/Progress-Report-Hungarys-Fenced-Borderlands.

120 "The Future of Schengen," European Commission Council on Foreign Relations, https://www.ecfr.eu/specials/scorecard/schengen_flash_ scorecard; "Temporary Reintroduction of Border Control," Migration and Home Affairs—European Commission, on December 6, 2016, ec.europa.eu/home-affairs/what-we-do/policies/borders-and-visas/ schengen/reintroduction-border-control_en; Ibid, Erlinger, "Brussels Attacks Fuel Debate Over Migrants in a Fractured Europe," *New York Times,* https://www.nytimes.com/2016/03/23/world/europe/belgium-attacks-migrants.html.

121 "Back to Schengen: Council Adopts Commission Proposal on Next Steps towards Lifting of Temporary Internal Border Controls," European Commission, May 12, 2016, ec.europa.eu/commission/presscorner/detail/en/IP_16_1723; Romina McGuinness, "Schengen REJECTED by France as Country Extends Border Checks Due to Terror Threat," *Express*, April 5, 2018, https://www.express.co.uk/news/world/941983/Schengen-France-identity-check-terrorist-threat-passport-European-Commision.

122 Ibid.; "Temporary Reintroduction of Border Control," European Commission Migration and Home Affairs website reflecting through 2020, https://ec.europa.eu/home-affairs/what-we-do/policies/borders-and-visas/schengen/reintroduction-border-control_en.

123 Ibid.; Romina McGuinness, "Schengen REJECTED by France as Country Extends Border Checks Due to Terror Threat," https://www.express.co.uk/news/world/941983/Schengen-France-identity-check-terrorist-threat-passport-European-Commision.

124 Alex Massie, "How Terror Threatens the EU," *Slate*, March 25, 2016, slate.com/news-and-politics/2016/03/brussels-brexit-and-the-future-of-the-european-union.html; Ned Simons, "Brexit Will Keep UK Safer from Isis Terror, Says Justice Minister Dominic Raab in EU Referendum Speech," HuffPost, March 29, 2016, consent.yahoo.com/collectConsent?sessionId=1_cc-session_9203db61-c117-4a1b-b5ff-00156279087f; Alan Riley and Francis Ghilès, "Brexit: Causes and Consequences," Barcelona Centre for International Affairs, October 2016, https://www.cidob.org/publicaciones/serie_de_publicacion/notes_|internacionals/n1_159/brexit_causes_and_consequences; Robert Hutton, "The Roots of Brexit," Bloomberg, May 8, 2015, https://www.bloomberg.com/quicktake/will-uk-leave-eu.

125 Olayinka Ajala, "Brexit and the Fight against Terrorism in the United Kingdom," E-International Relations, May 31, 2018, www.e-ir.info/2018/05/31/brexit-and-the-fight-against-terrorism-in-the-united-kingdom/; Riley and Ghilès, "Brexit: Causes and Consequences."

126 Matthew Goodwin and Caitlin Milazzo, "Taking Back Control? Investigating the Role of Immigration in the 2016 Vote for Brexit," *SAGE Journals*, June 8, 2017, journals.sagepub.com/doi/full/10.1177/1369148117710799.

127   John Mauldin, "3 Reasons Brits Voted For Brexit," *Forbes*, April 20, 2018, https://www.forbes.com/sites/johnmauldin/2016/07/05/3-reasons-brits-voted-for-brexit/#30e4ca9a1f9d.

128   Joanna Dawson, "Brexit: Implications for National Security," House of Commons Briefing Paper CBP7798, March 31, 2017.

129   "CSI Brexit 4: People's State Reasons for Voting Leave or Remain," Nuffield College's Center for Social Investigation, April 24, 2018, https://ukandeu.ac.uk/wp-content/uploads/2018/07/CSI-Brexit-4-People's-Stated-Reasons-for-Voting-Leave.pdf.

130   Dion Nissenbaum and Julian E. Barnes, "Brussels Attacks Fuel Push to Close Off Militants' Highway," *Wall Street Journal*, March 24, 2016, https://www.wsj.com/articles/brussels-attacks-fuel-push-to-close-off-militants-highway-1458781674.

131   "Offensive against the Syrian City of Manbij May Be the Beginning of a Campaign to Liberate the Area Near the Syrian-Turkish Border from ISIS," Meir Amit Intelligence and Terrorism Information Center, June 23, 2016, https://www.terrorism-info.org.il/Data/articles/Art_21025/E_112_16_894662560.pdf.

132   Jim Michaels, "U.S.-Backed Syrian Forces Gave Defeated ISIL Militants Safe Passage," *USA Today*, August 17, 2016, https://www.usatoday.com/story/news/world/2016/08/16/us-backed-syrian-forces-gave-defeated-isil-militants-safe-passage/88862834/.

133   Emma Graham-Harrison, "US Airstrikes Allegedly Kill at Least 73 Civilians in Northern Syria," *Guardian*, July 20, 2016, https://www.theguardian.com/world/2016/jul/20/us-airstrike-allegedly-kills-56-civilians-in-northern-syria; Ryan Devereaux, "Civilian Death Toll from Coalition Airstrikes in Syria Could Be Single Largest in U.S.-Led War on ISIS," *Intercept*, July 19, 2016, https://theintercept.com/2016/07/19/civilian-death-toll-from-coalition-airstrikes-in-syria-could-be-single-largest-in-u-s-led-war-on-isis/.

134   Viktoria Dendrinou, "Brussels Attacks Expose Europe's Scant Progress on Security," *Wall Street Journal*, March 24, 2016, https://www.wsj.com/articles/brussels-attacks-expose-europes-scant-progress-on-security-1458829690.

135   Ruth Bender, "Germany Accuses Asylum Seeker of Aiding Paris Attacks Leader," *Wall Street Journal*, July 7, 2016, https://www.wsj.

com/articles/germany-accuses-asylum-seeker-of-aiding-paris-attacks-leader-1467904592.

[136] Matthias Verbergt, Natalia Drozdiak, and Dion Nissenbaum, "Brussels Suicide Bomber Slipped Terror Net," *Wall Street Journal*, March 24, 2016, https://www.wsj.com/articles/brussels-suicide-bomber-slipped-terror-net-1458779556.

[137] "Europol Setting Up Team of 200 Investigators to Deploy to Migration Hotspots," Europol, press release, May 12, 2016, https://www.europol.europa.eu/newsroom/news/europol-setting-team-of-200-investigators-to-deploy-to-migration-hotspots.

[138] Derek Scally, "Dortmund Attack: No Links Found between Suspect and Bombing," *Irish Times*, April 13, 2017, https://www.irishtimes.com/news/world/europe/dortmund-attack-no-links-found-between-suspect-and-bombing-1.3047395.

[139] Erik Kirschbaum, "In Election Year, Germany to Tap Asylum-Seekers' Phones for ID Checks," Reuters, February 20, 2017, https://www.firstpost.com/world/in-election-year-germany-to-tap-asylum-seekers-phones-for-id-checks-reuters-3293238.html; "New Surveillance Law: German Police Allowed to Hack Smartphones," DW News, June 22, 2017, https://www.dw.com/en/new-surveillance-law-german-police-allowed-to-hack-smartphones/a-39372085; "'Massive Encroachment on Privacy': German MPs Pass Stringent New Rules for Asylum Seekers," RT News, May 19, 2017, https://www.rt.com/news/389000-germany-refugees-new-rules/; "German Minister Advocates Rule Change to Allow Surveillance of Children," DW News, March 6, 2017, https://www.dw.com/en/german-minister-advocates-rule-change-to-allow-surveillance-of-children/a-39103269.

[140] Viktoria Dendrinou, "Brussels Attacks Expose Europe's Scant Progress on Security," *Wall Street Journal*, March 24, 2016, https://www.wsj.com/articles/brussels-attacks-expose-europes-scant-progress-on-security-1458829690.

[141] "Europol Warns: Danger of Terrorism in Europe Is Rising," *Der Spiegel* translated, June 27, 2017, https://www.spiegel.de/politik/ausland/europol-warnt-terrorgefahr-in-europa-steigt-a-1154567.html.

[142] "The Fight against Terrorism, Cost of Non-Europe Report," European Parliamentary Research Service, May 2018, pp. 19–22, https://

www.europarl.europa.eu/RegData/etudes/STUD/2018/621817/
EPRS_STU(2018)621817_EN.pdf.

143   Todd Bensman, "ISIS Commander Arrested in Hungary Held Refugee Passport Enabling Unrestricted Air Travel," PJ Media, March 25, 2019, https://pjmedia.com/homeland-security/todd-bensman/2019/03/25/isis-commander-arrested-in-hungary-held-refugee-passport-enabling-unrestricted-air-travel-n101439.

144   Viktoria Dendrinou, "Brussels Attacks Expose Europe's Scant Progress on Security," *Wall Street Journal.*

145   Johan Ahlander and Mansoor Yosufzai, "Sweden Intensifies Crackdown on Illegal Immigrants," Reuters, July 13, 2017, https://www.reuters.com/article/us-sweden-immigration-crackdown/sweden-intensifies-crackdown-on-illegal-immigrants-idUSKBN19Y0G8.

146   "The Fight against Terrorism," pp. 40–42.

147   Ibid.

148   Bender, "Germany Accuses Asylum Seeker of Aiding Paris Attacks Leader."

149   Matthew Karnitschnig and Jacopo Barigazzi, "EU and Turkey Reach Refugee Deal," Politico, March 20, 2016, https://www.politico.eu/article/eu-and-turkey-finalize-refugee-deal/.

150   Elena Becatoros, "3 Years On, What's Become of the EU-Turkey Migration Deal?" Associated Press, March 20, 2019, https://apnews.com/2eb94ba9aee14272bd99909be2325e2b.

151   Keith Walker and Timothy Jones, "Germany's List of 'Safe Countries of Origin' and What It Means," DW News, February 15, 2019, https://www.dw.com/en/germanys-list-of-safe-countries-of-origin-and-what-it-means/a-46262904.

152   Matteo Civillini and Lorenzo Bagnoli, "Skyrocketing Costs for Returning EU Migrants," *EU Observer*, May 5, 2017, https://euobserver.com/migration/137720.

153   "Germany Plans to Fast-Track Deportations of Failed Asylum-Seekers," DW News, November 18, 2018, https://www.dw.com/en/germany-plans-to-fast-track-deportations-of-failed-asylum-seekers/a-46347915.

154   "Germany: More Than Half of Deportees Go Missing," DW News, July 15, 2018, https://www.dw.com/en/germany-more-than-half-of-deportees-go-missing/a-44685328.

155 Rod Nordland and Mujib Mashal, "Europe Makes Deal to Send Afghans Home, Where War Awaits Them," *New York Times*, October 5, 2016, https://www.nytimes.com/2016/10/06/world/asia/afghanistan-eu-refugees-migrants.html?action=click&module=RelatedCoverage&pgtype=Article&region=Footer.

156 Mujib Mashal, "Europe Is Called 'Willfully Blind' to Risks Afghan Deportees Face," *New York Times*, October 5, 2017, https://www.nytimes.com/2017/10/05/world/asia/afghan-refugees-deported.html.

157 Patrick Kingsley, "By Stifling Migration, Sudan's Feared Secret Police Aid Europe," *New York Times*, April 22, 2018, https://www.nytimes.com/2018/04/22/world/africa/migration-european-union-sudan.html; "Libyan Militia Chief Admits Deal with Tripoli to Stem Migrant Flow," *Times* (UK), September 1, 2017, https://www.thetimes.co.uk/article/libyan-militia-chief-admits-deal-with-tripoli-to-stem-migrant-flow-ahmed-dabbashi-brigade-migrant-crisis-italy-538lwtgf5.

158 Holly Ellyatt, "'Pack Your Bags,' Italy's New Leaders Tell 500,000 Illegal Migrants—but It'll Cost Them," CNBC, June 5, 2018, https://www.cnbc.com/2018/06/04/pack-your-bags-italys-new-leaders-tell-500000-illegal-migrants--but-itll-cost-them.html; Declan Walsh and Jason Horowitz, "Italy, Going It Alone, Stalls the Flow of Migrants. But at What Cost?," *New York Times*, September 17, 2017, https://www.nytimes.com/2017/09/17/world/europe/italy-libya-migrant-crisis.html?module=inline.

159 "Council of Europe Alarmed by Italy's Migrant Policy," Associated Press, February 7, 2019, https://www.usnews.com/news/world/articles/2019-02-07/council-of-europe-alarmed-by-italys-migrant-policy.

160 Frontex Risk Analysis for 2020, p. 30.

161 Ibid., p. 44.

162 Kevin Uhrmacher, Kevin Schaul, and Michael Scherer, "Where 2020 Democrats Stand on Immigration," *Washington Post*, April 8, 2020, https://www.washingtonpost.com/graphics/politics/policy-2020/immigration/.

163 Peter Nesser, "Military Interventions, Jihadi Networks, and Terrorist Entrepreneurs: How the Islamic State Terror Wave Rose So High in Europe," *Combating Terrorism Center Sentinel* 12, issue 3 (March 2019), ctc.usma.edu/military-interventions-jihadi-networks-terrorist-entrepreneurs-islamic-state-terror-wave-rose-high-europe/.

164 Michelle Hackman, "Joe Biden Would Likely Use a Familiar Tool – Executive Powers – to Reverse Trump Immigration Policies," *The Wall Street Journal*, August 23, 2020, https://www.wsj.com/articles/joe-biden-would-likely-use-a-familiar-toolexecutive-powersto-reverse-trump-immigration-policies-11598108400; Ian Schwartz, "All Democrats At Main Debate Agree Illegal Immigrants Should Get Health Care Coverage," RealClear Politics, June 27, 2019,https://www.realclearpolitics.com/video/2019/06/27/all_dem_candidates_raise_hand_when_asked_if_illegal_immigrants_should_get_health_care_coverage_at_debate.html; Nidhi Prakash, "Joe Biden's Campaign Reversed And Said He's Supporting A Moratorium On Deportations," BuzzFeed News, February 22, 2020, https://www.realclearpolitics.com/video/2019/06/27/all_dem_candidates_raise_hand_when_asked_if_illegal_immigrants_should_get_health_care_coverage_at_debate.html; "The Biden Plan For Securing Our Values As A Nation of Immigrants," The Joe Biden Campaign, https://joebiden.com/immigration/#

Chapter Two

1 "Potential Terrorist Threats: Border Security Challenges in Latin America and the Caribbean," Hearing Before the House Foreign Affairs Committee, Subcommittee on the Western Hemisphere, 114th Cong., 2nd sess., March 22, 2016 (statement of the Honorable Alan D. Bersin, Assistant Secretary for International Affairs and Chief Diplomatic Officer, US Department of Homeland Security), https://docs.house.gov/meetings/FA/FA07/20160322/104726/HHRG-114-FA07-Wstate-BersinA-20160322.pdf.

2 Callimachi, "How ISIS Built Machinery of Terror."

3 Democrat Party Platform, 2016, https://democrats.org/wp-content/uploads/2018/10/2016_DNC_Platform.pdf.Na

4 Scott Eric Kaufman, "'Stories Like These Are Good at Scaring People': Congressman Shoots Down Right-Wing ISIS Myth in Pitch-Perfect Facebook Post," Salon, April 16, 2015, https://www.salon.com/2015/04/15/stories_like_these_are_good_at_scaring_people_congressman_shoots_down_right_wing_isis_myth_in_pitch_perfect_facebook_post/.

5 "Napolitano: DHS Is Working with Mexico on 'Special Interest Aliens' Threat along the U.S.-Mexico Border," *CNS News*, January 17, 2012,

https://www.cnsnews.com/news/article/napolitano-dhs-working-mexico-special-interest-aliens-threat-along-us-mexican-border.

6   FBI FY 2006 Budget Request: Hearing Before the House Comm. On Appropriations, 108th Cong. (Mar.8, 2005), (Question and Answer between Rep. John Culberson and Robert Mueller, Director, Federal Bureau of Investigations). Mark Sherman, "Al Qaeda entering US with fake ID, Mueller says, Associated Press, March 9, 2005, https://www.timebomb2000.com/xf/index.php?threads/ot-fbi-warns-of-special-interest-aliens.142290/.

7   "Travels of President George W. Bush," US Department of State, 2015, history.state.gov/departmenthistory/travels/president/bush-george-w.

8   George W. Bush, *Decision Points* (New York: Crown Publishing Group, 2011), 302.

9   Christopher Wilson, "The Lessons of Post-9/11 Border Management," Wilson Center, November 18, 2015, https://www.wilsoncenter.org/article/the-lessons-post-911-border-management.

10 "Motive Sought in New York Subway Bomb Plot," CNN, August 2, 1997, http://www.cnn.com/US/9708/02/brooklyn.bomb.pm/index.html?_s=PM:US.

11 Edward Alden, *The Closing of the American Border: Terrorism, Immigration and Security Since 9/11*, 1st ed. (New York: HarperCollins, 2008), 40.

12 Chad C. Haddal, "People Crossing Borders: An Analysis of Border Protection Policies," Congressional Research Service Report No. R41237, May 13, 2010, p. 4, https://fas.org/sgp/crs/homesec/R41237.pdf.

13 Marc R. Rosenblum, Jerome P. Bjelopera, and Kristin M. Finklea, "Border Security: Understanding Threats at U.S. Borders," Congressional Research Service Report No. R42969, February 21, 2013, p. 2.

14 The official names and creation dates of the commissions are as follows: (1) Gilmore Commission, known officially as the Advisory Panel to Assess Domestic Response Capabilities for Terrorism Involving Weapons of Mass Destruction, created on October 17, 1998 (Pub. L. 105–241); (2) Bremer Commission, known officially as the National Commission on Terrorism, created on October 21, 1998 (Pub. L. 105–277); and (3) the Hart-Rudman Commission, known officially as the U.S. Commission on National Security/21st Century, created on

September 2, 1999; Ibid.; Border Security: Immigration Enforcement between Ports of Entry.

15 David W. Moore, "Eight in 10 Americans Support Ground War in Afghanistan," Gallup, November 1, 2001, https://news.gallup.com/poll/5029/eight-americans-support-ground-war-afghanistan.aspx; "Immigration," Gallup.com, January 31, 2020, news.gallup.com/poll/14785/immigration.aspx; Lydia Saad, "Americans More Pro-Immigration Than in Past," Rey Koslowski, "Immigration and Insecurity: Post-9/11 Fear in the United States, Social Science Research Council's Insights from the Social Sciences, https://items.ssrc.org/border-battles/immigration-and-insecurity-post-911-fear-in-the-united-states/; Lydia Saad, "Americans More Pro-Immigrant Than in Past," Gallup, April 23, 2019, https://news.gallup.com/poll/163457/americans-pro-immigration-past.aspx.

16 Thomas Eldridge, Walter Hempel Ginsburg, Janice L. Kephart, and Kelly Moore, *9/11 and Terrorist Travel: Staff Report of the National Commission on Terrorist Attacks upon the United States*, Center for Homeland Security and Defense, 2004, https://www.hsdl.org/?abstract&did=449288.

17 Alden, *Closing of the American Border*, 36–37.

18 Peter Andreas, *Border Games: Policing the U.S.-Mexico Divide* (Ithaca, NY: Cornell University Press, 2012, Kindle Edition), 58–60.

19 Homeland Security Act of 2002, Pub. L. No. 107–296, Title IV, Subtitle A, Sec. 401 (2001), https://www.dhs.gov/xlibrary/assets/hr_5005_enr.pdf.

20 Intelligence Reform and Terrorism Prevention Act of 2004, Pub. L. 108–458, Sec. 7201, b1, https://www.govinfo.gov/content/pkg/PLAW-108publ458/html/PLAW-108publ458.htm.

21 *Establishment of the Human Smuggling and Trafficking Center: A Report to Congress*, US Department of Homeland Security, June 16, 2005 (see Executive Summary and Introduction), https://www.legislationline.org/download/id/1266/file/183109be7c5dcc7e7af02aa74602.pdf.

22 Secure Fence Act of 2006, H.R. Rep. No. 6061, Sec. 2(b) (2002), http://www.gpo.gov/fdsys/pkg/BILLS-109hr6061enr/pdf/BILLS-109hr6061enr.pdf.

23 "National Strategy for Combating Terrorism," National Archives and Records Administration, September 2006, georgewbush-whitehouse.archives.gov/nsc/nsct/2006/.

24 "Executive Summary," US Customs and Border Protection, National Border Patrol Strategy, U.S. Department of Homeland Security, 2005, http://cw.routledge.com/textbooks/9780415996945/gov-docs/2004.pdf.

25 "United States Border Patrol, Border Patrol Agent Nationwide Staffing by Fiscal Year," https://www.cbp.gov/sites/default/files/assets/documents/2019-Mar/Staffing%20FY1992-FY2018.pdf.

26 Textual materials retrieved for supervised examination included the files of the following members of the White House Domestic Policy Council: Deputy Chief of Staff Joshua B. Bolton, Special Assistant to the President Ryan W. Bounds, Special Assistant to the President Todd Braunstein, Special Assistant to the President Jay Lefkowitz, and Special Assistant to the President Kristin Hughes. Other examined textual materials came from the Bush Record Policy Memo files of White House Staff Secretary Thomas von der Heydt.

27 Ryan Bounds, "Information Memorandum for the President, Immigration Reform Legacy," memorandum to President, undated from 2009 file folder. Official records of George W. Bush's presidency are housed at the George W. Bush Presidential Library and administered by the National Archives and Records Administration (NARA) under the provisions of the Presidential Records Act (PRA)

28 Haddal, "People Crossing Borders," 10–12.

29 Blas Nuñez-Neto, Alison Siskin, and Stephen Viña, "Border Security: Apprehensions of 'Other than Mexican' Aliens," Congressional Research Services Report No. RL33097, 2005, p. 19, http://trac.syr.edu/immigration/library/P1.pdf.

30 "Supervision of Aliens Commensurate with Risk," Department of Homeland Security, Office of Inspector General, Report 11-81, p. 5, https://www.oig.dhs.gov/assets/Mgmt/OIG_11-81_Dec11.pdf.

31 "Second Phase of National Security Entry-Exit Registration System Announced," US Department of Justice, press release, November 22, 2002, http://www.justice.gov/ archive/opa/pr/2002/November/02_ag_649.htm.

32 Muzaffar Chishti and Claire Bergeron, "DHS Announces End to Controversial Post-9/11 Immigrant Registration and Tracking Program," Migrationpolicy.org, May 17, 2011, https://www.migrationpolicy.org/

article/dhs-announces-end-controversial-post-911-immigrant-registration-and-tracking-program.

33 "DHS Removes Designated Countries from NSEERS Registration (May 2011)," Department of Homeland Security, September 29, 2015, https://www.dhs.gov/dhs-removes-designated-countries-nseers-registration-may-2011.

34 "Supervision of Aliens Commensurate with Risk, Report OIG-11-81," Department of Homeland Security Office of Inspector General, December 2011, https://www.oig.dhs.gov/assets/Mgmt/OIG_11-81_Dec11.pdf.

35 "Special Interest Alien Use of the California-Mexico Border, August 2009," Department of Homeland Security joint assessment with the California State Terrorism Threat Assessment Center. This document was obtained while the author was working as a journalist in Texas.

36 "Update: 2006 SIA Trends Reveal Vulnerabilities Along Route to US," National Counterterrorism Center Report NSAR 2007–21. The author obtained this report while working as a journalist in 2007.

37 Memorandum from US Border Patrol Chief David V. Aguilar, for All Sector Chief Patrol Agents, Subject: Arrests of Aliens from Special Interest Countries, November 1, 2004, https://cis.org/sites/default/files/2018-08/Aguilar_memo.pdf.

38 "Jihadism in Southern Thailand: A Phantom Menace," International Crisis Group, Report No. 291, November 8, 2017, https://www.crisisgroup.org/asia/south-east-asia/thailand/291-jihadism-southern-thailand-phantom-menace

39 David J. Bier and Alex Nowrasteh, "45,000 'Special Interest Aliens' Caught Since 2007, but No U.S. Terrorist Attacks from Illegal Border Crossers," Cato Institute, December 18, 2018, https://www.cato.org/blog/45000-special-interest-aliens-caught-2007-no-us-terrorist-attacks-illegal-border-crossers.

40 "MYTH/FACT: Known and Suspected Terrorists/Special Interest Aliens," Department of Homeland Security, January 7, 2019, https://www.dhs.gov/news/2019/01/07/mythfact-known-and-suspected-terroristsspecial-interest-aliens.

41 "Special Interest Alien Use of the California-Mexico Border, Appendix 1: Fiscal Year 2007–08 Special Interest Alien Apprehension Data, August 2009," Department of Homeland Security joint assessment with the

California State Terrorism Threat Assessment Center. This document was obtained while the author was working as a journalist in Texas.

42   Brian M. Rosenthal, "Border Surge Harming Crime Fighting in Other Parts of Texas, Internal Report Finds," *Houston Chronicle,* February 25, 2015, https://www.houstonchronicle.com/news/article/Border-surge-harming-crime-fighting-in-other-6099660.php, embedded within: www.scribd.com/document/256933420/Border-Surge-Report?ad_group=131678X1600845Xfbe3797e67e41bd57956eb30539c121a&campaign=SkimbitLtd&keyword=660149026&medium=affiliate&source=hp_affiliate.

43   Michael McCaul, "Chairman McCaul: The Terrorist Exodus Has Begun and We're Not Ready for It," Fox News, March 9, 2016, https://www.foxnews.com/opinion/chairman-mccaul-the-terrorist-exodus-has-begun-and-were-not-ready-for-it.

44   "ISIS Suspect Reveals Plans to Open Up Route from Syria to U.S. through Mexico," Fox News, April 22, 2016, updated December 1, 2016, https://www.foxnews.com/world/isis-suspect-reveals-plans-to-open-up-route-from-syria-to-u-s-through-mexico.

45   United States v. Hamza Naj Ahmed, Mohamed Abdihamid Farah, Abdirahman Yasin Daud, and Guled Ali Omar; Case 0:15-cr-00049-MJD-HB (US District Court, District of Minnesota, April 20, 2016), Response by the United States to Defendant Daud's Motion in Limine to Bar Government from Labeling Defendant with Prejudicial Terms, Document 469.

46   "Current and Projected National Security Threats to the United States," Hearing Before the Select Committee on Intelligence, US Senate, 109th Cong. (February 16, 2005), https://www.govinfo.gov/content/pkg/CHRG-109shrg22379/html/CHRG-109shrg22379.htm.

47   "Update: 2006 SIA Trends Reveal Vulnerabilities along Route to US, National Counterterrorism Center Special Analysis Report 2007-21, May 11, 2007." Obtained while author worked as a journalist.

48   Brian Bennett, "Bin Laden Apparently Sought Operative with Valid Mexican Passport," *Los Angeles Times*, May 2, 2012, latimesblogs.latimes.com/world_now/2012/05/papers-bin-laden-sought-operative-to-cross-into-us-from-mexico.html.

49   Jana Winter, "Online Posts Show ISIS Eyeing Mexican Border, Says Law Enforcement Bulletin," Fox News, August 29, 2014, last updated

November 23, 2015, https://www.foxnews.com/us/online-posts-show-isis-eyeing-mexican-border-says-law-enforcement-bulletin.

50 *Dallas News* Administrator, "Watchdog: DPS Hush about Findings of Islamic State on the Border," *Dallas Morning News*, August 27, 2019, https://www.dallasnews.com/news/watchdog/2015/09/17/watchdo,-dps-hush-about-findings-of-islamic-state-on-the-border/.

51 "Cybersecurity, Terrorism, and Beyond: Addressing Evolving Threats to the Homeland," Hearing Before the Homeland Security & Governmental Affairs Committee, US Senate, 113th Cong. (September 10, 2014), https://www.hsgac.senate.gov/hearings/cybersecurity-terrorism-and-beyond-addressing-evolving-threats-to-the-homeland.

52 Anne Speckhard and Ardian Shajkovci, "PERSPECTIVE: ISIS Fighter Claims Attack Plot Via Mexico, Underscoring Border Vulnerability," Homeland Security Today, June 3, 2019, www.hstoday.us/subject-matter-areas/terrorism-study/perspective-isis-fighter-claims-attack-plot-via-mexico-underscoring-border-vulnerability/; Todd Bensman, "What to Make of a Report on ISIS Plans to Breach the U.S.-Mexico Border?" Center for Immigration Studies, June 19, 2019, cis.org/Bensman/What-Make-Report-ISIS-Plans-Breach-USMexico-Border.

Chapter Three

1 Chris Roberts, "Transcript: Debate on the Foreign Intelligence Surveillance Act," *El Paso Times*, August 22, 2007, https://www.eff.org/files/filenode/att/elpasotimesmcconnelltranscript.pdf.

2 Letter from Trey Gowdy (R-SC), Chairman of the House Committee on Oversight and Government Reform, to Honorable John V. Kelly, Deputy Inspector General, US Department of Homeland Security, December 20, 2018, https://republicans-oversight.house.gov/wp-content/uploads/2019/01/2018-12-20-TG-to-DHS-IG-re-Abdulahi-Hasan-Sharif.pdf.

3 "Man Charged in Edmonton Attacks Crossed into U.S. from Mexico, Records Show," Canadian Broadcast Corporation News, October 4, 2017, https://www.cbc.ca/news/canada/edmonton/edmonton-attacks-abdulahi-sharif-hasan-attempted-murder-border-crossing-united-states-1.4330527; Jonny Wakefield, "Everything We Know about the Man Charged in Edmonton's Truck Attack from the Woman Who Knows Him Best," *Edmonton Journal*, September 28, 2018, https://

edmontonjournal.com/news/crime/who-is-abdulahi-hasan-sharif-one-year-later-everything-we-know-about-the-alleged-edmonton-attacker/.

4   "Edmonton Attack Suspect Had 'Genocidal Beliefs,' Says Former Co-worker Who Reported Him to Police," Canadian Broadcast Corporation News, October 2, 2017, https://www.cbc.ca/news/canada/edmonton/abdulahi-hasan-sharif-somali-edmonton-1.4316074.

5   Ibid.

6   Michelle Shephard and Julien Gignac, "Suspect in Edmonton Attack Faces Terrorism, Attempted Murder Charges," *Toronto Star,* October 1, 2017, https://www.thestar.com/news/canada/2017/10/01/edmonton-police-investigate-acts-of-terrorism-after-cop-stabbed-and-van-hits-pedestrians.html.

7   Alexandra Zabjek, "Edmonton Police Investigate 'Acts of Terrorism' after Officer Stabbed, Pedestrians Run Down," Canadian Broadcast Corporation News, October 1, 2017, https://www.cbc.ca/news/canada/edmonton/jasper-downtown-edmonton-pedestrians-struck-1.4315545.

8   Ibid.

9   Jonny Wakefiled, "Everything We Know about the Man Charged in Edmonton's Truck Attack from the Woman Who Knows Him Best," *Edmonton Journal,* September 28, 2018, https://edmontonjournal.com/news/crime/who-is-abdulahi-hasan-sharif-one-year-later-everything-we-know-about-the-alleged-edmonton-attackerun.

10 Andrew R. Arthur, "Inspector General Must Investigate Somali Terror Suspect," Center for Immigration Studies, October 9, 2018, https://cis.org/Arthur/Inspector-General-Must-Investigate-Somali-Terror-Suspect.

11 Author interview with James Dinkins, February 26, 2020.

12 Reid Wilson, "Texas Officials Warn of Immigrants with Terrorist Ties Crossing Southern Border," *Washington Post*, February 26, 2015, https://www.washingtonpost.com/blogs/govbeat/wp/2015/02/26/texas-officials-warn-of-immigrants-with-terrorist-ties-crossing-southern-border/.

13 Written testimony of DHS Office of Policy Acting Assistant Secretary for Border, Immigration and Trade Michael Dougherty; CBP Office of Field Operations Deputy Executive Assistant Commissioner John Wagner; and ICE Homeland Security Investigations Assistant Director for National Security Investigations Division Clark Settles for a House Committee on Homeland Security Task Force on Denying Terrorist

Entry into the United States hearing titled "Preventing Terrorists from Acquiring U.S. Visas," March 5, 2017, https://www.dhs.gov/news/2017/05/03/written-testimony-cbp-ice-plcy-house-committee-homeland-security-task-force-denying.

14   This information is derived from a Law Enforcement Sensitive Texas Department of Public Safety intelligence assessment that was provided, unauthorized, to several media outlets. For this item, the DPS document cites in endnote 109 unclassified intelligence Report "4 0061329 14," https://www.scribd.com/document/256933420/Border-Surge-Report.

15   United States v. Anthony Joseph Tracy (4th Circuit Court, Eastern District of Virginia, 2011), Document 132.

16   United States v. Tracy, Detention Hearing Transcript, Document 72, 34; CIPA Hearing Transcript, Document 72, 9.

17   United States v. Tracy, CIPA Hearing Transcript, Document 72.

18   "ICE Removes Pakistani Man Sentenced for Role in Human Smuggling Conspiracy," US Immigration and Customs Enforcement, press release, December 19, 2018, https://www.ice.gov/news/releases/ice-removes-pakistani-man-sentenced-role-human-smuggling-conspiracy.

19   Dylan Baddour and W. Gardner Selby, "Duncan Hunter Makes Unconfirmed Claim," Politi-fact, October 10, 2014, https://www.politifact.com/factchecks/2014/oct/10/duncan-hunter-2/duncan-hunter-makes-unconfirmed-claim-border-patro/

20   Stephen Dinan, "Smuggling Network Guided Illegals from Middle East Terror Hotbeds to U.S. Border," *Washington Times*, June 2, 2016, https://www.washingtontimes.com/news/2016/jun/2/smuggling-network-guided-illegal-immigrants-from-m/; Stephen Dinan, "Sharafat Ali Khan Smuggled Terrorist-Linked Immigrants," *Washington Times*, April 12, 2017, https://www.washingtontimes.com/news/2017/apr/12/sharafat-ali-khan-smuggled-terrorist-linked-immigr/.

21   Stephen Dinan, "Pakistani Mastermind of Plot to Smuggle 'Terrorism' Immigrants to U.S. Sentenced," *Washington Times*, October 17, 2017, https://www.washingtontimes.com/news/2017/oct/17/sharafat-ali-khan-sentenced-terrorism-illegal-immi/.

22   Evan Simon, "How 'the Terrorist Watch List' Works," ABC News, June 17, 2016, https://abcnews.go.com/US/terrorist-watch-list-works/story?id=39931316.

23 "Terrorist Identities Datamart Environment," National Counterterrorism Center, 2017, https://www.dni.gov/files/NCTC/documents/features_documents/TIDEfactsheet10FEB2017.pdf.

24 Julia Ainsley, "Only Six Immigrants in Terrorism Database Stopped by CBP at Southern Border from October to March," NBC News, January 7, 2019, https://www.nbcnews.com/politics/immigration/only-six-immigrants-terrorism-database-stopped-cbp-southern-border-first-n955861.

25 Whistleblower Reprisal Complaint in the matter of Brian Murphy, Department of Homeland Security Office of Inspector General, page 6, September 8, 2020, https://int.nyt.com/data/documenttools/homeland-security-whistleblower/0819ec9ee29306a5/full.pdf

26 Unclassified U/FOUO intelligence assessments produced by U.S. Customs and Border Patrol materials and reviewed by the author.

27 Guillermo Contreras, "Jordanian Pleads Guilty to Smuggling Yemen Immigrants into the U.S. via the Texas Border," *San Antonio Express-News*, April 30, 2019, https://www.mysanantonio.com/news/local/article/Jordanian-pleads-guilty-in-Texas-to-smuggling-13806703.php; Todd Bensman, "Mexico-Based Smuggler Trafficked Six People From Terrorist Hotbed Over U.S. Border," *Federalist*, November 6, 2019, https://thefederalist.com/2019/11/06/mexico-based-smuggler-trafficked-six-people-from-terrorist-hotbed-over-u-s-border/.

28 Ibid.

29 Bob Price, "Three Men from Yemen Apprehended after Illegal Border Crossing in Arizona," Breitbart News, May 18, 2020, https://www.breitbart.com/border/2020/05/18/three-men-from-yemen-apprehended-after-illegal-border-crossing-in-arizona/.

30 Comments recorded by the author attending the press conference on April 29, 2019, in San Antonio, Texas, and as published in "Why the Case of Jordanian-Mexican Smuggler Who Transported Yemenis over the Texas Border Is Important," Center for Immigration Studies, May 1, 2019, https://cis.org/Bensman/Why-Case-JordanianMexican-Smuggler-Who-Transported-Yemenis-over-Texas-Border-Important.

31 Thomas J. Lueck and William K. Rashbaum, "New York Cites a Terror Threat," August 1, 2004, *New York Times*, https://www.nytimes.com/2004/08/01/nyregion/new-york-cites-a-terror-threat.html.

32 Ibid.

33 In 2006, the author was granted access to the document and permission to cite information from it.

34 In 2007, the author conducted a telephone interview with Martinez and quoted him in the article "Have Terrorists Crossed?," the Investigative Project on Terrorism, March 25, 2008, https://www.investigativeproject.org/625/have-terrorists-crossed.

35 FBI official interview with the author circa 2006; Bensman, "Have Terrorists Crossed?"

36 Matter of S-J-M Application Form 1-601, Application for Waiver of Grounds of Inadmissibility, U.S. Citizenship and Immigration Services, Non-Precedent Decision of the Administrative Appeals Office, January 11, 2018, https://www.uscis.gov/sites/default/files/err/H6%20-%20Waiver%20of%20Inadmissibility%20-%20Unlawful%20Presence%20-%20212%20(a)(9)(B)/Decisions_Issued_in_2018/JAN112018_01H6212.pdf; Denise Bell, "Tier III Terrorist Organizations: The Role of the Immigration Court in Making a Terrorist Determination," Immigration Law Advisor, US Department of Justice Executive Office for Immigration Review, July 2016, https://www.justice.gov/eoir/file/880381/download; Aqueel Ahmed v. Eric Holder et al. (US District Court, Eastern District of Pennsylvania, 2014) civil action 13-3017, Memorandum, http://www.paed.uscourts.gov/documents/opinions/14d0204p.pdf; United States v. Farida Goolam Mohommed Ahmed (US District Court, Southern District of Texas, McAllen District), Preliminary Examination/Detention Hearing Transcript, case 04-CR-3156-M (July 27, 2004); Murtaza Ali Shah, "MQM-London Leaders Interrogated in Washington," *International News*, October 24, 2018, https://www.thenews.com.pk/print/384705-mqm-london-leaders-interrogated-in-washington.

37 Access to investigative materials provided to the author in 2006.

38 "Al Qaeda Operatives Captured by CIA Provided Intelligence Behind New Orange Heightened Terrorist Threat Alert," *Homeland Security Today Magazine*, August 5, 2004, https://www.prweb.com/releases/2004/08/prweb147272.htm.

39 Elizabeth Aguilera, "Detained Tunisian Cleric Previously Deported from Canada and France," *San Diego Union-Tribune*, January 27, 2011, https://www.sandiegouniontribune.com/sdut-illegal-immigrant-said-jaziri-was-deported-from-ca-2011jan27-story.html.

40   "Outspoken Montreal Imam Ordered Detained until Deportation," Canadian Broadcast Corporation News, October 17, 2007, https://www.cbc.ca/news/canada/montreal/outspoken-montreal-imam-ordered-detained-until-deportation-1.658787.

41   United States v. Kenneth Robert Lawler, Mario Javier Alonso-Viera, Case 3:11-cr-00378-H (Southern District of California, January 12, 2011), Criminal Complaint, Document 1.

42   Ibid.

43   United States v. Kenneth Robert Lawler, Mario Javier Alonso-Viera, Case 3:11-cr-00378-H (Southern District of California, April 13, 2011), Stipulation of Fact and Joint Motion for Release of Material Witness and Order Thereon, Document 44.

44   Rim Hana, "Said Jaziri Regains His Seat at the House of People's Representatives 'HPR,'" Tunisie Numerique, October 21, 2019, https://news-tunisia.tunisienumerique.com/tunisia-audio-said-jaziri-regains-his-seat-at-the-house-of-peoples-representatives-hpr/.

45   This information is derived from a Law Enforcement Sensitive Texas Department of Public Safety intelligence assessment that was provided, unauthorized, to several media outlets. For this item, the DPS document cites in endnote 111 as "HIR/CBP 0295-11," https://www.scribd.com/document/256933420/Border-Surge-Report.

46   Ibid.

47   Information provided verbally to the author by intelligence community sources with direct access.

48   Stephen Dinan, "Agents Nab Pakistanis with Terrorist Connections Crossing U.S. Border," *Washington Times*, December 30, 2015, https://www.washingtontimes.com/news/2015/dec/30/pakistanis-terrorist-connections-nabbed-us-border/.

49   Tatiana Sanchez, "Hunter Raises Questions about Pakistani Border Arrests," *San Diego Union-Tribune*, January 6, 2016, http://www.sandiegouniontribune.com/news/border-baja-california/sdut-pakistanis-arrested-border-patrol-2016jan06-story.html.

50   *Border Patrol: Checkpoints Contribute to Border Patrol's Mission, But More Consistent Data Collection and Performance Measurement Could Improve Effectiveness,* Government Accountability Office, GAO-09-824, https://www.gao.gov/products/GAO-09-824.

51 United States v. Mahmoud Youssef Kourani, 2:03-cr-80481, (Eastern District of Michigan, Southern Division, November 19, 2003), p. 3 Indictment; Warren Richey, "Are Terrorists Crossing the US-Mexico Border? Excerpts from the Case File," *Christian Science Monitor*, January 15, 2017, https://www.csmonitor.com/USA/Justice/2017/0115/Are-terrorists-crossing-the-US-Mexico-border-Excerpts-from-the-case-file.

52 Pauline Arrillaga and Olga R. Rodriguez, "The Terror-Immigration Connection," Associated Press, July 3, 2005, http://www.nbcnews.com/id/8408009/ns/us_news-security/t/terror-immigration-connection/#.X0bQRi2z10v.

53 "U.S. Designates Al-Manar as a Specially Designated Global Terrorist Entity Television Station Is Arm of Hizballah Terrorist Network", U.S. Department of Treasury, press release, March 23, 2006, https://www.treasury.gov/press-center/press-releases/Pages/js4134.aspx.

54 This information is derived from a Law Enforcement Sensitive Texas Department of Public Safety intelligence assessment that was provided, unauthorized, to several media outlets. For this item, the DPS document cites in endnote 114 as "Information shared by HIS agents, 2012," https://www.scribd.com/document/256933420/Border-Surge-Report.

55 United States v. Mujeeb Rhaman Saify, Case 2:19-mj-04081-MAH (US District Court, District of New Jersey, March 27, 2019), Document 13, Notice of Motion.

56 United States v. Mujeeb Rhaman Saify, Case 2:19-mj-04081-MAH (US District Court District of New Jersey, February 5, 2019), Criminal Complaint.

57 This information is derived from a Law Enforcement Sensitive Texas Department of Public Safety intelligence assessment that was provided, unauthorized, to several media outlets. For this item, the DPS document cites in endnote 110 Customs and Border Protection Field Intelligence Report "FIR-MCS-12-1207179," https://www.scribd.com/document/256933420/Border-Surge-Report.

58 Colleen Long, "Appeals court determines asylum seeker has right to hearing," the Associated Press, March 7, 2019, https://apnews.com/d980fdcf8ace4f6499ba5c92f46bb2dd.

59 "Two Alleged Operatives of the Tamil Tigers Terrorist Organization Extradited to Brooklyn," FBI New York Field Office, press release, December 27, 2012, https://archives.fbi.gov/archives/newyork/press-

releases/2012/two-alleged-operatives-of-the-tamil-tigers-terrorist-organization-extradited-to-brooklyn.

60 "Canadian National Charged with Alien Smuggling Conspiracy and Attempting to Bring Aliens to the United States," US Department of Justice Office of Public Affairs press release, August 19, 2020, https://www.justice.gov/opa/pr/canadian-national-charged-alien-smuggling-conspiracy-and-attempting-bring-aliens-united.

61 "Somali National Sentenced to More Than 8 Years in Federal Prison for Making False Statements in Terrorism Investigation," US Immigration and Customs Enforcement, press release, July 25, 2013, https://www.ice.gov/news/releases/somali-national-sentenced-more-8-years-federal-prison-making-false-statements.

62 United States v. Abdullahi Omar Fidse and Debkah Abdallah Sheikh (5th Circuit Court, Western District, Texas, 2011), Detention Order, Document 26; Unsealed Indictment, Document; United States v. Fidse and Sheikh, Narrative from Immigration and Naturalization Service, Document 11, Exhibit 1, Narrative from Immigration and Naturalization Service; United States v. Fidse and Sheikh, Defendant's Motion to Dismiss for Due Process Violation, Document 58; United States v. Fidse and Sheikh, Document 26; Document 214 (filed February 13, 2015).

63 United States v. Fidse, Case 13-50734 (US Fifth Circuit Court of Appeals, August 2014); United States v. Fidse, Case 5:11-cr-00425-FB (Western District of Texas, August 2011).

64 United States v. Abdullahi Omar Fidse and Debkah Abdallah Sheikh (5th Circuit Court, Western District of Texas, 2011), Detention Order, Document 26; Unsealed Indictment, Document; United States v. Fidse and Sheikh, Narrative from Immigration and Naturalization Service, Document 11, Exhibit 1, Narrative from Immigration and Naturalization Service; United States v. Fidse and Sheikh, Defendant's Motion to Dismiss for Due Process Violation, Document 58; United States v. Fidse and Sheikh, Document 26; Document 214 (filed February 13, 2015).

65 United States v. Fidse and Sheikh, Case 5:11-cr-00425-FB (Western District of Texas, June 2011), Detention Order; United States v. Fidse and Sheikh, Case 5:11-cr-00425-FB, (Western District of Texas, May 2011), unsealed indictment.

66   United States v. Fidse, Case 13-50734 (U.S. Fifth Circuit Court of Appeals, August 2014); United States v. Fidse, Case 5:11-cr-00425-FB (Western District of Texas, August 2011).

67   Testimony of Ms. Janice Kephart before the US Senate Judiciary Subcommittee on Immigration, Border Security, and Citizenship and the US Senate Judiciary Subcommittee on Terrorism, Technology, and Homeland Security, March 14, 2005, https://www.judiciary.senate.gov/imo/media/doc/Kephart%20Testimony%20031405.pdf.

68   The laws governing asylum protection were first established in statute with the passage of the Refugee Act of 1980, Pub. L. No. 96-212, § 201, 94 Stat. 102, 102–06 (1980); (codified at 8 U.S.C. §§ 1101(a)(42), 1157-1159). The Refugee Act provided, for the first time, a US refugee policy that stated that aliens who are present in the United States and who meet the definition of a refugee can apply for asylum protection in the United States. The legal standard for a refugee and asylee is the same, but noncitizens must apply for refugee status from outside the United States and for asylum status from within the United States. The final regulations for implementing the Refugee Act of 1980 were issued in 1990.

69   United States v. Mohammed Ahmed Dhakane, Case 5:10-cr-0, Document i.Y3-1 (Western District of Texas, April, 8, 2011); "Somalian Charged with Making False Statements on Application for Asylum," US Attorney's Office, press release, March 4, 2010, https://archives.fbi.gov/archives/sanantonio/press-releases/2010/sa030410.htm.

70   "Court Filings: Terror-Linked Smuggler Brought Somali Terrorists into US through Southwestern Border," Texas Department of Public Safety Intelligence Analysis, February 15, 2011, via Wikileaks.org, https://wikileaks.org/gifiles/attach/124/124199_Terror%20Linked%20Smuggler%20Brought%20Somali%20Terrorists%20into%20US.pdf.

71   United States v. Muhammad Ahmad Dhakane (5th Circuit Court, Western District of Texas, 2010), Government Sentencing Memorandum, Document 57, https://www.scribd.com/document/51237749/Ahmed-Dhakane-DOJ-Sentencing-Memorandum; Richey, "Are Terrorists Crossing the U.S. Mexico Border?"

72   United States v. Dhakane, Transcript of Sentencing Hearing.

73   United States v. Dhakane, Government Sentencing Memorandum, Document 57.

74 Wes Bruer, "Terror Alert as US Uncovers Somali Human Smuggling Ring," *Long War Journal*, May 27, 2010, https://www.longwarjournal. org/archives/2010/05/terror_alert_in_us_uncovers_so.php.

75 United States v. Muhammad Ahmad Dhakane (5th Circuit Court, Western District of Texas, 2010), Government Sentencing Memorandum, Document 57, https://www.scribd.com/document/51237749/Ahmed-Dhakane-DOJ-Sentencing-Memorandum.

76 United States v. Dhakane, Government Sentencing Memorandum, Document 57.

77 Todd Bensman, "What Terrorist Migration over European Borders Can Teach about American Border Security," Center for Immigration Studies backgrounder, November 6, 2019, https://cis.org/Report/ Terrorist-Migration-Over-European-Borders.

78 Andrea Thomas and Mohammad Nour Alakraa, "Syrian Accused of Islamic State Links Arrested in German Refugee Camp," *Wall Street Journal*, December 17, 2015, https://www.wsj.com/articles/ syrian-accused-of-is-links-arrested-in-germany-1450367997.

79 Valentina Pop and Ruth Bender, "Germany Ill-Prepared for Terror Fight, Critics Say," *Wall Street Journal*, December 22, 2016, https:// www.wsj.com/articles/germany-ill-prepared-for-terror-fight-critics-say-1482356048; "Germany Bomb Threat: Jaber al-Bakr Caught by Three Syrians," BBC World News, October 10, 2016, https://www. bbc.com/news/world-europe-37606947.

80 Johannes Saal, "The Islamic State's Libyan External Operations Hub: The Picture So Far," *Combatting Terrorism Center Sentinel* 10, issue 11 (December 2017), https://ctc.usma.edu/the-islamic-states-libyan-external-operations-hub-the-picture-so-far/.

81 "ISIS Christmas Bomb Plot: Munir Mohammed and Rowaida el Hassan Jailed," Sky News, February 23, 2018, https://news.sky.com/ story/is-christmas-bomb-plot-munir-mohammed-and-rowaida-el-hassan-jailed-11262570.

82 "Pair Jailed for UK Homemade Bomb Attack Plan," BBC News, February 22, 2018, https://www.bbc.com/news/uk-england-derbyshire-43158741.

83 Jorge Cancino, "More Than 90 Percent of Migrants from the First Central American 'Caravan' Passed Asylum Interview," Univision News, October 24, 2018, https://www.univision.com/univision-

news/immigration/more-than-90-of-migrants-from-the-first-central-american-caravan-passed-asylum-interview; "Credible Fear Workload Report Summary, FY 2019 Total Caseload," US Citizen and Immigration Service, https://www.uscis.gov/sites/default/files/document/data/PED_CredibleFearStatsFY2019ThruMarch.pdf; Stephan Dinan, "DHS Triples Rate of Asylum 'Fear' Denials as New Policy Kicks In," *Washington Times*, January 14, 2020, https://www.washingtontimes.com/news/2020/jan/14/dhs-doubles-denial-rate-credible-fear-asylum-claim/.

84 "Crushing Immigration Judge Caseloads and Lengthening Hearing Wait Times," TRAC Immigration Database, Syracuse University, https://trac.syr.edu/immigration/reports/579/.

85 Miriam Jordan, "Syrians Seek U.S. Asylum via Mexico," *Wall Street Journal*, February 20, 2014, https://www.wsj.com/articles/syrians-seek-u-s-asylum-via-mexico-1392948076?tesla=y.

86 Maria Recio, "Syrian Families Turned Themselves in to Authorities at Texas-Mexico Border," *Fort Worth Star-Telegram*, November 19, 2015, https://www.star-telegram.com/news/state/texas/article45480042.html.

87 Lauren Frayer, "The Long, Perilous Route Thousands of Indians Have Risked for a Shot at Life in U.S.," National Public Radio, July 9, 2020, https://www.npr.org/2020/07/09/814957398/the-long-perilous-route-thousands-of-indians-have-risked-for-a-shot-at-life-in-us.

88 "Court Filings: Terror-Linked Smuggler Brought Somali Terrorists into US through Southwestern Border," Texas Department of Public Safety Intelligence Analysis, February 15, 2011, via Wikileaks.org.

89 Todd Bensman, "Attorneys Speak Out on Mexican Deportations," *Global Post*, May 30, 2010, https://www.pri.org/stories/2009-07-14/attorneys-speak-out-mexican-deportations.

90 United States v. Rakhi Gauchan, Complaint, Document 3.

91 "Man Charged in Edmonton Attacks Crossed into U.S. from Mexico, Records Show," Canadian Broadcasting Corporation, October 4, 2017, https://www.cbc.ca/news/canada/edmonton/edmonton-attacks-abdulahi-sharif-hasan-attempted-murder-border-crossing-united-states-1.4330527; Todd Bensman, "The First Border-Crosser to Attack in North America: Finally, an Update," Center for Immigration Studies, October 3, 2018, https://cis.org/Bensman/First-BorderCrosser-Attack-North-America-Finally-Update.

92   Wakefield, "Everything We Know about the Man Charged in Edmonton's Truck Attack"; "Andrew R. Arthur, "Zadvydas Claims More Victims: Edmonton Attacker Released under 2001 SCOTUS Ruling," Center for Immigration Studies, October 12, 2017, https://cis.org/Arthur/Zadvydas-Claims-More-Victims.

93   United States v. Assadi, Indictment.

94   "Iranian Convicted of Running Profitable Alien Smuggling Operation in South America," US Department of Justice, October 3, 2002.

95   United States v. Fessahazion, Plea Agreement, Document 23.

96   Ibid., 32–33.

97   Jordan, "Syrians Seek U.S. Asylum via Mexico."

98   Todd Bensman, "Travelers from Muslim Countries Still Jumping U.S. Borders," PJ Media, February 20, 2009, https://pjmedia.com/blog/todd-bensman/2009/02/20/obama-think-twice-before-rolling-back-bushs-border-crackdowns-n17635.

99   "U.S. Asylum System: Agencies Have Taken Actions to Help Ensure Quality in the Asylum Adjudication Process, but Challenges Remain" (GAO-08-935), Government Accountability Office, September 2008, https://www.gao.gov/assets/290/281570.pdf.

100 Ibid.

101 Ibid.

102 Cheryl K. Chumley, "Four GOP Reps Press for GAO Probe of 'Rampant' Asylum Fraud," *Newsmax*, February 25, 2014, https://www.newsmax.com/Newsfront/asylum-fraud-probe-GAO/2014/02/25/id/554724/.

103 Anonymous authors, "USCIS Needs Direct Access to Law Enforcement Power to Curb Rampant Immigration Fraud," Center for Immigration Studies, May 6, 2019, https://cis.org/CIS/USCIS-Needs-Direct-Access-Law-Enforcement-Power-Curb-Rampant-Immigration-Fraud.

104 *Asylum: Additional Actions Needed to Address Fraud Risks* (GAO-16-50), Government Accountability Office, December, 2015, https://www.gao.gov/assets/680/673941.pdf.

105 United States v. Fidse and Sheikh, Defendant's Motion to Dismiss for Due Process Violation; Unsealed Indictment, Document 3.

106 United States v. Fidse and Sheikh, Detention Order, Document 26.

107 Lauren Frayer, "The Long, Perilous Route Thousands of Indians Have Risked for a Shot at Life in U.S.," National Public Radio, July 9, 2020,

https://www.npr.org/2020/07/09/814957398/the-long-perilous-routethousands-of-indians-have-risked-for-a-shot-at-life-in-us.

108 Todd Bensman, "U.S. Lays Out Welcome Mat for Middle Eastern and 'Extra-Continental' Migrants While Mexico Blocks Them: A Crazy Immigration Policy Disconnect," Creative Destruction Media, February 5, 2020, https://creativedestructionmedia.com/analysis/2020/02/05/u-s-lays-out-welcome-mat-for-middle-eastern-and-extra-continental-migrants-while-mexico-blocks-them-a-crazy-immigration-polic-y-disconnect/.

109 Kevin Sieff, "The U.S. Is Putting Asylum Seekers on Planes to Guatemala—Often without Telling Them Where They're Going," Washington Post, January 14, 2020, https://www.washingtonpost.com/world/the_americas/the-us-is-putting-asylum-seekers-on-planes-to-guatemala--often-without-telling-them-where-theyre-going/2020/01/13/0f89a93a-3576-11ea-a1ff-c48c1d59a4a1_story.html.

110 "Procedures for Asylum and Withholding of Removal; Credible Fear and Reasonable Fear Review, Federal Register of the National Archives," June 15, 2020, p. 36269, https://www.federalregister.gov/documents/2020/06/15/2020-12575/procedures-for-asylum-and-withholding-of-removal-credible-fear-and-reasonable-fear-review#citation-14-p36269.

Chapter Five

1 "Combatting Transnational Criminal Threats in the Western Hemisphere," Hearing Before the House Foreign Affairs Committee, Subcommittee on the Western Hemisphere, 115th Cong., 2nd sess., May 23, 2018 (statement of Rear Admiral Brian Hendrickson, director of Network Engagement Team, US Southern Command), https://foreignaffairs.house.gov/hearing/subcommittee-hearing-combatting-transnationalcriminal-threats-in-the-western-hemisphere/.

2 "Feda Ahmed Combatant Status Review Board memo to Ahmed's Personal Representative," The Guantanamo Docket Project of the New York Times, https://www.nytimes.com/interactive/projects/guantanamo/detainees/1013-feda-ahmed/documents/5

3 "Feda Ahmed Combatant Joint Task Force-GTMO Assessment Memorandum for Commander, United States Southern Command,"

October 18, 2004, The Guantanamo Docket Project of the *New York Times*, https://www.nytimes.com/interactive/projects/guantanamo/detainees/1013-feda-ahmed; "Timeline of Guantanamo Detainee Documents Lawsuit," Associated Press, March 3, 2006, https://www.foxnews.com/story/timeline-of-guantanamo-detainee-documents-lawsuit

4   Ibid, "Feda Ahmed Combatant Joint Task Force-GTMO Assessment Memorandum for Commander, United States Southern Command."

5   Ibid.

6   Joint Task Force-GTMO Assessment Memorandum For Commander, United States Southern Command, Department of Defense, September 10, 2004, as posted to *New York Times* The Guantanamo Docket Project website, https://www.nytimes.com/interactive/projects/guantanamo/detainees/1013-feda-ahmed/documents/11

7   Ibid, "Feda Ahmed Combatant Status Review Tribunals Summary."

8   Ibid, Joint Task Force-GTMO Assessment Memorandum For Commander.

9   Ibid.

10 Ibid.

11 Ismael Lopez, "Nicaragua Arrests Four Men Suspected of Ties to the Islamic State," Reuters, June 25, 2019, https://www.reuters.com/article/us-nicaragua-security-isis-idUSKCN1TQ345; "Alert Intelligence Report: ISIS Terrorists Would Be in Mexico to Try to Cross into the US," Zeta Libre Como El Viento, April 4, 2020, https://zetatijuana.com/2019/06/reporte-de-inteligencia-alerta-terroristas-del-isis-estarian-en-mexico-para-intentar-cruzar-a-eu/.

12 Olga Rodriguez, "Central America on guard for al-Qaida," Associated Press, August 21, 2004, https://www.chron.com/news/nation-world/article/Central-America-on-guard-for-al-Qaida-1959787.php.

13 Alfonso Chardy, "Former Miramar al-Qaida Leader Hid Near U.S.-Mexico Border, New Documents Show," *Miami Herald*, February 14, 2016, https://www.miamiherald.com/news/nation-world/national/article60356051.html.

14 Ismail Khan, "Pakistani Military Kills al Qaeda Leader," *New York Times*, December 6, 2014, https://www.nytimes.com/2014/12/07/world/pakistan-kills-senior-qaeda-leader-wanted-by-fbi.html?searchResultPosition=3.

15 *Country Reports on Terrorism 2019: Panama*, US State Department, June 2020, https://www.state.gov/reports/country-reports-on-terrorism-2019/panama/

16 Calah Schlabach, "Torn between Humanitarian Ideals and U.S. Pressure, Panama Screens Migrants from Around the World," Arizona State University, Walter Cronkite School of Journalism, Cronkite Borderlands Project, https://cronkitenews.azpbs.org/2020/07/02/humanitarian-flow-panama-migrants/.

17 "Se Identificatron a 19 extranjeros vinculados con terrorismo: INM Vinculados con Terrorismo: INM," *El Sol de Mexico,* November 3, 2019, https://www.elsoldemexico.com.mx/mexico/sociedad/informe-2014-2018-19-extranjeros-migrantes-vinculados-terrorismo-inm-4405229.html.

18 Jana Winter, "Feds Issue Terror Watch for the Texas/Mexico Border," Fox News, June 25, 2015, https://www.foxnews.com/us/feds-issue-terror-watch-for-the-texas-mexico-border.

19 "Costa Rica Detains Somali with Alleged Terrorism Links," Reuters, March 23, 2017, https://www.reuters.com/article/us-costa-rica-suspect-idUSKBN16U2CP.

20 *Country Reports on Terrorism 2017, US State Department,* page 207, https://www.state.gov/wp-content/uploads/2019/04/crt_2017.pdf.

21 Ibid; Arizona State University, Walter Cronkite School of Journalism, Cronkite Borderlands Project, https://cronkitenews.azpbs.org/2020/07/02/humanitarian-flow-panama-migrants/.

22 Todd Bensman, "Central American Countries Are Helping Middle Easterners Illegally Enter the United States," *Federalist,* January 2, 2019, https://thefederalist.com/2019/01/02/central-american-countries-helping-middle-easterners-illegally-enter-united-states/.

23 "ICE, Brazil Federal Police arrest alleged leader of major human smuggling organization, U.S. Immigration and Customs Enforcement news release, September 10, 2020, https://www.ice.gov/news/releases/ice-brazil-federal-police-arrest-alleged-leader-major-human-smuggling-organization; *Country Reports on Terrorism 2019: Brazil,* US State Department, June 2020, https://www.state.gov/reports/country-reports-on-terrorism-2019/brazil/.

24 Ibid, *Country Reports on Terrorism 2019: Brazil.*

25 Ibid.

26   Ernesto Londono and Leticia Casado, "Egyptian Sought in F.B.I. Qaeda Query Says He Has Nothing to Hide," *The New York Times,* August 18, 2019, https://www.nytimes.com/2019/08/18/world/americas/brazil-fbi-al-qaeda.html

27   Ibid.

28   "Exclusive: Border Patrol Circulates Intel Alert Titled 'Suspected Suicide Bomber En Route to the U.S.,'" Breitbart News, January 9, 2020, https://www.breitbart.com/border/2020/01/09/exclusive-border-patrol-circulates-intel-alert-titled-suspected-suicide-bomber-en-route-to-the-u-s/.

29   Julia Edwards, "U.S. Seeks Latin American Help amid Rise in Asian, African Migrants," Reuters, August 16, 2016, https://www.reuters.com/article/us-usa-immigration-mexico-exclusive/u-s-seeks-latin-american-help-amid-rise-in-asian-african-migrants-idUSKCN10R0DD.

30   *Country Reports on Terrorism 2018*, US State Department, p. 198, https://www.state.gov/wp-content/uploads/2019/11/Country-Reports-on-Terrorism-2018-FINAL.pdf.

31   Pauline Arrillaga and Olga R. Rodriguez, "Porous Border Is Seen as Terrorist Threat," Associated Press, July 3, 2005, https://www.latimes.com/archives/la-xpm-2005-jul-03-adna-border3-story.html.

32   *Country Reports on Terrorism 2016,* page 291, https://www.state.gov/wp-content/uploads/2019/04/crt_2016.pdf

33   *Country Reports on Terrorism 2016*, US State Department, https://www.state.gov/reports/country-reports-on-terrorism-2016/.

34   Kristina Wong, "US Military Eyes 'Extremist Islamic Movement' in Latin America," *The Hill,* June 1, 2016, https://thehill.com/policy/defense/281948-top-us-military-commander-in-latin-america-worried-about-extremist-islamic.

35   Written testimony of US Immigration and Customs Enforcement Homeland Security Investigations Executive Associate Director James Dinkins for a Senate Committee on Homeland Security and Governmental Affairs hearing titled "Border Security: Frontline Perspectives on Progress and Remaining Challenges," April 10, 2013, https://www.dhs.gov/news/2013/04/10/written-testimony-us-immigration-and-customs-enforcement-senate-committee-homeland.

36   Internet site last accessed September 9, 2020: https://www.justice.gov/criminal-hrsp/file/997546/download

37 Department of Homeland Security Immigration and Customs Enforcement power points obtained by the author in 2007.

38 "International Law Enforcement Cooperation Leads to Brazilian Takedown of Significant Human Smugglers," US Department of Justice, Office of Public Affairs, August 20, 2019, https://www.justice.gov/opa/pr/international-law-enforcement-cooperation-leads-brazilian-takedown-significant-human; "Brazil Police Crack Down on Group Sending Africans to US," Agencia Brasil, August 20, 2019, https://agenciabrasil.ebc.com.br/en/geral/noticia/2019-08/brazil-police-crack-down-group-sending-africans-us.

39 "Brazil Police Crack Down on Group Sending Africans to US," US Department of Justice, Office of Public Affairs, August 20, 2019, https://www.justice.gov/opa/pr/international-law-enforcement-cooperation-leads-brazilian-takedown-significant-human.

40 Daniel Mello, "Brazil Police Crack Down on group sending Africans to US," Agencia Brazil, August 20, 2019, https://agenciabrasil.ebc.com.br/en/geral/noticia/2019-08/brazil-police-crack-down-group-sending-africans-us

41 Ibid, "ICE, Brazil Federal Police arrest alleged leader of major human smuggling organization, U.S. Immigration and Customs Enforcement news release, September 10, 2020.

42 Ibid.

43 *Country Reports on Terrorism 2014:* US Department of State, 2015, http://www.state.gov/j/ct/rls/crt/2014/239409.htm.

44 Luisa Feline Freier, *Open Doors (for Almost All): Visa Policies and Ethnic Selectivity in Ecuador* (London: London School of Economics, Center for Comparative Immigration Studies, 2013).

45 Todd Bensman, "Ecuador Still Helping Unknowns from All Over the World Get to the U.S. Border," *Federalist*, October 21, 2019, https://thefederalist.com/2019/10/21/ecuador-still-helping-unknowns-from-all-over-the-world-get-to-the-u-s-border/; "Ecuador Expands List of Countries Whose Citizens Need a Special Tourist Visa," Cuenca High Life, August 13, 2019, https://cuencahighlife.com/ecuador-expands-list-of-countries-whose-citizens-require-a-special-tourist-visa/.

46 Todd Bensman, "Panama and Costa Rica Doing Smugglers' Work with 'Controlled Flow' Policy," Center for Immigration Studies, December 27, 2018, https://cis.org/Bensman/Panama-and-Costa-Rica-Doing-

Smugglers-Work-Controlled-Flow-Policy; Todd Bensman, "Central American Countries Are Helping Middle Easterners Illegally Enter the United States," *Federalist*, January 2, 2019, https://thefederalist. com/2019/01/02/central-american-countries-helping-middle-easterners-illegally-enter-united-states/.

[47] United States v. Mohammed Kamel Ibrahim and Sampson Lovelace Boateng (US District Court for District of Columbia, 2007), Transcript from Sentencing Hearing.

[48] Todd Bensman, "VIDEO: CIS in Panama and Costa Rica: How America Filters Potential Terrorists in Distant Lands," Center for Immigration Studies, December 12, 2018, https://cis.org/Bensman/VIDEO-CIS-Panama-and-Costa-Rica-How-America-Filters-Potential-Terrorists-Distant-Lands.

Chapter Six

[1] John F. Kelly, Posture Statement of General John F. Kelly, United States Marine Corps Commander, United States Southern Command," Before the 114th Congress Senate Armed Services Committee (March 12, 2015), https://www.armed-services.senate.gov/imo/media/doc/Kelly_03-12-15.pdf.

[2] United States v. Irfan Ul Haq, Case 1:11cr-00056-JDB (US District Court for the District of Columbia, September 12, 2011), Factual Proffer in Support of Guilty Plea, Document 48.

[3] "Three Plead Guilty to Conspiracy to Provide Material Support to the Pakistani Taliban," US Department of Justice, press release, September 12, 2011, https://www.justice.gov/opa/pr/three-plead-guilty-conspiracy-provide-material-support-pakistani-taliban.

[4] "Pakistani Citizen Sentenced to 50 Months in Prison for Conspiracy to Provide Material Support to the Pakistani Taliban," US Department of Justice, press release, FBI Miami Division, January 5, 2012, https://archives.fbi.gov/archives/miami/press-releases/2012/pakistani-citizen-sentenced-to-50-months-in-prison-for-conspiracy-to-provide-material-support-to-the-pakistani-taliban.

[5] United States v. Irfan Ul Haq, Case 1:11-cr-00056-JDB, Motion for Downward Departure and Memorandum in Aid of Sentencing, Document 86, filed January 3, 2012.

6   United States v. Irfan Ul Haq, Case 11-00056 (JDB), (US District Court for the District of Columbia, September 12, 2011), Document 48, Factual Proffer in Support of Guilty Plea.

7   United Staves v. Moktar Hossain and Milon Miah, Case 5:18-cr-00912 (US District Court, Southern District of Texas, Laredo Division, May 18, 2019), Government's Response to Defendant's Motion to Suppress, Document 42.

8   United States v. Rakhi Gauchan (5th Circuit Court, Western District of Texas, 2014), Criminal Complaint, Document 3; Indictment; Government Motion for Upward Departure, Document 27.

9   United States v. Mehrzad Arbane (11th Circuit Court, Southern District of Florida, 2003), Case Complaint.

10   United States v. Maher Jarad (US District Court for District of Columbia, 2007), Indictment.

11   United States v. Assadi, Government Trial Memorandum.

12   United States v. Neeran Zaia et al., 35 F.3D 567 (6th Circuit Court, US District Court for the District of Columbia, 1994), Indictment.

13   Ibid.

14   United States v. Mohamed Abdi Siyad, Case 3:18-mj-04365-JLB (US District Court, Southern District of California, August, 8, 2018), Document 1, Criminal Complaint.

15   United Staves v. Moktar Hossain and Milon Miah, Case 5:18-cr-00912 (US District Court, Southern District of Texas, Laredo Division), Indictment, Document 62, July 30, 2019.

16   United States v. Gauchan, Criminal Complaint, Document 3.

17   United States v. Anthony Joseph Tracy (4th Circuit Court, Eastern District of Virginia, 2011), Document 132.

18   Todd Bensman, "Out of Iraq: An Illegal Flight of the Chaldean Christians to America," *San Antonio Express-News*, May 2007, https://www.toddbensman.com/breaching-america-part-v-out-of-iraq-an-illegal-flight-of-chaldean-christians-to-america/.

19   Todd Bensman, "Why the Case of Jordanian-Mexican Smuggler Who Transported Yemenis over the Texas Border Is Important," Center for Immigration Studies, May 1, 2019, https://cis.org/Bensman/Why-Case-JordanianMexican-Smuggler-Who-Transported-Yemenis-over-Texas-Border-Important.

20   Pauline Arrillaga and Olga Rodriguez, "Investigation: Smuggler Pipelines Channel Illegal Immigrants into the U.S," Associated Press, July 3, 2005, https://journalstar.com/news/smuggler-pipelines-channel-illegal-immigrants-into-u-s/article_c16b7442-f775-5d57-8bfb-4022ffba9bec.html.

21   United States v. Assadi, Case 1:2002-cr-00030 DCDCE Government Motion for Upward Departure.

22   "Jordanian National Sentenced for Conspiracy to Bring Aliens into the United States," US Department of Justice, Office of Public Affairs, press release," October 29, 2019, https://www.justice.gov/opa/pr/jordanian-national-sentenced-conspiracy-bring-aliens-united-states.

23   United States v. Merhay, Government Motion for an Order to Seal, Document 2.

24   United States v. Muhammad Hussein Assadi, 223 F.Sup.2d (2008), Government Trial Memorandum.

25   United States v. Ashraf Ahmed Abdallah (US District Court for the District of Columbia, 2001), Indictment.

26   United States v. Kaushik Jayantibhai Thakkar (5th Circuit Court, Southern District of Texas, 2012), Plea Agreement.

27   United States v. Mohammed Kamel Ibrahim and Sampson Lovelace Boateng (US District Court for District of Columbia, 2007), Factual Proffer, Document 18.

28   Ibid; Arrillaga and Rodriguez, "Investigation."

29   United States v. Neeran Hakim Zaia el al., Case 1:04-cr-00401-RMC, Document 86, Government's Opposition to Defendants' Motion to Interview Complainants, November 15, 2005.

30   United States v. Assadi, Indictment.

31   US Immigration and Customs Enforcement, "Ghanaian Pleads Guilty to Conspiracy and Alien Smuggling Charges," US Department of Homeland Security, April 22, 2008, http://amandala.com.bz/news/ghanaian-alien-smuggler-pleads-guilty-in-us-court/?upm_export=print

32   United States v. Abdallah, Indictment.

33   United States v. Gauchan, Indictment.

34   United States v. Boateng, Factual Résumé.

35   United States v. Jarad, Indictment.

36   "Iranian Convicted of Running Profitable Alien Smuggling Operation in South America," Department of Justice, October 3, 2002.; "Iranian

Convicted in Smuggling Case," The Associated Press, October 3, 2002, https://apnews.com/6b4c5ce2590498257144a6cf48637e56

37 United States v. Lorian et al., Criminal Complaint.

38 Kelly, "Posture Statement."

39 United States v. Sharafat Ali Khan, Case 1:16-cr-00096-RBW, Transcript of Hearing Before Honorable Reggie B. Walton, p.15, September 1, 2017.

40 "Foreign National Extradited and Pleads Guilty to Human Smuggling Conspiracy," Department of Justice, press release, April 12, 2017, https://www.justice.gov/opa/pr/foreign-national-extradited-and-pleads-guilty-human-smuggling-conspiracy; "Foreign National Sentenced to 31 Months in Prison for Leadership Role in Human Smuggling Conspiracy," Department of Justice, press release, October 17, 2017, https://www.justice.gov/opa/pr/foreign-national-sentenced-31-months-prison-leadership-role-human-smuggling-conspiracy; United States v. Sharafat Al Khan, Case 1:16-cr-00096-RbW (US District Court for the District of Columbia, June, 3, 2016), Criminal Complaint, Document 1, https://cis.org/sites/default/files/2018-08/Sharif%20Khan%20complaint.pdf; United States v. Sharafat Al Khan, Case 1:16-cr-00096-RbW, Government's Memorandum in Aid of Sentencing, Document 38 (June 30, 2017), https://cis.org/sites/default/files/2018-08/Khan%20sentencing%20memorandum.pdf.

41 United States v. Mohammed Hussein Assadi, Government's Trial Memorandum.

42 United States v. Dhanraj Samuel (5th Circuit Court, Southern District of Texas, 2009), Criminal Complaint Affidavit.

43 United States v. Zeayadale Malhamdary (9th Circuit Court, District of Arizona, 2005), Second Superseding Indictment, Document 42; United States v. Malhamdary, Case Sentencing Memorandum.

44 United States v. Boateng, Defendant's Memorandum in Aid of Sentencing.

45 "Iranian Convicted in Smuggling Case," The Associated Press, October 3, 2002, https://apnews.com/6b4c5ce2590498257144a6cf48637e56.

46 United States v. Lorian, Criminal Complaint.

47 United States v. Zeayadale Malhamdary (9th Circuit Court, District of Arizona, 2005), Second Superseding Indictment, Document 42.

Chapter Seven

[1] Jeff Shields, "2 Charged in Smuggling Ring," The South Florida Sun Sentinel," September 14, 2002, https://www.sun-sentinel.com/news/fl-xpm-2002-09-14-0209130797-story.html

[2] "Canadian National Charged with Alien Smuggling Conspiracy and Attempting to Bring Aliens to the United States," US Department of Justice Office of Public Affairs release, August 19, 2020, https://www.justice.gov/opa/pr/canadian-national-charged-alien-smuggling-conspiracy-and-attempting-bring-aliens-united

[3] Tim Craig, "Kabul Libre! One New Afghan Trail to the West Goes through Cuba," *Washington Post*, April 17, 2016, https://www.washingtonpost.com/world/asia_pacific/kabul-libre-one-new-afghan-trail-to-the-west-goes-through-cuba/2016/04/16/da214926-0188-11e6-8bb1-f124a43f84dc_story.html.

[4] United States v. Tracy, Government Affidavit in Support of Complaint.

[5] *Trend Analysis Report on Iran Migration*, US Customs and Border Protection Office of Alien Smuggling Interdiction, July 2011.

[6] Todd Bensman, "A Talk with an Iranian Migrant in Costa Rica En Route to the U.S. Border," Center for Immigration Studies, December 20, 2018, https://cis.org/Bensman/Talk-Iranian-Migrant-Costa-Rica-en-Route-US-Border.

[7] "Mafia at RNP Sold Identities to Syrians and Palestinians," *La Prensa*, May 22, 2016, https://www.laprensa.hn/honduras/962558-410/mafia-en-rnp-vendió-identidades-a-sirios-y-palestinos#ifrndnloc.

[8] "Five Syrians Detained at Honduras Airport," *La Prensa*, November 18, 2015, https://www.laprensa.hn/honduras/902692-410/detienen-a-cinco-sirios-en-aeropuerto-de-honduras.

[9] Alan Gomez, "Report: U.S.-Bound Syrians Arrested in Honduras with Fake Passports," *USA Today*, November 18, 2015, https://www.usatoday.com/story/news/world/2015/11/18/report-us-bound-syrians-arrested-honduras-fake-passports/76016812/.

[10] Arrillaga and Rodriguez, "Investigation."

[11] Tom Diaz and Barbara Newman, *Lightning Out of Lebanon: Hezbollah Terrorists on American Soil* (New York: Random House, 2006), 221.

[12] United States v. Zeayadale Malhamdary (9th Circuit Court, District of Arizona, 2005), Second Superseding Indictment, Document 42.

13 United States v. Zeayadale Malhamdary (9th Circuit Court, District of Arizona, 2005), Plea Agreement, Document 74.

14 Todd Bensman, "Afghanis Caught with Genuine Mexican Passports Bought in Mumbai: A U.S. Security Vulnerability in Mexico's Foreign offices?" *San Antonio Express News*, March 2008, https://www.toddbensman.com/how-smugglers-use-the-middle-east-based-consulates-of-latin-american-nations/.

15 Todd Bensman, "Iraqi Border Jumpers," *Global Post*, May 30, 2010, https://www.toddbensman.com/iraqi-border-jumpers/.

16 United States v. Ibrahim and Boateng, Factual Résumé.

17 United States v. Ahmad Dhakane, FBI Verbatim Translation, Document 68–69.

18 United States v. Annitta Devi Gerald (5th Circuit Court, Southern District of Texas, 2009), Criminal Complaint.

19 Luis Guilherme Barrucho and Camilla Costa, "Brazil Welcomes More Syrians Than Countries on the European Refugee Route," BBC News Brazil, September 9, 2015, https://www.bbc.com/portuguese/noticias/2015/09/150904_brasil_refugiados_sirios_comparacao_internacional_lgb; Franco Bastida, "Brazil Opens Arms Wider to Syrian Refugees Than Many EU Nations," *Panama Post*, September 7, 2015, https://panampost.com/franco-bastida/2015/09/07/brazil-opens-arms-wider-to-syrian-refugees-than-many-eu-nations/?__cf_chl_jschl_tk__=8878c9555872c1a103acc305cb4d14b7e27dca34-1587995553-0-AU9bvduDarjn1cGQLgAl_iQkd1X_L9SkAIB8C_TnJ8HrvmiZeFEvFluUQWwUvl6KhZ07.

Chapter Eight

1 Tim Craig, "The Taliban Once Ruled Pakistan's Swat Valley. Now Peace Has Returned," *Washington Post*, May 9, 2015, https://www.washingtonpost.com/world/the-taliban-once-ruled-pakistans-swat-valley-now-peace-has-returned/2015/05/08/6bb8ac96-eeaa-11e4-8050-839e9234b303_story.html?noredirect=on.

2 "Supervision of Aliens Commensurate with Risk," OIG-11-81, Department of Homeland Security, Office of Inspector General Report 11-81, December 2011, p. 18, https://www.oig.dhs.gov/assets/Mgmt/OIG_11-81_Dec11.pdf.

3   David V. Aguilar, "Arrests of Aliens from Special Interest Countries", US Customs and Border Protection memorandum, November 1, 2004, https://cis.org/sites/default/files/2018-08/Aguilar_memo.pdf; "Special Interest Alien Use of the California-Mexico Border," Department of Homeland Security joint assessment with the California State Terrorism Threat Assessment Center, August 2009. This document was obtained while the author was working as a journalist in Texas. The NCTC intelligence report "2006 SIA Trends Reveal Vulnerabilities along Route to US," obtained by the author while working as a journalist, listed the countries as follows: Afghanistan, Algeria, Bahrain, Bangladesh, Djibouti, Egypt, Eritrea, Indonesia, Iran, Iraq, Jordan, Kazakhstan, Kuwait, Lebanon, Libya, Malaysia, Mauritania, Morocco, Oman, Pakistan, the Philippines, Qatar, Saudi Arabia, Somalia, Sudan, Syria, Tajikistan, Tunisia, Turkey, Turkmenistan, the United Arab Emirates, Uzbekistan, and Yemen, as well as the territories of Gaza and the West Bank. DHS/ICE also recognized Thailand as an SIA country. In 2003, the American Immigration Lawyers Association obtained and published on its website (no longer available) a "countries of interest" list that included fifty-two countries. They were Afghanistan, Algeria, Angola, Argentina, Armenia, Bahrain, Bhutan, Brazil, Congo, Cyprus, Democratic Republic of Congo, Egypt, Eritrea, Ethiopia, Georgia, India, Indonesia, Iran, Iraq, Israel, Jordan, Kazakhstan, Kenya, Kuwait, Kyrgyzstan, Lebanon, Liberia, Malaysia, Mongolia, Morocco, Myanmar, Nepal, Oman, Pakistan, Panama, Paraguay, Philippines, Qatar, Republic of Yemen, Saudi Arabia, Somalia, Sri Lanka, Sudan, Syria, Tajikistan, Tunisia, Turkey, Turkmenistan, United Arab Emirates, Uruguay, Uzbekistan, and Venezuela.

4   Ibid, Supervision of Aliens with Commensurate Risk OIG-11-81 report.

5   Adam MacAllister, Dan Spengler, Kyle Larish, and Nam-young Kim, "Special Interest Aliens: Achieving an Integrated Approach," *Small Wars Journal*, undated, https://smallwarsjournal.com/jrnl/art/special-interest-aliens-achieving-an-integrated-approach.

6   Information provided to author by the FBI and ICE Office of Intelligence while author was employed by the Texas Department of Public Safety Intelligence and Counterterrorism Division; Todd Bensman, "Eight Recommendations to Congress and the White House to Counter Potential Terror Travel to the U.S. Southern Border," November 1,

2018, https://cis.org/Report/Eight-Recommendations-Congress-and-White-House-Counter-Potential-Terror-Travel-US-Southern

7   Todd Bensman, "Breaching America Part IV: Made It to America," The San Antonio Express-News, May 2007, https://www.toddbensman.com/breaching-america-part-iv-made-it-to-america/.

8   May 2019 Interview with the author of retired FBI Special Agent James G. Conway.

9   Todd Bensman, "Breaching America Part III: Mexico: Stuck in the Middle," The San Antonio Express-News, May 2007, https://www.toddbensman.com/part-iii-mexico-stuck-in-the-middle/.

10   "Detention and Removal of Illegal Aliens," OIT-06-33, Department of Homeland Security, Office of Inspector General, April 2016, https://www.oig.dhs.gov/assets/Mgmt/OIG_06-33_Apr06.pdf.

11   Ibid.; "Breaching America Part IV: Made It to America."

12   "Supervision of Aliens Commensurate with Risk, U.S. Department of Homeland Security Office of Inspector General, December 2011, https://www.oig.dhs.gov/assets/Mgmt/OIG_11-81_Dec11.pdf.

13   "Costa Rica and Panama Arrest Dozens on Suspicion of People Smuggling," Reuters News, July 30, 2019, https://www.nytimes.com/2019/07/30/world/americas/costa-rica-panama-people-smuggling-arrest.html.

14   "Bangladeshi National Arrested in South Texas for His Role in Conspiracy to Bring Illegal Aliens into the US," US Immigration and Customs Enforcement, press release, September 4, 2019, https://www.ice.gov/news/releases/bangladeshi-national-arrested-south-texas-his-role-conspiracy-bring-illegal-aliens-us.

15   Nils Gilman, Jesse Goldhammer, and Steve and Weber, *Deviant Globalization: Black Market Economy in the 21st Century* (New York: Continuum, 2011; New York: Random House, Kindle Edition), 276–345.

16   Moisés Naím, *Illicit: How Smugglers, Traffickers and Copycats Are Hijacking the Global Economy* (New York: Random House, 2005, Kindle Edition), 327.

17   John Rollins, "Ten Years after the Terrorist Attacks of 9/11: The Need for a Transnational Approach to Address Risks to US Global Security Interests," *Homeland Security Affairs*, no date given.

18   Ibid.; Rollins, "Ten Years after the Terrorist Attacks of 9/11."

[19] Richard M. Stana, *Alien Smuggling: DHS could Better Address Alien Smuggling along the Southwest Border by Leveraging Investigative Resources and Measuring Program Performance*, GAO Report 10-919T, July 22, 2010, https://www.gao.gov/new.items/d10919t.pdf.

[20] Richard A. Best Jr., "Securing America's Borders: The Role of the Intelligence Community," Congressional Research Service, December 7, 2010, https://fas.org/sgp/crs/intel/R41520.pdf.

Chapter Nine

[1] World Migration Report 2020, United Nations International Office of Migration, p. 3, https://www.un.org/sites/un2.un.org/files/wmr_2020.pdf.

[2] Todd Bensman, "'Extra-Continental' Migration: Migrants from Across the Globe, Exempt from Trump Policies, Waved Through the Border," Center for Immigration Studies Video Report, January 29, 2020, https://cis.org/Bensman/Video-ExtraContinental-Migration-Southern-Border.

[3] Richard Rumelt, "The Perils of Bad Strategy," *McKinsey Quarterly* (June 2011), 4, http://www.mckinsey.com/insights/strategy/the_perils_of_bad_strategy.

[4] Marc R. Rosenblum, "Border Security: Immigration Enforcement between Ports of Entry," Congressional Research Service, May 3, 2013, https://securityassistance.org/sites/default/files/R42138.pdf.

[5] Bruce Bueno de Mesquita and Alastair Smith, *The Dictator's Handbook: Why Bad Behavior Is Almost Always Good Politics*, 1st ed. (New York: PublicAffairs Books, 2011), 167.

[6] Avi Dicter and Daniel L. Byman, *Israel's Lessons for Fighting Terrorists and Their Implications for the United States* (Washington, DC: Brookings Institution, 2006).

[7] "Mexico Flies 300 Indian Migrants to New Delhi in 'Unprecedented' Mass Deportation," Reuters, October 17, 2019, https://www.usnews.com/news/world/articles/2019-10-17/mexico-flies-300-indian-migrants-to-new-delhi-in-unprecedented-mass-deportation.

[8] Bensman, "Breaching America, Part III: Mexico: Stuck in the Middle."

[9] "EU: New immigration liaison officers network puts more emphasis on EU-level coordination," Statewatch, June 4, 2019, https://www.statewatch.org/news/2019/june/eu-new-immigration-liaison-officers-network-puts-more-emphasis-on-eu-level-coordination/; "Regulation

2019/1240 – Creation of a European network of immigration liaison officers," EU Monitor, September 17, 2020, https://www.eumonitor. eu/9353000/1/j4nvk6yhcbpeywk_j9vvik7m1c3gyxp/vl0h7d71ilz7.

[10] John M. Nomikos, "Combating Illegal Immigration, Organized Crime and Terrorism in Greece and Italy," *International Journal of Intelligence and CounterIntelligence* 26, no. 2 (2013): 288–303, http://www. security-round-table.eu/esrt/Articles/John-Nomikos.php.

[11] "Immigration: 'Recalcitrant' Countries and the Use of Visa Sanctions to Encourage Cooperation with Alien Removals," Congressional Research Service, January 23, 2020, https://fas.org/sgp/crs/homesec/ IF11025.pdf.

[12] Matthew Herber and Jalel Harchaoui, "Italy Claims It's Found a Solution to Europe's Migrant Problem. Here's Why Italy's Wrong," *Washington Post*, September 26, 2017, https://www.washingtonpost. com/news/monkey-cage/wp/2017/09/25/italy-claims-its-found-a-solution-to-europes-migrant-problem-heres-why-italys-wrong/.

[13] Matina Stevis-Gridneff, "Europe Keeps Asylum Seekers at a Distance," *New York Times*, September 8, 2019, https://www.nytimes. com/2019/09/08/world/europe/migrants-africa-rwanda.html.

[14] Rod Nordland and Mujib Mashal, "Europe Makes Deal to Send Afghans Home, Where War Awaits Them," *New York Times*, October 5, 2016, https://www.nytimes.com/2016/10/06/world/asia/afghanistan-eu-refugees-migrants.html?action=click&module=Related Coverage&pgtype=Article&region=Footer.

[15] Patrick Kingsley, "By Stifling Migration, Sudan's Feared Secret Police Aid Europe," *New York Times*, April 22, 2018, https://www.nytimes. com/2018/04/22/world/africa/migration-european-union-sudan.html; "Libyan Militia Chief Admits Deal with Tripoli to Stem Migrant Flow," *Times* (London), September 1, 2017, https://www.thetimes.co.uk/ article/libyan-militia-chief-admits-deal-with-tripoli-to-stem-migrant-flow-ahmed-dabbashi-brigade-migrant-crisis-italy-538lwtgf5.

[16] Matthew Karnitschnig and Jacopo Barigazzi, "EU and Turkey Reach Refugee Deal," Politico, March 20, 2016, https://www.politico.eu/ article/eu-and-turkey-finalize-refugee-deal/.

[17] Elena Becatoros, "3 Years On, What's Become of the EU-Turkey Migration Deal?" Associated Press, March 20, 2019, https://apnews. com/2eb94ba9aee14272bd99909be2325e2b.

18 Stevis-Gridneff, "Europe Keeps Asylum Seekers at a Distance," the *New York Times*, September 8, 2019.

19 Lori Hinnant, "500 Refugees Trapped in Libya to Be Evacuated to Rwanda," Associated Press, September 10, 2019, https://apnews.com/0021fca830be418196063c12d0ee8647; Adam Nossiter, "At French Outpost in African Migrant Hub, Asylum for a Select Few," *New York Times*, February 25, 2018, https://www.nytimes.com/2018/02/25/world/africa/france-africa-migrants-asylum-niger.html.

20 Bernd Riegert, "Could Hungary's Transit Zones for Refugees Be a Model for Germany," DW News; April 7, 2018, https://www.dw.com/en/could-hungarys-transit-zones-for-refugees-be-a-model-for-germany/a-44511989.

21 Jason Kao and Denise Lu, "How Trump's Policies Are Leaving Thousands of Asylum Seekers Waiting in Mexico," *New York Times*, August 18, 2019, https://www.nytimes.com/interactive/2019/08/18/us/mexico-immigration-asylum.html.

22 Jonathan Blitzer, "How Trump's Safe-Third-Country Agreement with Guatemala Fell Apart," the *New Yorker*, July 15, 2019, https://www.newyorker.com/news/news-desk/how-trumps-safe-third-country-agreement-with-guatemala-fell-apart.

23 Abigail Poe, Adam Isacson, Lisa Haugaard, and Sarah Kinosian, "Time to Listen: Trends in U.S. Security Assistance to Latin America," Law.org, http://securityassistance.org/publication/time-listen-trends-us-security-assistance-latin-america-and-caribbean.

24 Freier, *Open Doors (for Almost All)*, 17–18.

25 Caitlin Dickerson, "Trump Effect Wears Off as Migrants Resume Their Northward Push," *New York Times*, January 10, 2018, https://www.nytimes.com/2018/01/10/us/border-crossings-trump-effect.html; Amanda Holpuch, "The Invisible Wall: How Trump Is Slowing Immigration without Laying a Brick," *Guardian*, December 23, 2016, https://www.theguardian.com/us-news/2017/dec/23/donald-trump-mexico-border-wall-invisible-immigration.

Afterword

1 Robert D. McFadden, "Nicholas Winton, Rescuer of 669 Children from Holocaust, Dies at 106, *New York Times*, July 1, 2015, http://

www.nytimes.com/2015/07/02/world/europe/nicholas-winton-is-dead-at-106-saved-children-from-the-holocaust.html.

2   Lydia Warren, "The Astonishing Story of How a Humble London Stockbroker Saved 669 children—most of them Jews—from Czechoslovakia on the eve of World War II," *Daily Mail*, http://www.dailymail.co.uk/news/article-2615101/The-astonishing-story-humble-London-stockbroker-saved-669-children-Jews-Czechoslovakia-eve-World-War-II.html.

ABOUT THE AUTHOR

Todd Bensman currently serves as the Texas-based Senior National Security Fellow for the Center for Immigration Studies (CIS), a Washington, D.C. policy institute for which he writes, speaks, and grants media interviews about the nexus between immigration and national security. He has testified before Congress as an expert witness and regularly appears on radio and television outlets. Separately, he writes about homeland security for a variety of online publications, and teaches terrorism and intelligence analysis as a university adjunct lecturer. For nine years, through August 2018, Bensman led counterterrorism intelligence for the Texas Department of Public Safety's Intelligence and Counterterrorism Division in its multi-agency fusion center. Before his homeland security service, Bensman was a journalist for twenty-three years, covering national security after 9/11 as a staff writer for major newspapers and reporting in twenty-five countries. His reporting on migration from Islamic countries and cross-border gun smuggling to cartels earned two National Press Club awards (2008 and 2009), an Inter-American Press Association award, and two Texas Institute of Letters awards. His reporting on corruption spurred numerous federal investigations, indictments, and convictions.

Bensman holds an M.A. in Security Studies from the Naval Postgraduate School, Center for Homeland Defense and Security (2015, Outstanding Thesis designee). He also holds an M.A. in Journalism from the University of Missouri School of Journalism (2009). He holds an undergraduate degree in Journalism from Northern Arizona University. In 2017, he completed a 350-hour State of Texas Command College leadership program sponsored by the Texas Department of Public Safety.